RIPPLES OF
THE UNIVERSE

CLASS | NEW
2 | STUDIES
0 | IN
0 | RELIGION

EDITED BY Kathryn Lofton AND John Lardas Modern

RIPPLES OF THE UNIVERSE

Spirituality in
Sedona, Arizona

SUSANNAH CROCKFORD

The University of Chicago Press
Chicago and London

The University of Chicago Press, Chicago 60637
The University of Chicago Press, Ltd., London
© 2021 by The University of Chicago
Published 2021
Printed in the United States of America

30 29 28 27 26 25 24 23 22 21   1 2 3 4 5

ISBN-13: 978-0-226-77791-7 (cloth)
ISBN-13: 978-0-226-77807-5 (paper)
ISBN-13: 978-0-226-77810-5 (e-book)
DOI: https://doi.org/10.7208/chicago/9780226778105.001.0001

Library of Congress Cataloging-in-Publication Data

Names: Crockford, Susannah, author.
Title: Ripples of the universe : spirituality in Sedona, Arizona / Susannah
    Crockford.
Other titles: Spirituality in Sedona, Arizona | Class 200, new studies in religion.
Description: Chicago ; London : The University of Chicago Press, 2021. |
Series: Class 200 : new studies in religion | Includes bibliographical references and
    index.
Identifiers: LCCN 2020051232 | ISBN 9780226777917 (cloth) | ISBN 9780226778075
    (paperback) | ISBN 9780226778105 (e-book)
Subjects: LCSH: Spirituality—Arizona—Sedona. | Spirituality—Social aspects—
    Arizona—Sedona. | Occultism—Arizona—Sedona. | Religion and culture—
    Arizona—Sedona. | Sedona (Ariz.)—Religious life and customs.
Classification: LCC BL2527.S44 C76 2021 | DDC 204.09791/57—dc23
LC record available at https://lccn.loc.gov/2020051232

♾ This paper meets the requirements of ANSI/NISO Z39.48-1992
(Permanence of Paper).

For the people of Sedona, love and light

_____

CONTENTS

FIGURE 1. Sedona, Arizona.

INTRODUCTION

Everything Is Energy

We're an empire now, and when we act, we create our own reality.

—KARL ROVE, in Mark Danner, *Words in a Time of War*, 2007, p. 17

Energy is a very subtle concept. It is very, very difficult to get right.

—RICHARD FEYNMAN, in "What is Science?," presented at the fifteenth annual meeting of the National Science Teachers Association, in New York City, 1966

PROLOGUE: INTO THE VORTEX

"LOOK HOW CUTE YOU ARE," PURRED Vixen du Lac as she met me in the parking lot of the Super 8 motel to take me in her dark green Subaru to the Cosmic Portal. Sixty-five years old, with wispy frosted blond hair and plump pink lips, she was very friendly. It was my first day in Sedona, and Vixen had met me off the shuttle bus from Phoenix. Driving at breakneck speed, using her knee on the steering wheel, making rattling and clicking noises to the music on the radio, chattering frenetically, she introduced me to Sedona. It was a paradise I would find hard to leave, a sacred place, "a space between spaces." Frequency allows you to connect to everything that already is. She was an esoteric scientist, working on sonic harmonics. An MIT scientist tested her with a magnetometer and found she was on the same frequency as the vortexes. You should not drink tap water unless it had been mechanically and energetically purified. They were spraying chemtrails a lot today. The year 2012 was an important one, the ascension was imminent. The crystal ships were coming to take us back to the stars.

The Cosmic Portal was what Vixen called her house. I had contacted her via her website two weeks previously. She responded promptly, offering a variety of packages with ascending prices for my "special stay." The house itself was a small, one-floor building, with two bedrooms, two bathrooms, a fenced-in backyard of bare scrub and prickly pear cacti, and a garage. It was a building that in many respects resembled its neighbors in West Sedona. Inside, it was cluttered with crystals, stones, offerings, paintings, Buddha statues, roses made from toilet paper, little pink hearts with the letter "M" written on them, and two cats and a dog.

Vixen told me that the house was a temple, "energetically," she qualified, so as to foreclose the possibility that it was used as a house of worship. What she meant was that it was built on a vortex, the focal point of which was under the garage. This room was no longer used for cars but was renovated into an extension of the interior living space, becoming the place where she did her energy work. It was a meditation room, with many crystals of different colors, a vibrant painting with splashes of bright primaries, a couple of prints by the psychedelic artist Alex Grey, angel figurines, candles, incense, pipes, and two yoga swings hanging in the middle—to help tone your bum, she advised me. She stood me on the point between the yoga swings where the vortex was and asked, "Can you feel it?"

Vixen du Lac was born in the Bronx, in New York City. Prior to moving to Sedona, she ran a pet resort in Colorado. After the end of a difficult marriage and a robbery of her home, she arrived in Arizona with minimal belongings five years before I met her. In her own words, she had to start all over again with no money at age sixty. Before Colorado she had lived in Los Angeles, where she was a "great burlesque queen," who also acted in a few soft-core porn movies. In Sedona, she worked as a psychic and pet psychic, offering readings for a fee. When I was there, she did this from her home, but she had previously worked in one of the new age stores in the Uptown district. However, she made a distinction between herself, a real practitioner, and the "corporate" or "commercial" practitioners who were only in it for the money. She associated Uptown with the phony side of Sedona. Money corrupted spirituality, in her opinion, and she spoke often about how spirituality was not for sale. Although she rented out the spare room in her house to guests, she claimed not to make a profit, barely keeping a roof over her head. She saw herself as helping others, helping their "souls." She had been given her psychic gifts to help people, not profit from them.

However, the issue of money came up a lot in talking to Vixen and her associates. They would often say they were trying to manifest money. "Manifestation" was a term I came to hear often in Sedona, and it had the sense of effortlessly or miraculously creating things that were needed or desired. Manifestation created abundance, and although abundance could be anything—good health, love, crystals—it was most often used to refer to money. Vixen would often wax lyrical in one breath about how she did not have much to live off because her work was too important and it was wrong to charge people for something that was for the good of humanity, and then in the next breath about how she used to have so much more when she was in LA. She claimed to be able to sit back and sell her old movie merchandise, which had a cult following especially in Japan and Germany, or she could charge people for workshops and seminars in her house to make money, but she did not want to because what she had to do was too important. Profiting from spirituality was wrong, but manifesting abundance was somehow different, a more spiritual mode of exchange.

The importance of her mission was, for Vixen, derived from the imminent ascension. Also called the shift, this was a transformation to not only a higher state of consciousness but also a different ontological state. When I arrived in late July 2012, Vixen told me it was coming soon, coinciding with the end of the Mayan Long Count calendar on 21st December. Her mission was to help prepare people by holding performances of fire dancing, poetry, music, and humming as a way to help raise the frequency of the vibration of the energy. Those with a high enough vibration would ascend with the planet, perhaps taken up on crystal ships, a motif that often fluttered through her phrases without finding a coherent denotation. Stomach aches were a sign of ascension, she told me. Others I spoke to in Sedona informed me of various different ascension symptoms, such as getting very hot and then cold. A local musician sardonically quipped that people in Sedona had "ascension syndrome."

In any case, there were many murmurings that the planet was evolving and humans had to evolve with it or else . . . what? This was never entirely clear. There seemed to be a tension between a sense that everything was going to happen because of the divine powers of the universe and the sense that humans had to do something before it was all too late. It was unclear

FIGURE 2. West Sedona, with Thunder Mountain in the background.

to me whether the universe was going to take care of us or whether we had to save ourselves. If only those with high enough vibrational frequencies would survive the ascension or if those with lower vibrational levels would also come along for the ride. Would the crystal ships still come if no one watched Vixen hum?

A self-described walker between worlds, Vixen was not only a psychic. She also called herself a Pleiadian walk-in, which meant that she had an alien consciousness in her body that was from the Pleiades star system. The being had entered her some time ago, she was not specific about when, but thought that it was possibly during one of her surgeries. It gave her the mission of teaching people the truth through edutainment, which was why she made multiple attempts to put on performances to help educate and entertain audiences through music and breathing exercises. Through the breathing, which she called toroid breathing because that was the shape of the energy pattern it created, she said she became an individual vortex. This technique had cured her of hepatitis B, she claimed. When instructing others to do this, she told them to breathe through the neck, and when she did it she vocalized in a manner that reminded me of the *Star Wars* character Darth Vader. At the beginning of auditions, rehearsals, and during performances, she would stop and instruct everyone present to breathe in this manner, saying "mmm," what a "delicious" vibration. She called these her "projects" and each had its own website and Facebook page, with colorfully enigmatic names like Sonic Harmoniks, Occupy Self, and M3.

This mission continued, yet she was unclear whether the Pleiadian was still in her or not, and she always spoke in the first person, never the third. She told me that everyone is an alien being, as our souls have been incarnated on other worlds before we entered the bodies we have on this world. Everything is energy, and so the energy that constituted physical beings on Earth had been part of countless other beings on other planets and in other dimensions previously.

Places, too, had specific energy patterns. The energy of Sedona meant the population was very transient, Vixen told me; some people could not stay, they were spit out by Sedona. This evoked an image of Sedona as a person, discharging those she found unpalatable. Vixen told me there were layers upon layers in Sedona. People participating in hidden practices, who you would not know what they did unless you got the right introduction. She hinted that she worked with people on wondrous things that she could not discuss. You can stay on the outside very easily, she warned me; most tourists do, they only see the four main vortexes. I asked if there were more and she snorted, "Of course!" There were many. I asked if the whole city was a vortex and she said yes, with many different access points. What this meant was that it had a very intense level of energy. Yet each person had their own path and their own energy and created their own experience.

Vixen asserted that I would not be able to group people in Sedona, as they were all individuals. At the same time, she was not above giving advice on the right way to do things and the wrong people with whom to associate. The stores in Uptown offering crystals and psychic readings were "phony." And when it came time for me to move out of the Cosmic Portal and find a room to rent long-term, she advised me to use the Arizona Conscious Communications email list. If I sent out an email saying exactly what I wanted, it would come to me. At first, I thought she was suggesting that this particular list would be efficacious because so many people in the town subscribed to it. But it was not so, she was explaining to me how energy worked. By writing an email and sending it out, I was declaring to the universe what I wanted. In this way, I would manifest the exact room I desired. What you put out there came back to you.

This meant that if people were unable to stay in Sedona, it was because they were not meant to be there. Equally, if they were poor, it was because that was the experience they had created for themselves. Yet I wondered: if everyone was equally capable of creating any reality for themselves, why did some people have so much more than others? Indeed, Vixen herself was a person of humble means. She received food stamps, a program sponsored by the state government that provided those with low incomes a certain amount of money each month that could be used for food. A neighbor brought her food from the food bank, run by a local church that gave out free food boxes for those under a specified level of income. When these sources were exhausted, she would occasionally bounce checks to buy groceries. Her main source of income was renting out the spare room in her house to tourists, contravening a local ordinance in place at the time against short-term rentals and endangering her own tenancy. She lived precariously, trying to balance her material needs with her spiritual mission. Often in her rhapsodies, she would say she had less than $100 in her bank account or she was on her last $100. This was always suffixed with claims that she could make money, it would be easy, but she would rather be happy, in love, and continue with her mission. She reframed her poverty as a choice, an experience she had created for herself deliberately because it served a higher purpose than being personally wealthy.

Still, she complained about the food from the food bank because it was not organic, and she rarely seemed to eat. The first week I stayed with her, I realized that the only thing I saw her eat was some fried shrimp, and only five of those. She fed her dog more than she fed herself. Yet she took a lot of vitamin and supplement pills. There was a cupboard in her house full of supplements, and she seemed to take a handful of different pills each day. When I asked her about health insurance, as an indirect way to address her health issues, she told me she had no health insurance because she did not get much security due to the political situation, "you know, what's really going on." When I asked what that meant, she told me about the New World Order and the dark rulers of the underground, even providing a complicated chart of conspiratorial interconnections between various groups such as the Rothschilds, the Communist Party of America, and the Freemasons. Although that did not seem to me to explain her lack of health insurance, it pointed toward the darkness lurking on the underside of the love and light in Sedona. Things were not as they seemed; there were shadowy forces pulling the strings, trying to prevent the spiritual development of the people. As I journeyed deeper into the vortex, I began to see how intertwined the darkness and the light, the material and the spiritual, were.

SEEKING

Arriving in July 2012, I encountered Sedona on the cusp of a transition. Digital platforms, particularly YouTube, were increasingly used for dissemination of information and acquiring followers, just as local laws were changing to accommodate "sharing" sites, such as Airbnb and Uber. New economic and social potentials produced by these platforms played a part in transformations in the heterodox religiosity for which Sedona was known as a focal point. The label "new age" no longer held wide purchase for those involved in this heterodoxy. Talking to psychotherapists-turned-past life regressionists and kombucha-brewing crystal wearers, they told me they were not new agers, they were not woo woo. The two were transposable in Sedona: woo woo meant new age and new age was woo woo. Nobody chose to be associated with either. They were simply choosing what served them, consciously co-creating their reality for the highest good, leaving behind what did not serve them while all the time embodying light and love. This was spirituality.

Ask a scholar of religion what spirituality is, and how it is different from religion, and you will likely receive a tortuously nuanced reply.[1] Ask a well-heeled retiree in Sedona, and you might get a snort of derision. However, for those actively engaged in it, spirituality was a path, a route through life that they divined by aligning themselves with the frequency of the vibration of the energy of the universe. In Sedona, I found a constellation of ideas and practices clustered around the central concept of energy as an all-pervasive force. "The universe" was a pantheistic conception of divinity. Aligning with the energy of the universe meant going through progressive stages of enlightenment described as a spiritual path. And there was a millenarian belief that a new paradigm was replacing the old paradigm, also called variously the Age of Aquarius, the shift, or the ascension.[2]

Change was coming; that much was known. Change was already happening. The prevailing impression was that this change was positive. The overwhelming optimism I had already experienced in America generally was magnified in Sedona in an attitude epitomized in the common refrain "light and love," and the ascension meant more of this, for everyone. Anything negative could be overcome with a positive attitude that flipped the switch and illuminated only the bright side. Yet there was a darkness lining the edges of this bright side. It peered out through asides about "them" and mutterings about the "powers that be." A few weeks before the 2012 presidential election in November, I got the shuttle up from Phoenix airport to Sedona, and the van driver told me unprompted about his near-death experience after passing a blood clot through his heart, what the other side was like, and how God was energy, permeating every living thing. Then he darkly segued into the unfairness of the Affordable Care Act, the dangers of Obama's socialism, and how the true purpose of the United Nations was one world government. The country was headed for civil war, he told me, it would happen soon. At the time the juxtaposition of light and love with imminent catastrophe seemed jarring to me. As my fieldwork progressed, and then more acutely in the years that followed, I began to grasp the connection. The dark forecasts were the problem to which spirituality offered a solution.

Spirituality was a space between religion and science, incorporating both but adhering to the norms of neither. An ongoing continuation of nineteenth-century formations of secularism, it still rattled with the haunted metaphysics of American Protestantism.[3] However, the twenty-first century brought its own dynamics. New media forms, modes of exchange, and digital interconnections swirled in a conflux of currents that both promised new possibilities and undermined old assumptions. Widening gaps between the rich and the poor, a hollowing out of the middle class, and rapidly exacerbating ecological crises gave new impetus to the millenarian utopianism that spirituality offered. Within this fragile moment, the local spiritual scene of Sedona looked to the stars, beyond the political formation of the United States, to a planetary, even cosmic scale for renewal.

The small town of around 17,000 inhabitants[4] stands within a series of striking red rock canyons that earned it a reputation as both a spiritual center and a luxury tourist resort. The two crossed over in the wellness retreats and metaphysically marketed spa packages offered by high-end hotels and tour companies. Among the three to four million annual tourists, Sedona also drew thousands every year who were explicitly seeking spiritual experiences. Several of the rock outcrops around the town were named vortexes, sites of spiraling energy both subtle and powerful. A range of smaller businesses, such as crystal shops, psychic readers, and vortex tours, catered to this more niche demand. There were numerous stores in the Uptown shopping district that were called something to do with the new age, such as Center for the New Age or Crystal Vortex. Yet the people I knew who were involved in spirituality and lived there year-round had their homes primarily on the other side of the town, called West Sedona. They were not the purchasers of luxury spa packages, but the service providers working for the corporations that sold them. They disdained Uptown and its gaudy stores as too commercial and just for tourists, much as Vixen had. The crossover of religion and economics was not always a comfortable intersection to inhabit.

Many traveled to Sedona from the centers of population in the United States and northwest Europe to visit, some stayed longer, and a few made it their permanent home. This constant migratory flow in and out of the small town made my own presence and position there legible. As a white-coded European English speaker, I easily slipped into the category of acceptable immigrant. Another tourist who stayed on, drawn by the energy. My interlocutors found me helpful, a friend with a car and a flexible schedule, always ready to volunteer for their projects and practices. Vixen put me to work in backstage support for her performances. I was useful but not yet on a spiritual path myself. Another rootless visitor in a place of spiritual pilgrims.

Yet as much as it may be thought of as a pilgrimage site, spirituality in Sedona is not like Catholicism in Lourdes or Islam in Mecca.[5] Most of the residents of the town were not involved in spirituality. The economy was centered on tourism, it was a resort and retirement community, with high real estate prices, popular with second-home owners and snowbirds (people, often elderly, who move south during the winter months). Those that did come there because they felt called by the special energy lived on the margins, rarely grouped as the "spiritual community," barely considered in the decisions of local power brokers. A lack of group identity was not seen as a problem, though. Following the spiritual path was a personal pursuit for my interlocutors; each person's spiritual path was their own to discern. The individual was placed rhetorically at the center of this formulation of spirituality.[6] Its most striking difference from American Christianity was perhaps this lack of a notion of a collective of believers equivalent to a church, that joined together (like a congregation), agreed on a shared set of core principles (like a creed), and shared a portion of its resources (like a tithe). This marked a radical shift in American religion away from congregations as the focus of religious life.[7]

Spirituality takes inspiration from a different set of interlocking traditions in American religion than congregationalism. It grows from Transcendentalist, spiritualist, and esotericist roots, flowering alongside the growth of science and secularism, found in different locations in America and globally.[8] It continues the historical current of metaphysical religion in America, as a contemporary living phenomenon.

Despite these historical particularities, the universalizing tendencies in spirituality de-historicize and de-locate culturally specific practices, making it seem like a product of the multiform monster named Modernity. Its embeddedness in social and cultural institutions and discourses remains, however. Like science, like secularity, it seems to spring forth *sui generis* around the world as a rational answer to a world losing its religious and epistemological hegemonies. Yet it is precisely this self-asserted singularity that requires strongest interrogation. If the individual is the locus of spirituality, how does it spread, how does it grow, how does it garner support? Is this individualism, as rugged and mythical as that attributed to the Western frontier, merely a rhetorical flourish? And if not, what is "the individual"? What is its shape, and where are its boundaries? And crucially, who gets to claim the status of an individual, and who remains to be seen as a representative of their group?

In the present volume, the interconnections between spirituality and political economy, class and race flow from ethnographic vignettes recorded in Sedona and the surrounding areas.[9] Small stories, from out-of-the-way places, told by people who seem marginal, unimportant, and strange, connect to larger narratives of culture and history in a land marked by captivity and empire.[10] I present personal stories of spiritual paths wending their way through the unstable ground of the gig economy and the digital platforms that support it. Aligning with the energy of the universe to manifest reality is mirrored by a largely unseen infrastructure that enables goods and services to appear at the touch of a screen and labor to be further distanced from capital as workers are rebranded as subcontractors. Manifestation is the operative mode of spirituality and also the digitized gig economy.

I use this approach as a way to evoke the daily unfolding of a religious form that lacked centralized institutions, accepted scriptures, leading authorities, and many of the other defining features of "a religion" as defined in the Euro-American theologically inspired intellectual tradition.[11] Narratives illustrate the multivariate ways my interlocutors lived their spiritual paths, avoiding a false impression of unity, yet at the same time showing the interdependence of people who view themselves as individuals with a discrete, bounded sense of "self." This sense of self is a necessary precondition for the idea of a path that leads to a dissolution of the self as it (re)integrates with the universe. It is also a necessary precondition for a subcontractor working with minimal rights and benefits for a corporation that characterizes their labor as "sharing." Freedom is the promise, yet what results is the deferred empowerment of the self.

There remains an unsatisfying loose end in this talk of spirituality. What is spirituality? The problem with the term is perhaps not its lack of definition but its surfeit. Talking about spirituality seems to force scholars to rethink, to reflect on, to revise religion itself. Indeed, my interlocutors shared this impulse, strenuously differentiating spirituality from religion, by which they meant organized, institutional religion, and what they were often implicitly referring to was American Christianity, of the type in which many of them had grown up. They were often far more comfortable asserting what spirituality was not than describing what it was. When thinking of the complexities and variations of Christianity cross-culturally and historically, I am loath to impose any fixed definition beyond an acknowledgment of Jesus as the son of God. So it goes with spirituality. If Christianity is Jesus-talk, spirituality is energy-talk.

In this spirit, I situate spirituality within the already amorphous boundaries of religion and something far more capacious, the complexes of words and actions that gesture toward the human capacity to imagine other worlds.[12] The imaginal capacity of humans, so central to sociality, works through narratives, both personal and cultural, passed down from one generation to the next, codified in laws, left unsaid in customs, embodied in practices. Narratives create an invisible halo around certain people based on the roles they are assigned and not simply the way they comport themselves in that role. Your mother is still your mother, even if her mothering is found wanting. A priest has stature beyond the manner in which he fulfills his duties, sprung from the power and authority of the tradition that consecrates him.

The stories of spirituality are still new, with novel themes; sometimes they seem ridiculous, often lacking the aura of authenticity and seriousness of ancient religious stories. In Sedona, special status was assumed, sometimes ascribed, but never taken for granted. There was a constant negotiation of who could claim which power, which status, which role, and who would accept that. An incipient spiritual leader could rise high one day on the backs of his followers, who saw him as an enlightened starseed with the ability to instantly manifest his reality as he chose. The next day he could find himself alone, scorned by accusations that he was starting a cult, seeking only money and sexual favors, and was nothing more than a common narcissist. The ensuing chapters elucidate roles such as starseed, shaman, and dark cabal, and the status of food, vortexes, and ascension as they are forged into specific shapes, and the imagining of the world in Sedona takes a particular cast. To begin, I provide a basic sketch of the cosmologies taking form, suggested by long-term engagement in this milieu, as a way to unpack terms and concepts that are inflected differently in this context from the norm.

COSMOLOGIES OF SPIRITUALITY

Energy is the central organizing concept of cosmologies of spirituality in Sedona. Everything is energy; it composes the substance of everything in the universe. Energy vibrates at specific frequencies and this creates the appearance of mass. Mass is merely an illusion, an effect of living in the third dimension.[13] The dimension we are currently in, the third, is characterized by a morally valenced conception of density. Things that are dense are a heavy drag upon the spirit, keeping it down in the third dimension. Good energy, good vibrations, are characterized as light and uplifting. There is an emotional level to this correspondence. Sadness, anger, bitterness are all heavy, dense, third-dimensional emotions, whereas happiness, love, and trust have a higher vibration. Raising the frequency of vibration by being positive emotionally is one way of ascending through the progressive levels called dimensions, a process called ascension. Energy crisscrosses the earth in a grid pattern of "ley lines," the intersections of which are called vortexes and are figured as spirals. Sedona's position at one such intersection is the explanation often given for why it has such special energy and why so many spiritual seekers feel called there. This infusion of the landscape with special powers, even agency, is the subject of chapter three.

Ascension operates on both a personal level and a planetary level, referring to a movement toward higher dimensions with higher levels of spiritual development. Certain committed persons will ascend quicker than the planet as a whole. The ultimate aim of ascension is to achieve oneness with the universe, which is sometimes also called source or spirit. There are parallels with both Christian theological and gnostic conceptions of leaving the material behind for the sake of the spiritual. Energy is an attracting force: since like attracts like, something with good or high energy will attract the same. Energy is something felt rather than seen or touched. Psychics in particular would tell me they feel a person's energy and tell them where it is going rather than directly reading thoughts or seeing the future. Channelers and healers direct energy from the universe and use it to receive messages and heal, respectively. Energy cannot be destroyed, so death is the transference of energy to another form, either in this dimension or to a higher or lower one, a process referred to as reincarnation.

There is a motility to energy. It flows, it vibrates, and through these movements it creates the illusion of mass. This creative force of energy was termed manifestation. In simple terms, manifestation was creating or making something happen. This was how each person's choices created their own reality. Raising or lowering the frequency of the vibration manifested either positivity or negativity. The aim was to consciously manifest positivity, which would produce abundance. There was a specific monetary association with the term "manifesting abundance," to the extent that it was often used as shorthand for making money. How to earn money was a particular anxiety for those following a spiritual path because doing so in a negative way could have adverse consequences for one's spiritual development. The ideal, therefore, was to make money through spiritual practice, which meant there would be no separation between work and spirituality. Consequently there was a moral valence to different forms of economic exchange.

The spiritual path is at its core consciously choosing to raise one's vibration through action, thought, and speech. It was described as beginning within each person and then expanding outward in an almost osmotic process. As each person turns away from materialistic concerns toward their spiritual path, a new society is created with a new economy. This change comes about not through organized, collective action but through a critical mass formed of individuals acting independently that then triggers a change in collective reality.[14] By some this is termed the new paradigm; others call it the shift or ascension. It is a period of revolutionary change heralding the ascent of spirituality over materialism, cooperation over competition, peace over war, sharing over greed, heart over head, feeling over thinking, intuition over logic. Astrologically this is framed as the movement from the Age of Pisces to the Age of Aquarius.[15] The origin of this use of the term "new age" was in early twentieth-century Theosophical Society materials, particularly the pamphlets of Alice Bailey announcing the imminent beginning of the Age of Aquarius and return of Christ.[16] Those already on the spiritual path are the vanguard of this revolutionary change, which affects every aspect of their lives from where they live to how they eat to how they earn their money.

The term "energy" is ubiquitous in spirituality, used to refer to god, the universe, and everything. This capaciousness suggests energy is a symbol, one so expansive that it resembles a floating signifier, so filled by its contradictory semiotic potential that it overflows and empties out entirely. In the

cobwebbed history of anthropological theory, Claude Lévi-Strauss referred
to the archetypal floating signifier, *mana*, as a pure symbol that operated on
the strength of its semantic function regardless of its paradoxical nature.[17]
The *mana*-debate inaugurated in the early twentieth century by Émile
Durkheim, Marcel Mauss, and Henri Hubert located it as an *ur*-concept of
religion, a basic category of human consciousness, found universally, with
different linguistic glosses cross-culturally. Without adopting the social evo-
lutionist paradigm inherent in the work of these theorists, there are discernible similarities between *mana* in early sociological theory and energy in
spirituality. *Mana* is "a force, a being . . . an action, a quality, a state" all at the
same time.[18] Energy could easily be given each of these descriptors, but it fits
particularly well with Durkheim's explanation of *mana* as an "impersonal
force," which both has no definite location and is everywhere, and is both
a physical force and moral principle.[19] The term "energy" even features as a
synonym in the translation of Durkheim's discussion of *mana* and totem.
There is, perhaps, more than mere coincidental resemblance between social
theories of an *ur*-principle undergirding a universal category of religion and
the universalizing claims of energy as everything and everywhere.

Energy is not an undifferentiated ether, however. It has certain properties and characteristics. Vibration is the integral property of energy. Just as
everything is energy, all energy vibrates, and vibration occurs at different
frequencies. This enables the production of hierarchy. A high vibration is
associated with being more spiritual and having special powers, such as
invisibility or levitation. Changing vibration is a way of changing the self.
Walking the spiritual path was often described by my interlocutors as raising their vibration. Frequency is the speed of the vibration, and it is measured in hertz (Hz). It is often used in reference to sounds. My first host in
Sedona, Vixen du Lac, told me that 432 Hz is the heart frequency, so new
paradigm music is made on this frequency because as a loving frequency
it helps raise the vibration, whereas heavy metal and Christian music have
a low frequency, with no use of 432 Hz. This lowers the vibration and can
cause evil and self-harm. The concepts of energy, frequency, and vibration
are intimately connected and are often used interchangeably.

Energy, frequency, and vibration are characteristics of the universe, an
immanent pantheistic conception of divinity, which is also called source,
spirit, or more rarely God. Using the term "source" highlights that it is the
origin of everything; I also heard the words "zero-point" and "singularity"
used. It is an idea influenced by Neoplatonism of a single source out of which
all creation emanates. While energy is to some extent isomorphic with the

universe because the universe is everything and everything is energy, it is more nuanced than that. Energy is the ripples emanating out of source that create reality; the universe is composed of energy vibrating at different frequencies. The higher the frequency of the vibration of the energy, the closer to the universe, which is the highest vibration but at the same time contains all other vibrations. The spiritual path raises the frequency of vibrations, elevating beings and planets closer to the universe and reuniting with source.

The universe is not an agentive divinity, in the sense that it does not mete out punishment or answer prayers. Instead, it reflects back the energy that beings put out. Happy thoughts reflect back positive vibrations from the universe, negative thoughts reflect back negativity. Positivity and wellness are therefore morally valenced because through good speech and action beings are manifesting the reality of the dimension they inhabit. Yet while it is not agentive in this way, the universe is still held responsible for things: "the universe wants you to have this," "I asked the universe for such and such," "you need to trust in the universe." As a reflection of the self, trusting in the universe is trusting in the self. It is the self that is actually being held responsible. This is the principle of oneness. A common phrase among my interlocutors was "we are all one," meaning that we are all of the same substance, we are all divine, only our experience is different. The point of existence is to experience this difference. Life is a way for divinity to experience itself in infinite forms. In a channeling session, the channeler described what he was doing as "it's just me talking to myself as you."[20]

Existence is an illusion of separation. We perceive ourselves as separate beings composed of dense mass because of our incarnation in the third dimension. Different dimensions grant different perspectives and even different sensory abilities, which is why, for example, we cannot see aliens but they can see us. But beyond this illusion is an inherent oneness of all things. There follows from this principle a rejection of dualisms, such as good/evil, male/female, you/me, which is sometimes noticed by scholars when describing the new age.[21] These dualisms are an effect of living in this dimension, and as such, following the spiritual path means evolving beyond such notions. This proved difficult in practice, however, and there was often a tension between holding the cosmological principle of non-dualistic oneness in theory and the practicality of living separate, discrete existences in Sedona.

The principle of oneness is why everything is interconnected, because it is all part of the same energy of the universe. Nothing is random, everything means something, because everything is connected energetically. If a coincidence occurs, it is actually pointing to a larger "truth" or mission.

Coincidence is called synchronicity and interpreted as the universe sending messages.[22] Again, this is not to say that the universe is exercising agency but that the energy that vibrates out from source hits certain frequencies that resonate with particular beings. Paying attention to synchronicities is a way of reading the signs that suggest how to follow the spiritual path. This resonance is a sign that activating that particular frequency will bring that being into alignment with the energy of the universe. Alignment has the sense of being in harmony; sometimes the word "attunement" is also used, meaning being in tune with the frequency of the energy of the universe. The aim is to align the self with the universe through going on the spiritual path, which is a way back to oneness by raising the frequency of the vibration of the energy until it resonates in harmony with the universe in oneness. When this happens, the self will disappear, the illusion of separation will fade.

Successfully aligning the self with the frequency of the energy of the universe leads to ascension up through the dimensions toward source. The universe is composed of multiple dimensions. We live in the third dimension, which is a dense dimension of matter with a relatively low vibration where many of the abilities associated with higher vibrations, such as invisibility, levitation, or instant manifestation, are not possible except to certain high-vibrational beings. The density of the third dimension is the cause of misery and suffering in this world. It is theodicy, spirituality's answer to the question of why evil exists. Some beings in this dimension are able to simultaneously inhabit higher dimensions because of their high vibration. These are the spiritual teachers, ascended masters, and starseeds who have achieved awakening and begun their personal ascension, an experience outlined in chapter three.

The concept of dimension suggests the influence of twentieth-century theoretical physics, particularly quantum theory and multiverses, which will be discussed in more detail below. However, dimension is used as a religious motif meaning something analogous to planes of existence rather than as scientifically quantifiable phenomena. Dimensions are a way of accessing other realms of consciousness, sometimes through achieving altered states of consciousness, as the mind has to be altered to perceive other dimensions. Higher dimensions have been theorized by physicists, artists, and writers since the nineteenth century as a means to conceptualize a space that exists beyond ordinary human perception.[23] For example, biblical scholar and author Edwin Abbott wrote *Flatland* in 1884 about a square that discovers the third dimension through an encounter with a sphere, revealing hitherto imperceptible dimensions of existence.[24] Artist Marcel Duchamp suggested that the fourth dimension was not time in the physicists' sense but the unrepresentable domain beyond the "ordinary" world that encompassed it and was "the real" world.[25] Since 2D objects cast 1D shadows, and 3D objects cast 2D shadows, so a 3D shadow would be cast by a 4D object. The fourth dimension is conceivable but not representable because it requires more dimensions than we have access to in the 3D. The possibility of dimensions beyond ordinary perception has inspired mystical and spiritual speculation alongside theoretical elaboration by physicists. It brings together philosophies of non-duality, which argue that consciousness creates or affects material reality, that cross over and blur any neat boundaries between spirituality and science.

Spirituality is deeply influenced by modern science.[26] For my interlocutors, science describes the same reality as spirituality; however, scientists are limited by their methods, which rely on falsifiable, empirical data and peer-reviewed studies. As one of my Sedona friends put it, metaphysics is better than physics because it goes *beyond* physics. It is possible to know more through metaphysics because it can access non-empirical reality. Clearly the talk about energy, frequency, and vibration is heavily indebted to Einstein's special theory of relativity among others, but it is a religious understanding of it. The displacement of the big bang theory with that of multiverses, where our universe is just one bubble in an ever-expanding sea of universes with the potential for portals between bubbles, is reflected in the cosmology of multiple dimensions as stages of spiritual evolution with reincarnation between multiverses.[27] The cosmology of spirituality seems to echo quantum theory in a similar way to how the big bang theory echoes Christian theologies of creation *ex nihilo*. The concept of energy makes claim to personal effects from the impersonal laws of physics. How one man in Sedona found personal significance in the potential for portals to other dimensions is described in chapter two.

Within the third dimension, reality takes a specific form as mass. Beings thus have bodies: the fleshy, dense 3D corporeal formation of the self. The self is further subdivided into the higher self and the mind. The higher self is also called the soul. It has a higher vibration than the mind or body, and so exists in a higher dimension.[28] The higher self has guides that can be angelic, extraterrestrial, or extradimensional beings. These guides are simply personifications of the energy of the universe, providing a way to make it easier to divine the spiritual path. It is the higher self, along with its guides,

FIGURE 3. Two large crystals on display outside the Center for the New Age, Sedona. Crystals are seen as powerful conduits for spiritual energy. They are one of the most common types of material culture in Sedona.

which is eternal, reincarnating in different forms with different minds and bodies in each lifetime. It is a more positive version of the self because it is in a higher dimension and therefore closer to source.

The mind is also called the ego or the "monkey mind"; it is the most third-dimensional part of the self. While the body can be improved (as outlined in chapter four, it can be made lighter through right diet and exercise), the mind can only be silenced. The mind chatters; it doubts, it needs. All of the negative third-dimensional emotions are the product of the mind. The mind is what undermines self-confidence, it is what manipulates others. Walking the spiritual path is listening to the soul over the mind, learning how to quiet the mind, tune it out, often through meditation, and hear only the higher self, which speaks through intuition. Intuition is the guidance of the soul, located in the heart rather than the head. "Heart-wisdom" is intuition and comes from the higher self, whereas "head logic" or reason comes from the mind or ego. This is a radical inversion of scientific empiricism and the "Western" notion of rationality that elevates internal feelings over the dictates of logic and reason. The new paradigm is built on exactly this shift in thinking, the consequence of which is to cast into doubt many of the social transformations and ideas associated with "progress" and "civilization" and elevate a counter-narrative of conspiracy theories, which is the subject of chapter five.

Some in Sedona did not use these specific words as much as others; however, there was a commonality of concepts behind the different terms used. There is a linguistic flexibility allowed in spirituality, so whether it is called the universe, source, or spirit on one level does not matter because these words mean the same thing, they invoke the same essence. Words are to a certain extent epiphenomenal; what really matters is the energy of what is said. However, on another level, word choice is very important because words have power, they do things. Echoing Jeanne Favret-Saada's ethnography of witchcraft in the French Bocage region, to speak words is to invoke power, not merely give information.[29] This resemblance grows stronger in the common refrain in Sedona that words are spells, which is "why it's called spelling." In practice this meant practicing clean speech, avoiding the word "no," and not speaking negatively, especially about other people in the form of insults or gossip. The vibration of the word is very important. Words both create reality and are epiphenomenal, both constituting what happens and an imprecise gloss over the same essential energy of the universe.

Words have this double nature because while what we perceive in the third dimension seems differentiated, in fact everything comes from the same source and reveals the same higher "truth." What follows from this is that those involved in spirituality pick and choose freely from sources as inspiration, regardless of cultural, religious, or national heritage. Cross-cultural concepts are seen as equivalent; energy is equated with the Holy Spirit, *prana*, *chi*, and *mana*. We return here to the resemblance between energy and the impersonal forces of early sociological theory, which equated *mana* and *prana* with *orenda* in Iroquois, *manitou* in Algonquin, *wakan* in Dakota, *Brahman* from Hinduism, *naual* from Mexico and Central America, and many other terms cross-culturally.[30] This latter term hints at something more than a formal resemblance, perhaps a potential historical link, or common inspiration, for spirituality and early twentieth-century sociological theory. "Nagualism" was popularized by Carlos Castaneda, an author with anthropological training whose numerous works are best classed as mass-market fiction.[31] Castaneda was popular with my interlocutors in Sedona, alongside other authors whose work crossed over the popular-scholarly barrier such as Mircea Eliade and Joseph Campbell. Ideas about impersonal forces, shamans, naguals, and so forth bled through from scholarly works into popular works into personal spiritual paths. Differences attributed to culture, religion, or nation were seen as epiphenomenal. "Culture" was dismissed as merely an appearance of difference that masks the fundamental unity of all things.

While in theory the spiritual path can be influenced by any source, in practice some sources are more popular than others. Native Americans, Tibetan Buddhism, and Catholic Christianity all featured far more frequently in my interlocutors' spiritual paths and aesthetics than other sources. These sources are those seen as more "spiritual" in American culture generally. They are the cultures represented, and misrepresented, most frequently in spiritual literature and websites. While this tendency toward universalism strips spiritual practices and ideas of their cultural and historical specificity, it has its own specific historical trajectory. The universalist tendency in American spirituality traces to at least the works of poet Walt Whitman, one of the nineteenth-century religious liberals for whom the "sympathy of religions" was fundamental.[32] Sympathy was for Whitman and his peers a way of unifying and identifying with others, particularly of overcoming sectarian religious divides.

However, it is now a divisive principle, one that critics often cite as the reason spirituality is inauthentic and appropriating, especially of Native American religious culture.[33] Seeing cultures as freely chosen and free to choose from can obscure power relations. There is an imperialism to universalism. The entities that can pick and choose are those that rule and colonize. The critique of early sociological and anthropological theory as undergirding European colonialism is well known.[34] The idea that cultural differences can be dismissed and overridden is an exercise of power. The universal that is expanded as the norm is an American universal, subsuming all others into itself in not so much sympathy as imperial domination. It is a maneuver that exerts control in both a political and economic sense, allowing other cultures to become not only the inspiration for spiritual paths but also their means of economic support.

The expansiveness of the notion of energy should not obscure its implication in power relations. Energy negotiates equality and hierarchy, being both immanent in everything and also a means of transcendence. Raising the vibration of the energy is how to go beyond the fleshy, earthly third dimension. It is also a way of ranking, assessing the more from the less spiritual, the good from the bad. This reflects an ongoing tension in American social and political life. All people were created equal in America, but the Constitution initially included only white European-descended men in this concept of equality; slaves were excluded as well as women. This tension between equality and hierarchy has been part of the American cultural fabric from the founding of the nation. It is part of the same cultural narrative— the origin story of America—that enshrines a sense of preordained destiny alongside a principle of freedom of the individual.

EVERYTHING HAPPENS FOR A REASON

Browsing the gift section in the organic grocery store in Sedona, I came across a tall mug in turquoise with a picture of a dragonfly and the slogan "Everything happens for a reason, just believe." This was a frequently heard proverb in Sedona, among the spiritual and not, and among Americans I knew more widely.[35] It is a conventional inspirational quote pasted onto stock photos of beautiful landscapes and posted as a meme online. Its ubiquity reaches the status of cliché in American culture. What struck me about this phrase, and led me to buy the mug, was how it summed up a cosmological principle in spirituality while also pointing to an irony in that thinking. Everything happens for a reason because there is a grand design behind all of life's events.

Sometimes this principle is called a "soul contract," but even those who did not use this specific term spoke of an agreement that each soul makes before it incarnates that contains everything that will happen in the lifetime it is about to embark upon. Everything that happens has already been determined and accepted by the soul before each lifetime begins. However, once incarnated the mind does not have access to this contract. It forgets, separating from the soul through being born into third-dimensional density. The newly embodied being must then go about creating their reality as they choose. This is why the signs of the right path need to be discerned by paying attention to synchronicities and the heart wisdom of intuition. Alignment with the energy of the universe is not obvious. Awareness must be developed so that choices are consciously made. Intention must be clear, so that only what is consciously chosen is created, and not what is unconsciously chosen. Without clear intentions and awareness, the unconscious parts of the self, those that are less spiritually developed, could create reality in ways that are not necessarily positive.

Following the spiritual path is fulfilling the soul contract, but implied within this is the possibility that the contract will not be fulfilled. It could even be broken, and thus incarnation continues. So, on one level everything has been agreed to in advance, a form of providence, the belief that there is a divine plan for all things, but on another free will is operating, opening a space for individual agency. This is why I found the mug ironic. If everything happens for a reason, then there is no need to believe or doubt in anything because it has all been predetermined, yet it ends with "just believe," suggesting there is still that space of doubt and belief.

This interaction of providence and individual agency is not unique to spirituality but found throughout American Christianity and cultural narratives more broadly. It goes to a central philosophical question: why are things the way they are? To put it in an anthropological frame, how and why is social reality constituted? Is it the outcome of individual actions or agency, and therefore are we free to live as we choose? Or are there broader structures determining what happens? Are we in fact not free, but the determined products of larger forces? This question goes back to the European colonization of the continent. Puritan colonists saw the settlement of America as a special mission and providence from God.[36] Those promoting westward expansion of the American empire across Native American lands justified genocide through the doctrine of Manifest Destiny, claiming that God provided this land for white conquest. These ideas continue to hold currency in fundamentalist Christian doctrines and American civil religion.[37] "Everything happens for a reason" means that even bad things are not truly bad because they have a higher purpose, it is all a part of God's plan. Yet there are certain groups in America that seem to benefit from God's plan far more than others.

This history is not incidental. The brutality of America's creation is a heavy inheritance. It produces hierarchy indexed by both class and color, and perceived group membership determines possibilities and potentials. Yet the promise of America was meritocracy, that individuals could create their destinies through hard work and faith. The promise always seemed to be made with those able to fit into the historically slippery category of whiteness, as the majority of my interlocutors in Sedona could.[38] While the privileges and benefits of whiteness are many, there is also a sense of guilt bestowed by this inheritance, and perhaps an inherent but unexamined fear of inadequacy.

FIGURE 4. One of the many "new age" stores in Sedona.

Past-life stories offered an imaginative outlet from the strictures of American racial categories. Using a version of the Indian religious concept of karma, some in Sedona talked about working through the karma of misdeeds in the past.[39] My belly dance teacher, a white woman in her forties from Portland, Oregon, with flowing long blond hair and secure employment as the accountant for her grandmother's oil and gas royalties, told me that in a past life she had been a brutal Mongol warlord. In that lifetime she had crossed Asia raping and pillaging, creating ripples of karma throughout her lifetimes, which was why she had been raped herself in every subsequent lifetime. Imagining herself as a racial other, she located a source for her guilt and a cause for her suffering.

It is energy that connects actions in past lives with occurrences in subsequent lives. Living a lifetime like my belly dance teacher described, as a brutal warlord raping and pillaging, created such a huge wave of negative energy that it resonated through every subsequent lifetime. Her soul contract involved suffering the same fate as her previous incarnation's victims. She told me this as a backstory to the account of how she had been raped in her current lifetime by her stepbrother. Providential ideas provide a framework for interpreting misfortune, a way of explaining why a bad thing happened. They also provide a frame for why good things happen. The self-help literature that populates the mind, body, spirit category of publishing is rife with a strain of prosperity consciousness, which promotes visualization and affirmation as techniques for manifesting abundance.[40] Prosperity is a reflection of emotional well-being and advanced spiritual development in a framework that explains why some are successful and some are not. It echoes the prosperity gospel in American Christianity, in which success and wealth are signs of God's grace.[41] This line of thinking shifts the providential frame from being imposed by forces beyond one's control to being influenced by one's behavior. It means you are responsible for everything that happens, everything happens for a reason, and the reason is you.

The history of American prosperity thinking reveals its political implications. In the nineteenth century, proponents of New Thought advocated affirmations and related techniques for clearing the channels of the mind to allow the divine energy of the universe to flow freely, a process of harmonization that would ensure mental and physical health.[42] Repeating positive phrases every day was one way to open channels and thus remain healthy. In the mid-twentieth century, Reformed Church minister Norman Vincent Peale published *The Power of Positive Thinking*, providing ten steps to overcome inadequate attitudes that held one back from personal success. Adding a distinctly Christian inflection to New Thought, Peale popularized a system that can be discerned, with the universe in place of references to the Christian God, in the techniques for manifestation of abundance that I heard about in Sedona. While mainstream academic and religious approval eluded Peale, his popular influence remained. The American president Donald J. Trump went to Peale's church in New York and remains a fan of his work.[43] Positive thinking has become an ideology in American culture that suggests that health, wealth, and success at work are all determined by a positive attitude.[44] Moreover, those that have these attributes deserve them. When things happen for a reason but that reason is one's attitude, then positive thinking becomes a moral imperative.

Positivity is bodily as well as mental. The concept of wellness has sprung up to mandate good health as a moral virtue.[45] There is an ethical imperative to exercise, eat right, and look after the self. This imperative also features strongly in spirituality. Poor health and emotional negativity have a low vibration that is a sign of a lack of spiritual development. Feeling bad and expressing negativity are signs that you are a bad person. Any health crises are to be met as a challenge through which to learn and grow, not dwell and suffer. Right diet, naturopathic remedies, and physical practices such as yoga, as well as positive thinking, are the way to overcome these crises, not going to allopathic doctors or having adequate health insurance, as explored further in chapter four.

The primacy of wellness and positivity has political and economic effects. Through taking personal responsibility for the health of the body and mind, collective policies, such as regarding health coverage, are de-emphasized. Wellness is a way to make productive workers, as witnessed by the popularity of mindfulness training among large corporations. The sick are managed by progressively more punitive policies to induce them to wellness through personal action. Personal responsibility for health obviates the requirement for collective responsibility for healthcare. Collective engagement of social problems is then collapsed into personal quests for the good life. Positivity and wellness ideologies can occlude social problems through suggesting that the cause and remedy are located in the individual and not the social. The advantages accrued to certain collectivities (such as multinational corporations profiting from the sale of insurance, pharmaceuticals, and so on) by defining citizens and workers as individuals, with an individual mandate to take care of their personal health, is one reason the category of "the individual" needs to be treated with some skepticism. It also calls into question the internalization of wellness and positivity ideologies in spirituality. For whom are these positive thoughts creating positive effects?

Sickness, poverty, sadness become personal failures in the ideologies of positivity and wellness. Failure is taboo in America; a subject avoided lest speaking of it invokes its occurrence. These ideologies run strong in spirituality, to the extent that narratives of spiritual paths involve rewriting of economic declines and downward social mobility as spiritual development, as explored in chapters one and three. The energy drew them to Sedona; they often also had plenty to escape from in their former lives. Since it is up to each person to create their own reality as a positive one, it is their own fault if misfortune occurs. They are being too negative, bringing misfortune into their consciousness, and so causing bad things to happen. These ideologies are not separate from class structures and political economic realities in America, the inequalities of which are blurred by the thinking that the root of all problems and also the solutions are within the self.

THE REAL AND THE FAKE

Swami Steve was my meditation teacher in Sedona for almost a year. A bald, tanned man with a neat white beard, he held weekly meditation sessions that he called satsangs at his rented home in West Sedona that he called his ashram. Hailing from Boston, his strong accent made "heart chakra" sound like "hat chakra." He taught that the aim of meditation was to silence the inner dialogue of the mind. Spirituality was about maintaining awareness and presence. There were three stages: asleep, awake, and oneness. Steve became awake in 2001. While driving in California, he stopped at a beach, sat down and meditated, and "bam!" was how he described an experience of immediate awakening. At the time he worked as an engineer and was married with two children. He left his wife, children, and career after Krishna Prem came to see him. He subsequently spent a month in India and was made a sannyasin by Osho at his ashram in Pune.

Krishna Prem was one of the earliest American devotees of Osho, also known as Bhagwan Shree Rajneesh.[46] The Rajneeshis, as his group of adherents was known, were one of the Indian-inspired new religious movements flowering in America during the 1970s and 1980s out of the social and spiritual experimentation of the 1960s.[47] Swami Steve was a living embodiment of this heritage, bringing elements of the previous decades' spiritual experimentation into his meditation practice in Sedona. It was a period of trying on new cultures, especially from "the East," which was associated with mysticism and spirituality. Increasing affluence among middle-class white Americans buttressed the freedom to experiment. They were able to see themselves as individuals without cultural baggage, free to choose, with the power to take.

It would be easy to dismiss Swami Steve as a fake. He did not look or sound like the stereotype of a swami. A white man with a Boston accent talking about chakras at his satsangs in his ashram, he seemed to typify the cultural appropriation for which spirituality is so often critiqued. This critique was internalized among those involved in spirituality in Sedona. Swami Steve told me that 99 percent of Sedona spirituality was not really spiritual, but it kept people busy until they were ready for the real stuff. He called Sedona "candyland," a place of synthetic, sugary treats for the mind to distract from the real work of awakening.

There is another thread in Steve's narrative that I want to tease out: the man who had a successful career as an engineer, with two children, a home, and a wife. He described himself as living the American dream. This resonant cultural myth tells a story of how upward social mobility and economic security are available to those who work hard, regardless of their background. Embodied in literature by characters like Horatio Alger, who pulled himself up from humble origins by his bootstraps, the American dream tells a tale of meritocracy that denies the influence of a class structure or racial hierarchy.[48] Steve described how he lost faith in the American dream and turned to spirituality instead. It provided him with an alternative aspiration to the grind of constant material accumulation and economic prosperity. Continuing the zeitgeist of 1960s and 1970s spiritual experimentation, it gave a new way of imagining how the world could be.

During the increased affluence of the 1960s to the relative instability of the 1970s, economic conditions in America interacted with religious possibilities. The following decades witnessed the emergence of both neoliberalism and spirituality. Replacing Keynesian social capitalism of the early twentieth century, neoliberalism is a form of pure capitalism in which inequality has become extreme.[49] Neoliberalism is often used vaguely as a buzzword; however, it can be used with more precision as a series of policies implemented by national and local governments first in North America and Western Europe and then imposed globally, through which the social safety net was cut and the market was allowed to dictate the terms of exchange. There is a similarity of form with spirituality, in which four defining characteristics stand out: financialization, privatization, deregulation, and individual responsibility.

Financialization is the principle that everything is potentially monetizable and everything can be understood in terms of market calculations. In spirituality, people try to make their living off their spiritual practice, with no institutional support; their religion and even the self is monetizable. *Privatization* is when ownership of public assets is moved into private hands, shifting from a service that meets the needs of the public even if it loses money to an enterprise that must turn a profit for the benefit of shareholders. In a similar shift in animus from public to private, in spirituality practice is determined by individual practitioners, not a corporate body of a congregation with a leadership able to create rules governing that body, which is often named as part of a wider trend called the privatization of religion. *Deregulation* is the removal of government rules and regulations curtailing economic sectors. In spirituality there are few rules governing what is or is not valid practice that can be imposed by any overarching body. *Individual responsibility* means that everything that happens is attributed to individual agency. In economic terms, this means the poor are held responsible for their situation and not offered help through social welfare provision. In spirituality, as previously outlined, this produces prosperity consciousness and the "Law of Attraction," that you create your reality through your actions, words, and thoughts.[50] The frequency of the vibration of your energy affects everything that happens to you, so do not complain, do not critique, do not try to hold others responsible for what happens to you. Following the energy of the universe becomes a way of blaming the self and denying social impacts, which reifies existing power relations. The rich and powerful deserve to be so, as do the poor deserve their lot. Neoliberalism and spirituality share some formal or structural similarities, and they both emerged during the same historical moment of the late 1970s to early 1980s in the industrial capitalist liberal democracies of North America and Western Europe. This historical co-emergence suggests a deeper connection.

However, this is not a simple case of subscribing to the various sociological critiques of spirituality that it is a consumerist commodification of religion.[51] Rather, there is a similar set of social conditions during this period co-constituting transformations in both political economy and religion.[52] What these conditions could be is suggested by David Graeber, who analyzes the interaction of markets, currency, and economics with other social forms, suggesting that Eurasian history (including the United States, post-conquest) can be broken down into cycles of virtual credit currency in the form of IOUs alternating with currency in the form of metal coinage.[53] The most recent transition in this cycle started in 1971 when Richard Nixon abandoned the gold standard and the Bretton Woods agreement, precipitating another phase of virtual money in which the US dollar became the reserve currency for many states. This laid the foundation for the proliferation of neoliberal policies under the administrations of Ronald Reagan, George H. W. Bush, and Bill Clinton.

With the erasure of the materiality of money comes the proliferation of incorporeal modes of exchange, not only credit mechanisms but also securities, derivatives, and other financial instruments.[54] Lacking materiality, money has been accumulated on ever vaster scales, and the gap between those who have excessive wealth and the rest of the population has also expanded. This exacerbating inequality is enabled by the expansion of the size and influence of financial institutions, in which the market operates as the central organizing principle for all things. Spirituality is the complement to neoliberalism; the spiritual side of its pure capitalism. The financialization of everything in economic life has been accompanied by the spiritualization of everything in religious life. The immateriality of money takes on spiritual significance when money is seen as energy. Making money becomes manifesting abundance, and earning a wage can be imagined as consonant with spiritual development. The morality of exchange comes into question because how you make your money is part of how you develop spiritually.

An economic realm devoid of materiality but inundated by materialism came into being alongside spiritual forms that place particular and peculiar emphasis on the individual as the unit of religious action. In socially conservative fundamentalist Christianity, the personal relationship of the saved and born-again believer with God is central, and in spirituality, the personal spiritual path reunites the self with the universe. Both also have variants of prosperity discourse. Where each person creates their own reality, ultimate responsibility for what happens resides in their behavior and choices. However, what I wish to highlight through the epigraph to this introduction is that the ability to create reality is a mark of power. Gaining acceptance of your reality as valid is an exercise of power; equally, to have your reality invalidated is to be declared insane or otherwise have your claim to personal agency dismissed. Money, too, is an exercise of power. The sovereign determines which currency is valid. Consider how the American version of the sovereign, the president, declared dollars to no longer be convertible to gold. To be sovereign is to have the power to define. In spirituality, it is suggested that each person is a god or goddess; in effect, each person is sovereign in their own personal definition of the universe.

Yet any fall into solipsism will quickly land on hard limits. To suggest, to believe, that you are able to create your own reality according to your will is one thing. To make it happen is another. There is always a gap between theories of non-duality and the hard reality of matter. This gap is especially acute when an analogical leap is made between the theoretical proposition that at a subatomic level there is no mass to the religious proposition that thoughts, actions, beliefs shape and mold reality. If consciousness is crucial to how reality is experienced, human will and agency is central to that experience. Spirituality is a collection of practices that cultivate the will so that what occurs interior to consciousness aligns with what is experienced exterior in material reality.

Swami Steve's practice was meditation. Through meditation he became awake and aware, aligned with the energy of the universe so there was no gap between what he experienced externally and internally. Often in class, he would describe the benefit of meditation as allowing him never to be surprised. He walked down the street and a bottle rocket was suddenly exploded behind him by some teenagers, but he was so aware of everything through his meditation practice that he did not startle. Yet Steve remained constrained by hard material limits that he did not control. It was following his path that led Steve to abandon his career in engineering; it led him to

Sedona, where to maintain his ashram he sublet the rooms of a house he rented to others who sought to meditate and learn from him. Living outside institutional structures granted freedom, but also left him more exposed to the vicissitudes of the market and the state. After I left Sedona, he lost the ashram when he found he was unable to find reliable subletters for an extended period and advertised his services via social media as a handyman and housesitter instead. The ebbs and flows of fortune were common for those trying to pursue their spiritual path. While he may have rejected his previous life that he characterized as following the American dream, he was rejecting something that was no longer on offer. The term "American dream" was used by my older interlocutors, such as Steve, to characterize the life they had left behind, chasing material success by earnestly climbing the career ladder to pay their mortgage. But these were empty symbols of the past for my younger interlocutors. There was no career ladder to climb, little hope of owning their own home, or having enough long-term security to start a family. They lived in rented accommodation, worked on temporary contracts, hustling through various digital platforms, or picking up shifts in the tourism industry. Their lives were unstable, free of contractual obligations but undermined by lack of benefits, continually disrupted.

The new economy downshifted expectations and potentials, emptying out the middle class.[55] Following a spiritual path offered an alternative interpretation of these circumstances that neutralized critique. Spirituality denies class. There is no inequality; its appearance is an illusion of the third dimension. Cosmologies of spirituality have no space to map social inequality. Ascension dissolves class divisions and inequality; by taking care of the self spiritually, social inequality (and race and gender discrimination) will be overcome. Paying attention to such human concepts—we might call them social constructions—is, in the frame of spirituality, being bound by third-dimensional concepts. Instead, those on the spiritual path should pay attention to the self, purified of such limiting concepts. The self in spirituality is seen as separate from occupation or class or race. The effect is a doubling down on individual actions as a response to collective, social problems. Culture is epiphenomenal, manifestation overcomes its constructions.

Individualism must therefore be interrogated critically. In this context, the self is the core of the individual and society is composed of individuals. This view of society as an aggregate of individuals is the product of the historical tradition named individualism, a term coined by Alexis de Tocqueville in reference to the social atomization he observed in America.[56] The

FIGURE 5. A mural on the side of the Center for the New Age.

American citizen is individual, both an independent agent and a productive worker; one necessitates the other. The spiritual path fuses the independent agent and the productive worker into one divinized but also monetizable self. Being god of your own universe is also a way to make money. An understanding of the self as bounded, discrete, and constituted only by itself (and not through social relations with others) is a precondition for the individualism of the spiritual path. However, following the path means overcoming this formation of self. The path leads from the individual to the cosmic; aligning with the energy of the universe overcomes the gap between the self and external reality. Unifying with the oneness of the universe overcomes the illusion of separation, but how this is done remains mysterious. Manifestation is the technique and spiritual practice is the means. Yet this leaves an inability to think at middle scales, which renders the promised empowerment of the self deferred.

By projecting from the self to the universe, the middle scale between the local and the cosmic is skipped. Instead, there is a compression of spacetime, a bringing together of what is spatially and temporally distant. I call this metaphor of enfolding the analytic of the portal.[57] It is an opening, a rift, a nonlinear way through from previously divergent orientations of spacetime. Instead of moving in line with extant patterns, orientation in spacetime is ruptured.[58] The spiritual path led through a portal that disrupted spatial and temporal interconnection through offering the promise of transcending social constructions. Yet matter and meaning remain entangled.[59]

THE ROCKS WERE SCREAMING AT ME

Agency, Nature, and Space

It has come quickly, this crushing, industrial love of paradise. The pervert-free, less-trammeled, hundred-mile-view days were little more than two decades past, not so very long ago. Yet already my own history sounds like another country.

—ELLEN MELOY, *The Anthropology of Turquoise*, 2002, p. 74

PHOENIX IS THE MAIN ENTRY POINT to Arizona for many travelers arriving through one of Sky Harbor's four terminals. They encounter the span of a sprawling desert city rising from the dust on the backs of air-conditioning, water piped hundreds of miles from the north, and petroleum-fired transportation.[1] The grids of ochre dirt and artificial green form neighborhoods that form suburbs that form the swelling metropolis that eyes the encircling plains rapaciously. Heading north, I-17 climbs steadily from the low Sonoran desert of saguaros and creosote to the high desert of prickly pear cactus and sagebrush through undeveloped exits with inauspicious names such as Bloody Basin and Horsethief Basin that memorialize Arizona's cattle ranching past. Exit 179 leads through rolling hills to reveal the stunning red crags riveting the earth around the base of the Mogollon Rim, green trees swooping up over succulents grandly announcing the presence of fresh water. The town of Sedona settled smugly in the sandstone canyons, a modern-day tourist playground of turquoise and adobe gated communities, time-shares, hotels, and spas. On the outskirts, at the base of the hills, wherever the view is poorest, sit little manufactured houses and double-wide trailers, the lower-income homes that resemble the surrounding communities of Cottonwood, Cornville, and Jerome more closely than the high-value architectural gems that gird and mount the mesas and buttes of Sedona.

Running up through Oak Creek Canyon, following the path of the creek, the ponderosa pine grow thickly, and the human settlement thins to a few motels, campgrounds, and high-end restaurants and homes nestled at the ascending elevations. The narrow switchbacks choke with traffic every sunny weekend as visitors from every direction descend on the riparian coolness of Oak Creek Canyon, bathing in the natural swimming holes, bringing a cooler with the kids to sit on the banks and drink beer under the shade of the pines, a luxury absent in more southerly settlements. The canyons back onto the Mogollon Rim, the bottom edge of the Colorado Plateau, the tail end of the Rocky Mountains. Between the Rim and the base of the volcanic mountain ridge known in English as the San Francisco Peaks, named by Franciscan missionaries after their patron saint, squats the city of Flagstaff, the largest urban area in northern Arizona, home to a university, an observatory, and a ski resort. The railroad skirts the south side of Flagstaff; the Santa Fe Railroad follows the 39th parallel all the way to the Pacific and brought this settlement and the neighboring cities of Winslow, Holbrook, Williams, and Ash Fork into being. Parallel to the railroad runs its obsolescence: Route 66, the Mother Road of America's mythic itinerant past, now called I-40, although meandering dirt remnants of the old 66 still putter through the landscape alongside the newer road. North yawns the Grand Canyon, a four-hundred-mile gap in the earth; to the east, the Painted Desert and Petrified Forest; between them the expanse of the Navajo Nation, the largest Native American reservation in the continental United States.

This particular corner of Arizona has a number of spaces called sacred by different peoples at different times for different reasons. Sedona was considered a sacred site by everyone I spoke to; even people who were not interested in spirituality would mention that it was sacred to Native Americans or that its beauty was a sign of God's presence. Among those who followed a spiritual path, the vortexes were the most frequently cited reason for why they considered Sedona sacred.[2] Sedona is an example of the social production of the sacred in recent historical memory, a recorded and visible process of sacralization. The concepts of vortexes, energy, and nature are given specificity in this particular cultural context through the lens of spirituality.

The physical and sacred space is reinscribed with a new religious history, rewriting and co-opting Indigenous history and practice, and claiming what has been stolen and settled as rightful inheritance.[3]

The vortexes are swirling energy spirals calcifying certain rock formations and other locations in Sedona, imbuing these physical entities with agency. It is a tactile experience to my interlocutors; it can be felt. Since mass is an illusion created by energy vibrating at certain frequencies in cosmologies of spirituality, the presence of beautiful, even sublime features in the landscape inculcates the high vibration of energy in that area. The beauty of nature is a physical substantiation of the special energy. Vortexes, energy, and nature are interconnected and interdependent concepts in processes of sacralization in this context. The influences of Transcendentalism and the longer history of nature religion in America are evident.[4] This chapter interrogates the spatial connection between "the sacred" and "nature" in the social construction of American landscape, in which sacred space is closely identified with nature. It analyzes the capitalist material production of "nature" as a separate, preserved space that is not altered by humans that determine the priorities and regulations of land use. It inquires into the uneven distribution of resources for the production of nature in capitalism.

Sedona is rich in "natural amenities" such as forest, fresh water, canyons, and mountains.[5] This attracts tourists. The spiritual scene also acts as a tourist pull through the crystal stores in Uptown and vortex tours.[6] The beautiful landscape, talk of vortexes, and presence of other spiritual seekers are mutually reinforcing in creating the imaginary of Sedona as a sacred space composed of special energy. My interlocutors often began their spiritual path by visiting Sedona as a tourist. They were struck by the feeling of the place, its ambience. Then they moved to Sedona to live in the sacred, describing a mystical "call" from the energy of the land itself. Nature wants them there, but they find continual frustration from the human environment: too much traffic, onerous local ordinances, and overcrowding at well-known sites. Other people spoil nature.

The kind of nature desired has had the humans removed in a historical process of emptying the land of its previous or current human and non-human occupants.[7] It has been demarcated as an area for escape from others. It is an area where humans do not live, only visit, an imaginary space where something called "the environment" is separate from and needs to be protected from the impacts of the living creatures it encompasses. The government regulates spaces according to this utopian ideal through the National Park, National Forest, and National Monument system of land designations.[8] Conservation aims to fix this point into the landscape.[9] To create separate spaces for the sacred in the United States, this required the removal of people, both literally and figuratively, in a process of structural violence. The term "structural violence" brings awareness to the negative effects of social structures that systematically harm and disadvantage individuals. In ideating nature as sacred through the concept of energy, spirituality forms part of these inequitable social structures. Spirituality overwrites Indigenous land claims and sovereignty, building on the history of imperial aggression in the area that is reproduced in the fragility of the claims to that land and its sacredness.

VORTEXES EVERYWHERE

The vortexes are specific natural sites in Sedona that are different on an energetic level, according to my interlocutors. The energy of these sites is characterized as having a spiral pattern, described in the literature by local Sedona authors variously as spiritual or psychic or "subtle," and it is said to enhance spiritual practices, such as meditation, healing, and channeling.[10] Energy is used as a way of describing a sensorial relationship with certain geological formations.[11] It is figured as flowing in lines, called ley lines, that crisscross the earth in a grid, and the intersections of this grid form vortexes. These points are concentrations of energy, sometimes called "power spots" or likened to the chakras of the earth.[12] The energy of the vortexes is further categorized as being masculine or feminine, electromagnetic or electric, yin or yang.[13] These qualities are experienced, felt, rather than measured or seen, as a tingling sensation, a heightened emotional sensitivity, or a rush of new ideas and insights.[14] Vortexes make spirituality tangible. They offer a sacralization of nature in Sedona, as they are inextricably linked to the landscape. It is a sacrality that emanates from the earth itself.

There are four Sedona sites in particular named as vortexes: Cathedral Rock, Bell Rock, Airport Mesa, and Boynton Canyon. This was apparently engineered to service the needs of tourists, many of whom want to know specifically where the vortex is, in terms of a place on a map, a specific stop on their itinerary of Sedona.[15] Locals more often told me that the whole area was a vortex or that there were innumerable vortexes of varying sizes to be found around the town. The special energy spreads over the whole area, with the vortexes as different access points to it. In the first place I stayed—

FIGURE 6. Airport Mesa—the vortex is said to be on the mound.

"the Cosmic Portal"—I was told there was a vortex under the garage floor. Even though this was part of the built environment, it still contained a vortex that came from the earth beneath the house and not the garage floor itself. Still, the manner of discernment was the same; my host at the Cosmic Portal, Vixen du Lac, asked if I could "feel" it. She told me that vortexes were everywhere, not just in Sedona, and showed me pictures of the orbs that gathered around vortex sites.[16] She told me the special energy of vortexes has a way of making things happen how you need them to, which is often not how you wanted them to happen. How you want things to happen is a product of your ego, whereas manifestation creates what you truly need, and the vortex enhances the power of manifestation. The personal is connected to the cosmic through manifestation, which compresses the gap between consciousness and matter, between what you think and what happens.

Above all, vortexes are felt. A pressure on the third eye, maybe, the spot between the brow ridges, but everyone feels the energy differently. The idea of the sacred was based on feeling. My interlocutors felt that Sedona was special. "Vortex" and "energy" were just attempts to translate that into words. It was the emotional experience that validated it as a real thing. Feelings had their own ontological validity. If something was felt, it was real. There was no dismissal of "just a feeling"; a feeling was as real as something empirically perceived. This follows the primacy of intuition, heart wisdom, over logic.

The spaces that engender these feelings had their own histories, however. Philip, a videographer, told me that the original site of the Airport Mesa vortex was said to be on the flat top of the mesa, where the airport is located. This caused considerable disruption to the functioning of the small, private airport when people would walk along the runway with maps looking for the vortex. So the owners of the airport "moved" it. They got all the local vortex maps changed to say that the vortex is a rock outcrop about halfway up the road that leads to the airport. That is where the vortex is now located, and people go up there and say they feel the special energy. This suggests that only once a site is named as sacred is it then felt as such. Naming in this context is a magical act of transformation where the name "vortex" grants power in cosmologies of spirituality through its linkage with the concept of energy. Energy is not only a description of the sensorial relationship with the landscape, but a creative concept that allows people to color their experience there in a certain way. This particular story also implies that any aspect of landscape could be constructed as sacred. It was told for a specific reason: to undercut the accepted reality of the vortexes in Sedona, to make clear that the speaker was not taken in by this label as so many others in the town were.

This is not to suggest that Philip thought the notion of Sedona's special energy was invented, rather that the idea of there being four specific vortexes in Sedona was seen by people in the spiritual community as an introductory idea for those new to spirituality, especially tourists. It is simpler to direct a new arrival looking for a vortex to a specific location, such as Cathedral Rock, which is also the most photographed spot in Arizona, according to Forest Service data.[17] It is an easier climb than Bell Rock, a gentle incline with only a few spots of scrabbling over boulders that most visitors can achieve. It is the image of Sedona that is disseminated in tourist brochures and websites, attracting the 3–4 million tourists that visit each year. Unlike the other three of the "big four," the vortex has a specific locus, a dome of volcanic rock near the central spire, that can be climbed onto, rather than the vortex being the whole rock. It is a visible, impressive, iconic rock formation that can easily supply the answer to the question "What is a vortex?"

It is perhaps this iconicity that made it the frequent site of ceremonies and spiritual practice that I observed while in the field. Often on hikes up there, I would see people meditating or doing yoga on the volcanic dome; occasionally I spotted scattered human ashes. A monthly drum circle was held there, and I attended a number of ceremonies there for solstices and

FIGURE 7. Cathedral Rock, taken from the perspective of Red Rock Crossing.

other astrological or numerologically significant dates. When I asked about the name, my interlocutors likened the two tall columns of rock flanking a spindle to a cathedral. One of the local legends I was told was that it was originally called Court Rock by nineteenth-century settlers, and Court-house Butte, which is beside Bell Rock, was called Church Rock; the names were confused later on, and Court Rock became Cathedral Rock.[18] This story was deployed by those who wanted me to know they understood that the vortexes, and by extension the sacredness of Sedona, were a recent human invention. The name is a way of associating it with the sacral quality it gradually acquired.

The notion that Sedona is a maelstrom of invisible yet potent spiritual energy is also relatively recent and can be traced in historical accounts to the second half of the twentieth century. However, in accounts by local authors who are invested in spirituality, the vortexes are credited with a much older heritage. The vortexes were known to Native Americans, who held the whole area sacred, and were known about by psychics and mediums living in Sedona who did not publicize them.[19] Toraya Ayres described the emergence of "new age" activities in Sedona through the support of a realtor called Mary Lou Keller, who had a building on Hillside in the 1960s where she let people hold spiritual activities for free. In Keller's own account, the vortexes were known to Native Americans and then Ruby Focus, a group now called Rainbow Ray Focus that is still present in Sedona, came with channeled information about the vortexes and bought property adjacent to the Airport Mesa vortex through Keller in 1963.[20] She said this is the origin, despite other claims. The usual attribution in vortex guidebooks is to Dick Sutphen and Page Bryant, a pair of psychics who claimed to feel the vortexes in 1980s.[21] Sutphen made a career out of holding workshops on Sedona's vortexes aimed at developing psychic abilities, and published books about the vortexes and their powers. According to Ayres, Sutphen and Bryant only "publicized" the vortexes, along with Pete Sanders, another well-known Sedona psychic.[22]

There are two narratives here: one historical, which traces the vortexes through a sequence of local psychics who chose to talk about and publicize the vortexes in Sedona from the 1960s onward; the other mythological, claiming that the vortexes are a real and natural part of the landscape, their continuing existence going beyond recorded white American history to Native Americans. This can be seen as a claim intended to give the spiritual energy of Sedona authenticity and legitimate it through reference to the Indigenous peoples of the area.[23] After all, if the energy of Sedona is real, it stands to reason that others before the settling of Sedona by white Americans were aware of it, particularly a people reputed to be more spiritual than white Americans. In Sedona among people involved in spirituality, there was not a lot of interest in how the idea of the vortexes historically developed. There was more of an assumption that they were always there, a natural feature of the landscape, and people started to feel them as part of the shift in consciousness that began in the latter part of the twentieth century. Such lack of interest upholds cultural erasure. Stories of vortexes overwrote Indigenous stories, placing Native Americans and their prior claims to the land in the past.

There was more interest in how the vortexes came to be among long-term non-spiritual residents of the area. Mike was a carpenter who was born and raised in the area. He told me that he knew the guy who invented the vortexes, a man he described as "some burnt-out hippie in a rainbow bus, name of Glen or Greg or something," who decided there were spots of powerful energy. Mike conceded that they were all areas with great views and exposure; to him that was why they felt powerful. But this guy put a sign on the side of his bus that said "vortex tours" and he would take people around them. Soon after that tour buses started parking in Uptown. This story is probably apocryphal. I heard several different but similar versions of how the vortexes gained renown. Mike's version highlighted the social processes at the root of the vortexes. A man came, he felt certain sites were powerful, sites that were already much visited and emotionally affecting, and he named them, reified them, made them a thing, and then that thing could be described to others so they could find meaning in it too, and on another level, that thing could be packaged and then sold to others. The last point Mike made about tour buses in Uptown links to the growing acceptance of the vortexes on a corporate level. Not just businesses, but the city council of Sedona also found the idea of vortexes useful. Initially the town, which had an aging population of retirees who were mostly affluent, and its city council were hostile to these incomers, suspicious of the unkempt hippies. But then by the late 1980s, the town had come to accept them and started selling vortex maps and tours.[24] The chamber of commerce provided information about the vortexes and the spiritual businesses and retreats visitors could patronize on their trip to Sedona. The vortexes became another way to entice tourists to the area. Sedona as a sacred site became part of its "selling point."[25]

Yet it is insufficient to dismiss the vortexes as artifices cynically invented for the pursuit of profit. The experience of the vortexes could have life-changing effects. Amelia told the story of how in 2008, during the economic downturn, she lost everything: her home in San Francisco, her business as a decorator and interior designer, her corporate lifestyle, all her furniture. She lived in her car for thirteen months. She described this as a positive event because even though she had everything in terms of material success, she was not happy. When she lost everything, she found she was finally happy and grateful. Sometime after this experience she found herself receiving numerous signs about Sedona and the Grand Canyon, noticing references to them in the world around her, and then she was at a dinner and a friend of a friend said she wanted to go to the Grand Canyon but wanted someone to go with her. Amelia took this as a sign that she was meant to visit Arizona at this time, and accompanied her, going off on a solo trip to Sedona.

Amelia visited Cathedral Rock and went off trail, following the butterflies because she had always had "a lifelong thing" with butterflies. She was not sure about what vortexes were, so claimed she was not expecting anything, but then she had a "vortex experience":

> I stopped in my tracks and I just started crying with sheer joy, my physical body was still here in Sedona, but my spirit body was just so connected to the universe, it was pretty incredible. I was very aware of the divine being with me, very aware of just the omniscience of it all, it was pretty powerful.

This experience had a profound effect on her, and she decided that after pursuing her dream of living in France, she would move to Sedona, which she did in early 2012.

The experience at the vortex helped her intuit her personal spiritual path, which was to go to France, and then to Sedona. The beginning of this spiritual path started with a rupture, she lost her material things, and from that point she turned toward spirituality as a means of being happy, rather than pursuing her career as a means of being wealthy. The vortex experience was, analogically, a portal that transported her from one entanglement of meaning and matter—a successful corporate job in San Francisco—to another, discontinuous one, namely, following her spiritual path. However, in Amelia's narrative the importance of this life-changing event is downplayed, as she says it was only the "impetus" to change. Her interest in spirituality was a "lifelong situation," and she told the story of how she had a premonition of a friend's death in her twenties and how even at a couple of months old she would dream of things that were messages for her in her forties. She called herself an intuitive and psychic, and claimed to be sensitive to energy her whole life. It was only when she lost everything that she began to follow her true path of developing these gifts. Losing everything was the "trigger." Amelia emphasized the continuity of her interest in spirituality, for which the vortex experience was a realization and not causation.

The vortex experience can be seen as another trigger, or portal, along her spiritual path. Even though she had never heard of them and ostensibly expected nothing, it was the experience she had there that validated the idea that there was something special about those areas. While she maintained that every place has its uniqueness, there was a special energy in Sedona that was very powerful:

> I could feel the energy of Sedona a half hour outside, it was very power-
> ful . . . I've only left once and I felt quite ill, I thought I was car sick, but
> I was car sick for five days and I wasn't in the car for five days and as soon
> as I came back I felt fine again, so there is a lot of powerful energy here,
> yes, it's centralized, here and in other locations around the world.

Of all the other power spots in the world, Amelia told me she was drawn to this particular power spot because it was a reflection of her in that moment. Her spiritual path was an exploration of the self, and so the places she went to were reflections of who she was at that time.

When I met her, Amelia was in her forties and had been living in Sedona since February 2012. A thin, blond woman, extroverted and charismatic to the point of controlling, but warm and amiable. Her fresh, unblemished face made her seem younger than forty, except her eyes, which were drawn and lined. She made her living from selling Native American jewelry at Los Abrigados and other resorts in Sedona. She also considered herself a teacher, Reiki master, shamanistic practitioner, writer, and energy worker. She held private and group classes. While I was in Sedona, I attended some of her biweekly energy healing sessions and monthly shamanistic journey-ing sessions. For both she solicited a $10 donation. It was difficult for her to maintain herself financially in Sedona, she struggled to pay rent, and her patchwork of employment did not provide economic stability. She would place her business card on the table with crystals at the start of shamanic journeying sessions and energy healing sessions. The association of the card, the crystals, and the activity in the sessions was meant to raise her vibration in order to manifest abundance. Despite her continued economic troubles, she described living in Sedona in overwhelmingly positive terms. She framed her migration there as being "called" rather than being forced to move due to the loss of her business. This framing implied she was meant to be there, she was not an immigrant, she was not imposing or appropriating, although she made her living selling Native American cultural artifacts and called herself a shaman. Refusing to acknowledge the compromised moral position that working in the gig economy had placed her in, instead she called this her spiritual path, and as such it was "meant to be." In her terms, it was a reflection of who she was at that moment. Her circumstances therefore could not be any other way.

The vortex experience played a pivotal role in the way Amelia described her spiritual path. The content of this experience was a feeling that she interpreted as connecting her to a larger pattern in the universe, a network of energy to which the vortex gave access. On another level, the idea of vortexes can be seen as a portal into the practice of spirituality. They operate as a way of initiation, of coming into the cosmology of energy, the universe, and the spiritual path. They rarely played a larger role than this, except as a setting for ceremonies, a space in which spiritual practices took place. The vortexes are a socially produced sacred space; however, the experience of the vortexes is as a "natural" part of the landscape, an immanent invisible force of the earth and its particular energy. This energy was not restricted to the vortexes but characterized the area as a whole. The reality of this energy was further legitimized through reference to Native Americans. Native American religion and politics were reframed as spirituality, then used as an image of spiritual authenticity, a use reflected in Amelia's employment.[26] Despite her many claimed spiritual vocations, the one she subsisted on was the resale of Native American jewelry, using their cultural products to support herself just as she used their religious practices to buttress her spiritual path.[27]

Amelia can be seen as an example of downward social mobility, something that is often condemned as a personal failure in America, particularly when it involves loss of prestige and money. Amelia reframed this as a positive experience in spiritual terms through her ability to reconnect with nature once she lost all her material possessions and social status. What is interesting about this when thinking about the influence of the Transcendentalist glorification of nature on spirituality is that Transcendentalism occurred during a time when the middle class was emerging as a distinct social class.[28] Spirituality emerged during a time when the middle class was being squeezed by neoliberal policies undermining economic security. Nature seems to be prominent in American religion when the middle class is in transition. There is a need to retreat to nature, to that separate, sacred space, when economic relations in capitalism are unstable and in transition. In this context, spirituality reinscribes downward social mobility and reduced access to resources. It is a way of inverting a negative to a positive experience, and justifying social structural change through claiming that everything happens for a reason and that reason is for the best possible good. The construction of nature as sacred in spirituality reinforces the theme of providence through mystifying causation as the result of "natural" earth energies calling people to their spiritual path rather than losing or failing in an economic sense. Connecting nature with Native Americans and both with spirituality requires further interrogation, as it operates as part of the ongoing violent dispossession of Indigenous land and religion by white Americans.[29]

SPECIAL PLACES, SACRED SITES, NATIVE PEOPLES

Sedona is not a place to go to get a job or make a lot of money. There are few jobs available, even fewer that offer incomes that make it possible to pay the high rents charged.[30] The local economy is mostly tourism and real estate. Many of the homeowners are affluent people with second homes or retirees. People involved in spirituality were more likely to rent. Most of the young people I met did not stay in Sedona for more than a few months. Those that did tended to work in Sedona but live in the cheaper adjacent communities. Many of the older people I met who were involved in spirituality were hippies in the 1960s and 1970s who stayed and got absorbed by the tourist industry, so they could afford to live there. Yet regardless of the difficulties in staying there long-term, it was common for my interlocutors to respond to the question of why they came to Sedona by saying they were "called" there, as Amelia did.

In narratives like Amelia's, Sedona has agency. Agency causes events; as such, it can be the property of both humans and non-humans, even objects. Agents have positions in networks of social relationships, and it is this positionality that gives them a role in causation, a role that is attributed by humans because agency is relational.[31] Sedona's agency is attributed by those who figure it as a sacred place inhabited by special energy. The place is a personification of the special energy of the earth, and it reaches out and pulls people from their mundane existences into the spiritual path, thereby exerting agency at a pivotal moment in the turn to spirituality. Sedona causes people to follow their spiritual paths.

However, Sedona rejects as often as it attracts. A sentiment I heard often was summed up by Alice, who worked in a crystal store: "Sedona calls you and then when she's finished with you she spits you out." Alice was "called" from Wisconsin and a miserable job as a juvenile corrections officer, after visiting Sedona on vacation repeatedly over a period of ten years. She was referring to what environmental historian Adrian Ivakhiv calls "red rock fever," when the intensity of the energy amplifies to the extent that it overwhelms and expels people from Sedona.[32] I witnessed numerous people get "spit out" during my fieldwork. It was nearly always ascribed to the energy driving them away from Sedona to a different location, and never to the economic difficulties that trying to live in Sedona involved. The agency of Sedona was part of the sacralization process that mystified the political economic conditions of the town.

People move to Sedona for the nature, not the economy; they want to live in beautiful surroundings. Lifestyle migration, where movement is provoked by the desire for a better quality of life, is common.[33] Many such people are retirees, attracted by the year-round warm weather, a pattern repeated throughout the state of Arizona, where many communities are purpose built for retirees, with a lower age limit of fifty-five for occupation.[34] I met one such retiree in Sedona, Vivienne, who lived in Uptown next door to my friend Theresa. She lived alone in a large single-family ranch-style home that sat at the middle of a hill, the bottom of which still had lower-income dwellings, and the top of which was reportedly home to actor Sharon Stone and Beatrice Welles, director Orson Welles's daughter. This sort of spatial social stratification is common in Sedona. The other main hill, Airport Mesa, had million-dollar homes on the highest street (named "Panorama") with the best views. The homes toward the bottom of the hill were more likely to be manufactured houses with lower-income occupants. The beauty of the place was its selling point, so the priciest homes were the ones with the best views.

Vivienne was eighty years old when I spoke to her. She had lived in Sedona for twenty-four years, since 1988. Her husband, dead for a year, had worked his whole life for the Ford Motor Company, a job that had taken them to Argentina and Mexico and finally Kingman, a city in northern Arizona around 100 miles west of Flagstaff along I-40. From that experience, they knew they wanted to retire in Arizona, and they chose Sedona for its landscape. They both loved to hike, so they came to Sedona for a peaceful retirement in a beautiful place, a typical case of lifestyle migration. Nature was an object for them to come and enjoy. They pursued recreation there, not spirituality.

Vivienne was a Methodist and considered the vortexes a "fantasy," made up by "some woman years back" to attract tourists. It had no impact on her life or her decision to move there. Instead, Vivienne believed in a different fantasy: the American dream. She saw the recent history of America as one of teleological progress: things were getting better, people no longer suffered

from the infectious diseases that had killed so many during her childhood in
Alabama, infrastructure had improved greatly, and America despite its problems was still the greatest country on earth. This was the image of America
largely criticized and rejected by those involved in spirituality. Vivienne was
from a different generation. She had never had to work, and her husband
had remained employed his whole life by the same American car company.
There was still a Ford parked in the driveway when I visited. This was not
the economic experience of someone like Amelia. Vivienne could afford to
live where she wanted because she benefited from the prosperity of postwar
America. She still believed that prosperity was earned and deserved. She
represented not only the retirement population of Sedona, but the aging
upper middle class in America who had an economic privilege that was
being rapidly eroded. She could afford to enjoy the specialness of Sedona.

One way residents expressed this specialness was calling Sedona a bubble,
an island within a very different kind of area. It was seen as spiritually and
socially progressive, yet surrounded by socially conservative, Republican-
voting, "redneck" towns. The energy of Sedona was part of this bubble; as
mentioned above by Amelia, people would complain of feeling sick if leaving for a time. Conversely, the energy of being there could cause sickness,
I was told, and this was a sign that it was time to leave. Part of the mythology
of Sedona was that when it was time, in terms of the spiritual path, to leave,
Sedona conspired to make it difficult to stay. This is the getting "spit out" part
of the crystal store assistant's quote. The same energy that can draw people
in, and make things easy for them to stay, can also turn against them. In
practical terms what this meant was that people suddenly found they could
not find a job or place to stay, they lost their money, or their friends turned
against them. My housemate ran an eco-friendly cleaning company and
dealt with the rooms and homes of many people who were leaving. He said
many left in a hurry, they felt they just had to get out. One woman even said
the red rocks were "screaming" at her to leave. "Sedona" is a spiritual entity
with a specific energy. It has agency, in that it is a natural form imputed
with intentionality and causation. Sedona causes things to happen on the
spiritual path, drawing you in when the time is right and sending you on
your way again. It reveals the direction toward oneness on the spiritual path.

The intensity of Sedona was partly climatic and geological—the bright
blue skies, the red rocks, the stifling desert heat in the summer and mountain
snow in the winters—but the place tended toward a certain social intensity
as well as many "high-energy" people who were attracted there. The intense
level of energy was interpreted as meaning that Sedona was not a place to

live, but to do ceremonies. This lore was attributed to Native Americans by everyone who mentioned it. My kung fu friend Roger said the Hopi had said of Sedona, "You don't live in our church." Many in Sedona told me that the local Native American tribes came to Sedona to do ceremonies but did not live there. The Indigenous occupation of the land was erased through these stories, rewritten to support ideas of specialness and intensity.

Sedona is sacred to the Yavapai, the local tribe who occupied the land and were forcibly removed by the US Army to make space for the white settlers who came from the late nineteenth century. The oral history of the Yavapai told by elders Mike Harrison and John Williams stated that the area now known as Sedona is called *Wipuk*, the Middle of the World, and was the location where the first humans emerged from the earth. The Yavapai made "extensive seasonal use" of the area between the San Francisco Peaks and Oak Creek Canyon, and indeed did use it for prayer and ritual.[35] The issue they raised with the current development and use of Sedona was that they were concerned they would not be able to access the land for ritual use. Their sovereignty was undermined by white settlement.

There were differences of opinion about Sedona as a sacred space and as a developed place among scholars, elders, and individual tribal members, which leads to an important point: not all "Native Americans" are the same. The term is a homogenization of a diversity of different tribes, customs, and relations with white Americans and the settler state.[36] In northern Arizona the local tribes are the Yavapai, Apache, Navajo, Hopi, Hualapai, and Havasupai. The different tribes have had varied histories with white settlers; some, such as the Navajo and Apache, fought wars against the US Army, while others, such as the Hopi, did not.[37] These histories carry different weights. Contemporary tribal members have different relations with and opinions of white Americans, and this carries over to the social relations involved in spirituality. For example, Sun Bear, a member of the Ojibwe-Chippewa nation, actively sponsored non-Native use of Native American ceremonies such as the sweat lodge, something other tribal members, such as the Lakota Council, vehemently rejected.[38] These differences are elided under broad generalizations about "Native Americans."

What unites the tribes remaining in the United States on reservations is a history of trauma and oppression, explicit and premeditated genocide followed by cultural dispossession, resource appropriation, and broken agreements.[39] In northern Arizona, this violence played out in different ways for different tribes. The Yavapai were moved to a reservation near Camp Verde, a town to the west of Sedona in the Verde Valley, where they were merged with the Western Apache.[40] To the north of Flagstaff is the Navajo Nation, extending into southern Utah, Colorado, and New Mexico, which surrounds the much smaller Hopi reservation. The Navajo fought and were beaten by the US Army and then led by mountain man Kit Carson on a forced march to New Mexico, where many died of starvation and smallpox. They were later allowed to return to their ancestral land in the Four Corners area.[41] The Hopi reservation was created on their ancestral land, the villages atop a series of mesas in northeast Arizona; however, the Navajo Nation was created around them completely engulfing the Hopi and creating several areas of resource dispute between the two hostile groups.[42] The loss of diversity in talk of undifferentiated "Native Americans" allows for reification of an oppressed other, which in turn allows them to be seen as white Americans want them to appear.

Native Americans appeared frequently in explanations of Sedona's specialness, enabled by the fact that they had been forcibly removed from the town itself. "Native American" is an image used to symbolize a utopian vision of society. When those involved in spirituality talk about "the Native Americans," they are talking about their own idealized form of the Native, who is closer to nature, peaceful, and spiritual, one who is uncorrupted by "Western" civilization.[43] It is an image that does not exist, and bears little relation to the social reality of Native American tribes currently living in northern Arizona. It is an emblem of all the things they feel are missing in their own society. Opposing this image is its obverse: the disorderly and uncontrollable Savage, the drunken Indian. The Navajo and Hopi in Flagstaff and other towns bordering the reservations were impugned by white residents with a racist pejorative used for all Natives regardless of tribe that also carried implications of alcoholism, poverty, and poor health outcomes.

These twin images of "the Native" dominate the white American gaze of Native Americans. As Philip J. Deloria has argued, since the first landings of Europeans in North America Native Americans have been used as the other of white identity.[44] According to Deloria, white Americans tried to embrace both civilized order and the wildness of freedom to construct their own identity. In order to feel connected to the vast untamed landscape of their new land, they had to tame and destroy it to claim mastery. Native Americans were a remnant of what had existed before them, presenting both a challenge and an alternative to white domination and Manifest Destiny, creating a "two-hundred-year back-and-forth between assimilation and destruction" of the Indian people.[45] It is through this ambivalent and indeterminate other that white America understands and constructs its own identity. Dispossession of Native identity, through adopting practices, occupying land, and explicit claiming of Native ancestry, is part of the ongoing erasure and cultural genocide of Native Americans.[46] By placing Native Americans as part of nature, and in the past, white Americans erase the ongoing claims to sovereignty and land by Indigenous nations and relegate them to the status of racial inferiors and even temporal anomalies.[47]

Identity is produced in part through sacred sites, which carry the memory of significant events and embody the shared values of collectivities.[48] In the American West, this identity was constructed through patterns of selective remembering and forgetting, such as in the creation of the This Is The Place monument in Utah by the Church of Jesus Christ of Latter-Day Saints. This monument remembered the founding of the Salt Lake Valley settlement by Church of the Latter-Day Saints pioneers in such a way as to embrace them in a wider American identity as pioneers and tamers of the West while forgetting the history of persecution of Latter-Day Saints by Protestant Americans and the persecution of Native Americans by the LDS.[49] The Latter-Day Saints were able to lay claim to the land and identify with mainstream America through the removal of the Utes and Shoshone. Thomas E. Sheridan relates a similar story of the Santa Cruz Valley in southern Arizona, where the Tohono O'odham were dispossessed in order for developers to mine, farm, and then build retirement communities.[50] The vast and empty "space" of the American West was produced through the systematic violation and removal of Native American peoples by white Americans. Connecting the sacredness of Sedona to Native Americans must be read against this historical inheritance. Reinscription of Indigenous land as "America" is part of the spiritual invention of colonial nations, a history of spiritual domination.[51]

It is also problematic to claim that because land is sacred to Native Americans, its sacrality is therefore available for universal appreciation. Sacred space and time have specific conceptualizations in Native American religious life, especially when compared to American Protestantism, which spirituality still largely draws on. Native American religions have no sense of alienation from nature, all creation is good because there was no fall from grace, and sacred space and time are therefore characterized by continuity, not rupture.[52] Most tribes have a sacred center of their ancestral lands, which is permanent in that it came into being with creation and not with a historical event. It is identified with that tribe, who accept responsibility for it and relate all historical events within its confines; for example, Navajo land has four sacred mountains that mark its extent. This understanding of sacred space cannot be easily taken on and extended to people beyond the tribe because they do not have the same continuous relationship, responsibility, and identification with it. The close association with the land is why generally Native Americans do not reveal sacred spaces willingly or tell those not in the tribe about ceremonies held there.[53] To claim the vortexes as somehow "Native American" can be seen as an attempt at cultural assimilation, taking a space that is sacred to a specific group, the Yavapai, and claiming it for white Americans instead.

The recorded history of genocide of Native Americans was rarely addressed by those involved in spirituality. They seemed instead to prefer a mythological reconstruction of history that relocates Native Americans as ancient aliens. Sites sacred to Native Americans were often credited with being popular with extraterrestrials because both responded to the heightened energy of the spots. Some even made a link between aliens and Indigenous people who were either extraterrestrial races that landed on Earth or were visited by and given advanced knowledge or technology by extraterrestrials. The Hopi in particular were associated with the "star people," and a number of my interlocutors claimed there was a Hopi prophecy of the "fourth world" brought by the Blue Kachina that was another way of talking about the ascension to the fourth dimension. During a trip to Old Oraibi, a Hopi village on their reservation, a Sedona resident I was traveling with asked where the monument with the prophecy was located. She was met with only bemusement from the Hopi woman at the general store, who instead pointed the way to the memorial for Kit Carson. This alternate history of Native Americans, as star people landed on Earth for the spiritual renewal of those alive now, was a way of reinscribing "the Native" and "the alien," turning the native into the alien and conceptually dispossessing Native Americans of their prior right to the land.

Even for those who did not talk about aliens, Sedona was given an ancient pedigree because the energy came from the earth itself, and was known to people who inhabited the land before Native Americans. There was local lore that Sedona was built on an ancient Lemurian city, although in some versions it was just a temple, made of crystals. Nineteenth-century European occultists suggested that Lemuria was an ancient lost continent that coexisted with Atlantis and was destroyed by the same cataclysm as that continent.[54] Lemuria was an ancient society of advanced spirituality, the sister to Atlantis, which was an ancient society of advanced technology. The militaristic and materialistic Atlanteans caused the cataclysm that destroyed both continents. In some accounts, after the continents sank, the surviving Atlanteans and Lemurians scattered, mixed with, and transformed Indigenous peoples across the globe. According to my interlocutors, the crystal city under Sedona was powerful because it was built on the intersection of the ley lines that cross the earth, which Lemurians had knowledge of as a more spiritually advanced race. This alternate history rewrote the sacred geography of America, replacing the indigeneity of Native Americans with the earlier Lemurians. The people in Sedona following spirituality located themselves as their heirs, and through that claim they could imply that they belonged there. They could then perceive themselves as having a legitimate claim to the land. They could shrug off their historical inheritance as settlers or occupiers through making claim to be the spiritual descendants of the true first people.[55]

If the special energy of Sedona was caused by the physical properties of the land itself, then it would follow that the same phenomena could be observed elsewhere. The concept of ley lines as crisscrossing the earth with this special energy underpins the idea that there were other sacred sites, similar to Sedona, around the world. The most frequently mentioned were Mount Shasta in California, Maui in Hawaii, Machu Picchu in Peru, Glastonbury in England, and the Pyramids in Egypt.[56] It was common for my interlocutors to travel between them, with certain destinations being more popular, such as Maui and Mount Shasta, which were easier to get to and politically more stable.[57] The international network of sacred sites and the population of mostly young, seasonally or nominally employed people that worked in them spoke to the universalism of spirituality and the growing popularity of spiritual tourism. It was legible for them to align with the universe through any culture's sacred sites because they saw them all as manifested by the same energy. Everything is translatable in the universalist framework of spirituality. Things have essences, which are represented differently in different languages and places. Culture is epiphenomenal to the energy of the universe. Spirituality transcends all other forms of knowledge for those involved in it. What they "feel" through intuition is more important than what they "know" through reading, hearing, seeing.

The universalist framework of spirituality, based as it is on a pantheistic notion of energy, recalls the scholarly work of Mircea Eliade, who took an essentialist stance that religion is a natural characteristic of humanity. For Eliade, religion is concerned with human relations with the sacred, which is an inherent part of existence. Sacred spaces are an "irruption" of this integral power of the numinous, experiences he called hierophanies or theophanies.[58] Mountains are sacred, therefore, because the sacred is a real essence that breaks into the human, social world and large, imposing rocks are particularly able to convey this power. In social science, Eliade's approach has been eclipsed by that of Émile Durkheim, who saw religion as a social function created by people to integrate society.[59] For Durkheim, the sacred is produced by human activities and mirrors the social configurations that it knits together. Therefore, it is not important whether it is a mountain that is sacred or not; what matters is how the mountain functions to bring cohesion and stability to the society that considers it sacred. What unites these two approaches is a configuration of the sacred and its separation from the profane as central to religious life.

My interlocutors tended toward Eliade's position. When I asked if Sedona was sacred, they replied "of course" and moved on to other topics. For believers, the sacred simply is, it is immanent, it stems from the presence of divinity itself. Yet, as this chapter relates, there was still much debate on whether the vortexes were "real" or not. In recounting the historical production of the vortex sites, such as the change in position of the Airport Mesa vortex and the beginning of vortex tours, certain Sedona residents undermined the belief that the sacred is immanent. These stories emphasized the social construction of the sacred; the way it is created, changed, and negotiated by social agents. Indeed, by highlighting how it was useful to move the Airport Mesa vortex, they approximated a Durkheimian position. The vortexes were created by humans and became part of how Sedona functions socially. Eliade's understanding of the sacred is a believer's perspective; Durkheim's is a non-believer's.

Yet, recalling Vivienne, who did not believe in the vortexes, she still felt there was something special about Sedona. Why choose to retire in Sedona and not Kingman, where she already lived? The answer was that Sedona was a beautiful area, set in red rock canyons, with blooming orchards and foliage from the freshwater creek that ran down and through the canyons, and Kingman was a dry, high desert wasteland populated only because of its proximity to a major east-west highway, I-40. The sacred may be produced by human action, but humans are not indiscriminate in where they choose as sacred. Ivakhiv offered a third way between Eliade and Durkheim in arguing that nature was a participant in this process because the specific type of nature interacts with people's notions of divinity and sacrality, making some formations of rock and dirt more likely to be seen as inhabited by the divine than others.[60] What I emphasize is that this process is not neutral; the way space is made sacred is part of the structural violence of settler colonialism. For Sedona to be occupied by white Americans who can then "feel" its special energy, the material existence of Native Americans was devastated and they were rhetorically turned into spiritual essence that helped white people connect to the land they took. The sacred is easier to "feel" when there are fewer other humans in it.

DENATURED NATURE: HOW BEAUTIFUL
THE LAND IS WITHOUT OTHER PEOPLE

We sat at dinner discussing vortexes. Everyone gave their opinion. Lana's sister said it was powerful because so many people had meditated there, an accumulation in a specific space of the spiritual energy generated through the practice of meditation. Lana offered that she had heard they were "power spots" but did not think that was what made the area special. What attracted her was the landscape: it looked like the earth was naked, all cracked open, and on the surface, the interior of the earth was revealed in the canyons of Sedona. Nature and its expression in the landscape were central to Lana's spirituality. Being in nature and connecting with nature was how she experienced divinity, but moreover it was a way for her to "just be me." Lana called her practice "neo-shamanic"; however, she did not call herself a shaman. She was aware of the criticisms of Native Americans against white shamans, and so did not adopt any particular tribe's practice. She was fascinated by Native Americans, still, and had spent time with the Lakota, Yavapai, and Iroquois, learning some practices. There was a difference, she emphasized, between traditional and non-traditional Natives, and only the traditional ones on the reservation had valid information. The techniques she used she found herself through being outside in nature, and then trying them out and seeing what worked, she told me. This was then "validated," not "influenced," by learning about Native American practices. Her explanations performed a rhetorical sleight of hand, distancing herself from accusations of cultural appropriation while simultaneously setting herself up as the arbiter of what was "valid" information and which Native Americans were "traditional."

Lana worked as a corporate consultant, that was her paying job, and on the side she offered neo-shamanic retreats for free, although attendees had to pay the cost of their trip to Sedona. Most of the people who attended the retreats had also been corporate clients of hers at some point. The techniques she used in retreats were vision quests, medicine walks, talking sticks or "way of the council," prayer, and the creation of sacred space. This latter practice she called a "co-creation" of humans and nature. On a hike, she demonstrated it by saying, "Shhh . . . ," and we both quieted and all that could be heard was the wind and the birds. She said, "Remember to breathe," so I breathed deeply. A few moments went by and she touched my arm ever so softly and said, "We just created sacred space." But she also said there was a deficiency in the explanation, there was a facet she could not really explain, something ineffable. She wondered whether English had lost the words to speak about the sacred.

Vision quests, medicine walks, and using a talking stick to speak during a meeting or "council" are Native American practices. Lana's use of these practices was not explicitly linked to affiliation with any particular tribe, and like Amelia, seemed divorced from its original context and rewrapped in white American cultural expectations. The neo-shamanic practices of both had strong influences from the scion of Western shamanism Michael Harner.[61] Lana used the practices in both her neo-shamanic retreats and corporate consultancy work, and the value for her was that they worked across contexts. She told a story of reinterpreting a Native American long dance as a "team building simulation" on a corporate retreat to great success. For Lana, the practices were inspired by nature, this was the source for both Native Americans and her, and so it was not an appropriation of Native practice but something suggested by the land itself. This claim must itself be culturally situated. The conceptual separation of the land as pre-social and acultural is part of the capitalist alienation of nature as something separate from human action.[62] This distancing then allows for the "mastery" of nature through human actions acting upon nature-as-object.

Lana was in her sixties, originally from Pennsylvania, slight and strong. She had never married and had no children. Raised Catholic, along with her four siblings all younger than she was, she qualified her commitment as "lapsed." She was one of my few interlocutors who identified herself as politically active in support of a particular party, the Democrats. Her diet was vegan. An Outward Bound instructor in her twenties, this precipitated her love of exploring nature before she had any developed ideas about spirituality. Her corporate consultancy work was located mainly in Central Florida, and she owned a second home in Sedona where she held retreats. Lana told me she suffered from fibromyalgia, and was in pain when not moving, so she felt the constant compulsion to get out and move, especially hiking among the red rocks. Her adrenals and neurotransmitters were shot, so she could not sleep, and suffered from anxiety and dizziness, among other symptoms. She suffered for years with biomedical doctors only willing to give her sleeping pills. Then she went to a naturopath, who got her off the sleeping pills and replaced them with herbal remedies. These problems were caused by her high-powered corporate consultancy job, she believed, which was high stress and required long hours, frequent international travel, and changing time zones, conditions that encouraged poor sleep and diet. The way she did her job had destroyed her body. There were energetic problems of this job; she felt it drained her without giving back, so it was not an equal exchange. This was common, she said, a lot of professional women and executives get fibromyalgia from burning out and not taking care of themselves. She came to Sedona, partly, for healing. She believed the land itself was "energetic" and had healing effects.

The most common response to the question of what made Sedona special or different, from those involved in spirituality and those not, was that it was so beautiful. What made it beautiful was the complexion of nature—the red rocks, the big skies, the arboreal riparian area. This can be seen as part of a wider trend in American religion, something Catherine Albanese called "nature religion," where divinity is turned to in nature or nature is perceived as divinity.[63] This historical trajectory in American religion is found vividly in the works of the Transcendentalists, such as Ralph Waldo Emerson and Henry David Thoreau.[64] Like spirituality, Transcendentalism described a pantheistic notion of divinity revealed most immediately in nature, in which the divine emanates from a single source that communicates through intuition. Nature is appreciated as a microcosm of the macrocosm of the universe, a correspondence that suggests the shared roots of nature religion and esotericism.[65]

The significance of nature in America is political as well as religious, its immensity and grandeur fueling imperialist visions of Manifest Destiny as well as claims that it is a substantiation of the divine. It is particularly the concept of wilderness that is elaborated as sacred, as it combines "the sacred grandeur of the sublime with the primitive simplicity of the frontier."[66] This view of nature as sublime in the Kantian sense, most appositely in the form of wilderness, has spread widely throughout spirituality and beyond. As more people disengage from institutional religion as Lana had, appreciation of nature as a form of religiosity seems to be particularly appealing.

This speaks of a much larger current than spirituality in Sedona, the

FIGURE 8. The San Francisco Peaks.

investment of the American landscape with divinity. Arizona is a focal point for this process because its geological formations invoke potent symbols of American identity: the sublime and the frontier. Part of being in northern Arizona, rather than the desertified south, is living within "big nature." The area contains the San Francisco Peaks and the Grand Canyon, as well as Sedona. Thom, who was born in Flagstaff and grew up in the area, told me that these sites were connected. The Peaks were a "holy mountain" to the Navajo, bringing water and life to the land around it, the Grand Canyon was the "amphitheatre to the gods," and Sedona was the "great valley."[67] He went on to suggest that to see why this area is sacred, I should go up to the top of Mingus Mountain, from there see the whole valley, and see how the Peaks feed the rivers, and the snow from the summit and the springs create year-round flowing fresh water, one of the only places in the state that has this. The mountain is life; it brings water to the valley, making it fertile and green. All around it is desolate desert where nothing much grows, then suddenly there is this area, verdant and alive, and that is why it is sacred. To him, it seemed like God must have put this here, put all this life here. In Thom's view, it *is* God. God is all life, all things, and what we see as nature is in fact the face of God. This embodies the sentiment of nature religion, that the complexion of the landscape is an embodiment of divinity.

Such statements can be taken as arbitrary, the product of continuous association with a particular area over time that would be the same if this person grew up in Kingman or Tucson. However, there is perhaps more to it than pure social constructionism allows. The desert regions of southern Arizona are not susceptible to the same level of spiritual elaboration as the "big nature" in the north. The sublime according to Kant is an aesthetic experience defined by immensity; it overwhelms by its sheer scale.[68] The vastness of the Grand Canyon is therefore more than a massive hole in the ground that hinders development (as the first European surveyors thought).[69] Its scale is a way to approach the immensity of divinity. In both Transcendentalism and spirituality, the Kantian sublime is a pre-existing idea to be grasped by intuition. The sublime is an inherent aspect of the landscape waiting to be perceived—"felt"—by those sensitive to it. The Peaks are sacred because they give life through providing water and biodiversity to the area around the mountains; this life-giving power mirrors that of divinity.

Associating nature with divinity in this way seems straightforward; however, it is easy to overlook that what is meant by nature is not self-evident. Humans take the raw materials of the earth and sculpt it in specific ways; as a garden may be physically constructed to appear wild and untamed, so too is the concept of nature.[70] Nature as a concept connotes what exists beyond humans, yet humans continually select, cultivate, and represent nature in specific ways. Environmental historian William Cronon called nature a "contested terrain," at once universally real and culturally variable, seemingly self-evident yet difficult to speak about precisely.[71] He outlined the varied meanings imbued in the term "nature" that moralize, deify, technologize, and commodify something that is meant to be inherent, *prima facie*, and essentialist. As suggested above, in America the concept of wilderness is revered as the epitome of nature, wilderness is nature at its most natural. Cronon argued that it has become sacred as the symbol of the frontier and the birth of the nation. As the nation became more industrialized and urbanized, wilderness remained as the last bastion of the "real" America. It had to be protected in order to save America itself.[72] Its preservation required its circumscription. The wilderness has been legally defined through the creation of the National Parks since 1872; once it had been demarcated on a map, it could then be regulated by the federal government, through the National Park Service, the Forest Service, and the Bureau of Land Management. The way to experience wilderness is to drive there in a car on a highway, pay an entrance fee to a government agency, and walk along trails marked and maintained.

The human management of wilderness was reinforced to me during the government shutdown of late 2013 over the Affordable Care Act that changed the way healthcare was financed. The National Park Service was closed, and so the Grand Canyon was "closed." It was of course still there, a great gaping hole in the ground; however, the multitudes of disgruntled tourists that still came could not visit. The highway leading to the South Rim was blocked and the entrance gates left unmanned. In absolute terms it was still possible to see the Grand Canyon, by walking across the plateau to the chasm itself, but in social terms, it was inaccessible. Indicating the fragile ground the ideal of wilderness is built upon, the image is of "wild-ness": no civilization, no government, no humans even. Yet when humans thousands of miles away could not agree on whether government-subsidized health-care was a good idea, the wilderness was closed. Wilderness is not natural, it is a human concept, and when humans are no longer there, the wilderness ceases to exist. Perhaps in some ways, wilderness as a concept is like Sedona's vortexes. Its power can be felt by humans, they search for ways to access, protect, or commodify it, but ultimately, when the humans are not there, it is only rocks and trees and dirt.

The American conceptualization of wilderness can be located in pro-cesses of the material construction of nature, which are an integral part of industrial capitalism, a system that inevitably destroys nature because of the requirement for infinite economic growth predicated on the overuse of natural resources.[73] To compensate for this, pockets of "nature" called "wilderness" are saved in order to appreciate through touristic activities that push out the prior occupants and non-capital-generating land uses. The material production of nature is regulated by state and federal govern-ment policy and affected by disputes such as the government shutdown that caused the "closure" of the Grand Canyon. In determining who has access to the land and for what purposes, this process goes beyond an abstract cul-tural construction of nature. The material processes through which nature is produced constitute a form of structural violence. In making the Grand Canyon National Park, Native Americans were removed, highways and hotels were built, and access was made conditional on an entry fee, creating a pristine "natural" space that can be enjoyed only by those that can afford it. Access to nature in Sedona was similarly constructed and mediated by political economic relations. The sacralization of nature is also a naturaliza-tion of power.

TRANSCENDENCE

Living within "big nature" seemed a near ubiquitous desire among residents of Sedona, yet there seemed to be a countervailing current of rejection by the place. Sedona spat out those it did not want; they should not try to live in a hallowed landscape. Through this aphorism, Sedona was not only attributed agency but also imputed to have superhuman power. It had the power to decide who could live there and who could not, a denial of the all-too-human material processes that often forced people to move out of the town. It is this awe-inspiring power that evokes the concept of the sublime, a concept that also has a certain degree of ambivalence. The sublime is life, but it is also death. James Siegel analyzed student responses to the landscape around Cornell University in New York State and noted the recurrence of death images and thoughts of suicide in the non-suicidal.[74] The sublime is too much to comprehend; death allows for comprehension, providing fixity in the face of the abyss. Siegel remarked on the apocryphal reputation of Cornell as a suicide capital. The same was also said of Sedona. There were persistent rumors of people walking off onto the trails and taking their own lives, getting lost forever in the immensity of nature. The sublime is a way to comprehend what is ultimately incomprehensible, the source of life and death, a way to behold the "face of God."

Living within such immensity could be difficult in mundane ways. Lana told me about a controversy in Sedona about a woman named Dusty, whom she knew through one of the Sedona Facebook groups. Dusty, whom Lana admitted to me seemed "a bit off," was hired to be the personal assistant of a well-known Sedona resident, Misty. Misty headed a campaign against the Sedona airport, claiming the pilots were illegally dumping fuel as they took off, causing health problems among the residents, such as herself, who lived below the flight path. Misty's husband shot himself, and afterward she suffered from post-traumatic stress disorder. It was during this period that she hired Dusty to be her personal assistant for two weeks or so, while she was going through this trauma. However, she never paid her the promised wages. Then Dusty had a psychotic break at Misty's house; there was some sort of incident. Dusty had previously helped find the dead body of a missing woman who had killed herself, somewhere near Red Rock Crossing, through clairvoyance. Lana said she did not normally have time for people who call themselves psychics, but this woman really did help locate the body.

But after Misty denounced her, others did so too, calling her a predator and ostracizing her from the local community.

In its form, this story is quotidian small-town gossip. Disputes and misunderstandings boil over into mutual accusations of misconduct. Yet the striking detail for me, at the time I heard it, was the number of suicides contained within this anecdote, which hung at the sidelines, cast as backdrop. Suicide was the atmosphere for mundane social conflict in Sedona. Around the same time Peter, the focus of the next chapter, told me his erstwhile housemate had disappeared with a friend on a road trip to South Dakota, soon after another friend of hers had disappeared, possibly having committed suicide. The friend's body was missing, but everything was left in her house, and her dog was found alone on a trail. There was also a "suicide bridge," which was the location of a number of incidents.[75] The phenomenon was not restricted to Sedona; it was an occurrence in resort towns in the western United States frequent enough to earn a *National Geographic* report.[76] There was something jarring, for both residents and commentators, about seemingly high rates of suicide in towns reputed to be paradise. It was perhaps because these towns were thought to be paradisiacal that suicide seemed so incongruous, and it was therefore more commented upon. Why would anyone want to kill themselves in such a beautiful place?

I knew Jade through Vedic chanting sessions called kirtans as well as drum circles at the Brewery, and weekly parties we both attended at the house of a psychic belly dancer. Jade was a massage therapist and naturopath, who offered alternative methods for healing trauma. She had survived an unspecified trauma herself. Extremely thin, she suffered from an eating disorder. I first met her at a raw food potluck dinner, to which she brought quinoa salad that was not raw. She quipped that she had always been a rebel. She was someone who was around and about in Sedona at that time, a person present in the spiritual scene, part of the interconnected circles of people involved in spirituality. I connected her with a rideshare to Mexico for a Rainbow Gathering, and then to another acquaintance, Ben, to rent a room when she needed it. I considered her a friend.

Late in the summer, I was dropping Ben off at his place after a kung fu session. He said he had asked Jade to move out. I asked why, and he told me that she slept twelve hours a day, he could not make noise early in the morning without disturbing her, and he liked to get up early to meditate and practice his kung fu forms. Jade was too passive and *yin*; he used the word from the Chinese symbolism of yin and yang to describe her character. He went on to say that he really did not like her dog or the way she treated it. He felt she did not give it enough attention, and often left it on its own in the house, and besides, his aunt and mother, who owned the house, did not want pets there. In return, Jade apparently said she always felt like it was "Ben's house" and she was not welcome there. That evening, I saw her briefly at the drum circle at the Brewery, but she was dancing and did not notice me.

I left for a road trip to Oregon, and then Nevada, for a couple of weeks. When I returned, I was greeted with the news that Jade had died. It was on Facebook. There were posts on her profile page expressing shock and disbelief. Nowhere was the cause of death mentioned, or even that she had died. There was reference made to her leaving this physical plane, but that was it. Through speaking with others who knew her, it seemed that the eviction had been a shock that caused her to stop eating altogether, and then she disappeared. There were messages on her Facebook page asking her to get in contact with friends or family. Her medical condition was euphemistically mentioned. I then read in the local newspaper that she had been found by search and rescue off Thunder Mountain trail, near the Andante trailhead and Chimney Rock, having fallen from a cliff. Her death was widely believed to be a suicide.

There was a ceremony for her at the Thunder Mountain trailhead. Attendees brought candles, and as they entered, a local musician and psychic smudged them with sage and a large feather. Her family was there from Rhode Island and joined with her "Sedona family" for the ceremony. No one spoke about why or how she died. Only that she had left the physical realm of existence. This was important because death was not conceived of as a finality; her energy had transcended this physical dimension and would re-form in another dimension. The cycle of reincarnation continued. Jade would be reborn again in another body with a new mission, a new way for the universe to experience itself.

For a few weeks, mysterious deaths on the trails featured in animated conversations in Sedona. Apparently there were three suicides in the month before Jade's, and then in the same week as her, a man threw himself off Midgeley Bridge. Misty blamed the airport and the jet fuel dumping for all the suicides, claiming the toxic fumes caused mental illness. Another well-known resident offered exorcisms to help clear the energy field of anyone suffering from suicidal thoughts. I asked Benito, who was born in Sedona and spent his childhood there, why suicide seemed so frequent in Sedona. He told me it was because the people there were crazy, they would kill themselves not even because they were severely depressed but because they convinced themselves it was the right thing to do for a higher spiritual purpose. They go to Sedona expecting a lot, but it did not make them different, it just amplified how they already were.

This seemed like a bleak view cast over what must have been deeply personal trauma motivating these acts. The talk in those weeks reoccurred every few months or so with the next suicide, although Sedona did not have a higher-than-average suicide rate compared to the rest of Coconino County.[77] The discourse fueled the metaphor of Sedona feeding on those that lived there, chewing up and spitting out the unwanted. That so many deaths occurred on the trails that led through the canyons seemed to magnify this symbol. The landscape that drew so many in was swallowing those that could not cope with living within the sublime. The energy could be welcoming or it could be ruinous. Raising the frequency of the vibration of the energy granted transcendence beyond this dimension, and the result could be oblivion.

21ST DECEMBER 2012

"This Is My Story, Not Yours"

Willy Loman never made a lot of money. His name was never
in the paper. He's not the finest character that ever lived. But
he's a human being and a terrible thing is happening to him.
So attention must be paid. He's not to be allowed to fall into
his grave like an old dog. Attention, attention must be finally
paid to such a person—you called him crazy . . .

—ARTHUR MILLER, *Death of a Salesman*, 1949, p. 39

TO THE TOP OF BELL ROCK

ON THE MORNING OF 21ST DECEMBER 2012, small groups of bystanders
were scattered around the base of Bell Rock, one of Sedona's vortexes. Some
sat on deck chairs, others held binoculars. Representatives of the media
stayed in the parking lots at the two adjacent trailheads situated about half
a mile to the north and south of the rock, speaking into cameras that trained
their lens at the top. A fire engine, an ambulance, and Forest Service rangers
in pickup trucks sat waiting in the southern parking lot, called Bell Rock
Vista. Throngs of cars congested both of the adjacent lots. On the top was
a fluid group of 10–20 people that came and left during the day. A police
helicopter hovered in the sky. All of these spectators had come to this coni-

FIGURE 9. The view of Bell Rock from Peter Gersten's apartment.

cal red rock looking for something to happen, an event much hyped in the local and national media in the preceding weeks and months. However, it was not the vaunted special energy of the rock that drew them, but a socially created event. They were waiting to see if Peter Gersten would jump off the 479-foot rock to activate a portal that he would travel through to go to the source code that created this simulated reality and remove the virus that was currently threatening our existence.

The date 21st December 2012 was commonly held to be the end of the Mayan Long Count calendar and was identified by many in Sedona as a significant date when the ascension would begin or the world would end.[1] For Peter, it was the date his portal would open. It was a clear blue day, with few clouds and clement weather for December in northern Arizona. That morning at 10 am, Peter set off from his apartment in the Village of Oak Creek with a group of nine other people. Peter lived no more than twenty minutes from Bell Rock, and it was something of an obsession for him. He hiked it every day, sometimes twice a day, in the weeks running up to the 21st. He called his apartment a "shrine." It was decorated with images

FIGURE 10. Representations of Bell Rock in Peter's apartment.

and representations of Bell Rock in all manner of media: photos, paintings, drawings, copper, fabric, ceramics, stained glass, embossed brass, nails, on playing cards and oracle cards, on a box of tea bags. The window of the main room of his two-bedroom apartment looked out directly onto Forest Service land and the imposing shape of Bell loomed in the center. He believed he had been given this apartment the previous January by Sedona as part of his preparations for the 21st. Why else would he have been given such a prime location for ascending Bell unless he was meant to be up there on that date? He thought of "Sedona" as a high-energy life-form that oversaw his program in the simulation. It provided plot twists from which he learned more about his mission. If he was given a specific apartment, it was for a personally meaningful reason.

Many of the nine people who climbed up with him had ascended Bell Rock with Peter before. He had been on a mission since late August 2012 to take as many people to the top of Bell Rock as possible. He believed this would aid him in activating the portal because each person's frequency would help raise the vibration of the energy at the top, thus increasing the likelihood of the portal opening there. He had taken up friends, family members, and random strangers he met on the trails while hiking, but most of his companions had come through a website called www.couchsurfing .com. Peter listed on his hosting profile on this site that in exchange for a free place to stay, guests would have to climb to the top of Bell Rock with him, and he did not accept requests from people he did not think were fit or able enough to get to the top. He referred to people who successfully reached the top with him as "club members." They were always welcome to return to stay with him, and he would do anything he could to help them out because he saw the act of climbing Bell Rock with him as a benefit to his ultimate aim of activating the portal on 21st December. Indeed, he called the Couchsurfing website itself a portal to see who Sedona would send to him.

The nine people who climbed with him on the 21st all had different personal connections to Peter, yet collectively represented the sort of heterogeneity typical of social gatherings in Sedona. His nephew, Brad, had flown in from Miami, where he worked as a technical director in sports broadcasting and as a freelance videographer and photographer. His main concern was the safety of his uncle. He did not share Peter's beliefs and was worried by what might happen that day. Joseph, from Scottsdale, was a friend of Peter's who told me he was ex–Marine Corps and a filmmaker, although Peter later told me he never actually made any films except a YouTube video for Peter detailing his "leap of faith." He went on to work as a solar panel salesman. He did not pay taxes and owed the Internal Revenue Service $80,000, identifying himself as a tax protestor who did not accept the legitimacy of the IRS. He had an interest in channeling, having read *The Hathor Material*, and had tried the practice himself.[2] He believed a portal could open. Solomon was an old friend of Peter's, who had known him for twenty years. He was Italian American, retired, living mostly in Phoenix, who came up to Sedona a couple of days a week to relax. I knew him independently of Peter from kundalini yoga class. He took Peter's beliefs with good-hearted humor. Sally and Summer were two young women in their early twenties, in a relationship with each other, who had previously stayed with Peter through couchsurfing and climbed Bell Rock with him then. They met through contributing to the same blog that focused on spiritual concerns. They were both from the East Coast, and at the time they were driving around the country and making money from selling handmade jewelry. They had driven for fifteen hours from Texas and arrived that morning. Sally had previously told me they thought it was really important to be here on the 21st and see what happened with Peter. The other three people who accompanied Peter were a film crew from Arizona State University, who had been employed by two other ASU students who had couchsurfed with Peter and were making a documentary on eschatological beliefs in 2012. The two club members were in Mexico at the time covering the Rainbow Gathering held near Chichen Itza, and sent some colleagues of theirs to cover Sedona.[3] They were there purely as observers, and seemed the least invested in the whole affair. The remaining two people in the party were Peter himself, a seventy-year-old retired Jewish lawyer from New York City, and me.

It was Peter's intention to stay on Bell Rock for thirteen hours, from 11 am to 12 midnight. He thought the portal would open at either 11:11 am or 11:11 pm, so he had to be there for both times. He called 11:11 his "magic number." The winter solstice in 2012 was at 11:11 UTC (Coordinated Universal Time) on 21st December, which Peter claimed was the reason it was a significant date, not because the Mayan calendar ended then.[4] However, 11:11 UTC was actually 4:11 am Arizona time. Peter said he did not want to be up on the rock in the middle of the night, so he said it would open at 11:11 Arizona time, either am or pm, because it was his story and he was in this particular time zone. When the morning came, he was so excited that he said we should leave earlier than planned at 10 am, reaching the northern parking lot, Courthouse Vista, shortly afterward.

Bell Rock is 479 feet above ground level, and roughly conical or bell-shaped. From a bird's-eye view, its circular pattern of spiraling layers of sandstone and granite can be more easily seen. Peter told me this is why Bell Rock is obviously a vortex; the spiraling energy that signifies a vortex in Sedona is instantiated in the shape of the rock itself. The entire area is Forest Service land, meaning it is federally managed and certain official prohibitions exist. Technically, those using Forest Service land have to stay on the officially marked trails made and maintained by the Forest Service. These trails are marked by signs at junctions with the name of the trail and stone cairns girded with wire mesh, in order to help visitors in finding their way. It is common for both locals and tourists to go off trail, however, and to get to the titular top of Bell Rock, you have to go off trail. The stone cairns wend a path up the north side of the rock to about halfway and then stop. The north side is a gentle incline with many level plinths, making it an easy climb that most people are capable of achieving. Most vortex tours went this far and no farther. Many spectators that day stayed restricted to the north side. It was also within the province of the Forest Service to close the trails and thus restrict any access to Bell Rock. It had been one of Peter's fears leading up to the day that due to all the hype about his intentions, the Forest Service would close the land. However, this did not happen and it was freely accessible to all who could find their way to the top.

Peter knew the way up very well. He had been climbing Bell regularly since 2010, with increasing frequency as 21st December 2012 approached. His normal route left the Forest Service trail that circled the base on the west side, and followed a narrow unofficial trail that wound up loose scrabbly rock to the base. Then there was smooth curved sandstone with gentle gradients that could be easily stepped or climbed up by most people I saw attempt it. These gentle gradients came in waves, dotted with prickly pear cactus and juniper trees growing out of dirt patches among the rock. The junipers grew in twisted spirals, another sign that this was a vortex, according to some local people. About 200 feet up from the base was the first difficult part of the route. There was a sheer rock wall of about 6–7 feet that could be scaled using hand- and footholds, or a narrow crevice could be shimmied up, using the three sides of the passageway to brace but with a large boulder at the top that was awkward to climb around. Then there was a gradient steeper than below the crevice, but easy to walk up on two feet because of the viscosity of sandstone. It was taxing in terms of endurance, and we usually stopped and sat on a boulder halfway up and Peter took photos. At the top of this section was the part that caused the most problems for people I saw attempting the climb. It was a narrow crevice that had to be scaled on one side using hand- and footholds, then near the top you had to transfer all your weight over to the other side and haul yourself up with your hands. There was one part where you stood clutching the side of the rock face with nothing behind but a 450-foot drop, and that was psychologically challenging for many people. Then it was an easy climb up to the top, which was not actually the physical top. It was a rocky outcrop with three flat plinths beside the actual summit, which was normally impossible to climb without ropes and harnesses. Peter called the central part of the top that we first reached "the saddle," then there was an outcrop to the right with a flat top that was intimidating to climb. To the left was a rock outcrop with a hole in the top that Peter liked to get the couchsurfers to climb in and pose for photos. Farther round to the left heading toward the summit was what Peter called "the top," a circular plinth about 20 feet higher than the saddle, the highest point that could be climbed to unassisted.

On the 21st, Peter tried to change this well-worn route. He started us off climbing the north side along the Forest Service trail. Then he could not remember the way to the top from there, so we ended up skirting the base through the trees to the bottom of the sheer rock face or crevice section, and then going up his normal way. We walked in single file, Peter going first carrying his huge bag, packed with everything he might need for a prolonged stay, with someone else carrying the back. Brad, Joseph, Solomon, and I took turns helping him carry the other end of the bag. Solomon kept making joking references to Christ's ascent to Calvary as we walked up. As we began, he said, "Peter, your disciples follow you!," adding that twelve and thirteen did not show up. Then again, as he carried the bag, he cried, "We're carrying the cross here!" According to Sally, it did seem, as we followed him in single file with the bag first, that we were in a procession heading toward something significant. When we reached the top, there was an unfamiliar man talking on his mobile phone standing on the rock plinth to the right of us. He saw us, climbed down, and asked, "Are you Peter? I've been waiting to meet you."

This man, Jason, was one of seven people already at the top when we reached it that morning. He was from Phoenix, and he said he had been seeing 11:11 occur in his life for seven years, first on digital clock displays, and then it seemed ubiquitous. He felt drawn to come to Sedona and climb Bell Rock for the 21st. His mother was a psychic and had brought him to Sedona for visits for years, although this was his first time up Bell Rock. He was a thirty-year-old tattooist. His legs and arms were covered in tattoos, including an "11:11" on his forearm. He said that his whole life was on the designs on his legs. He had heard of Peter on the internet but never contacted him; he said he knew that a lot of weirdos would have contacted him and he was not like that. He was there of his own volition, not coordinated with Peter in any way, but drawn by the same impulse and feeling as Peter, he said. The other six people were over on the top doing qigong and yoga poses, including headstands and shoulder stands at the edge. Two of them had contacted Peter before and said they were there for him, although Peter told me he did not understand in what sense they meant. I spoke to them and they said they were here to support Peter and what he was doing, and then they said they were waiting for a spaceship. The others said they were there to see what happened. A number of other people both familiar and unfamiliar to Peter came up to the top in the lead-up to 11:11 am. One man, who said he was just there to meditate, was very smartly dressed. Peter whispered to me that he was probably an undercover policeman because his formal attire seemed out of place.

Peter had sent out an invitation on his website, now taken down, two years prior inviting people to come to Sedona on 21st December 2012 to

FIGURE 11. The summit of Bell Rock, behind Peter, a Yavapai County Sheriff officer, and the author standing on the plinth that Peter called the "top." © Brad Gersten

await an "extraordinary event."[5] He received a lot of online communication from a wide variety of people who had seen his video explaining his "leap of faith" or had read about him elsewhere on the internet or heard about him through word of mouth. Peter had had at least three interviews in the week preceding the 21st, for Phoenix newspapers and online radio shows, and there were articles about him in the press across Arizona, elsewhere in the United States, and internationally.[6] One man emailed Peter and offered to sell all his possessions and join him, if he got reassurance from Peter that the portal truly would open. Peter told him not to come if he needed reassurance, it had to be a personal decision based on faith. It had become something of a media event. Peter commented to me on the hype, and complained that all they cared about was the "leap of faith." They just wanted to see something happen, they wanted to see if he would jump, and then laugh at him if he did not. Throughout the day he received calls and texts from unknown numbers asking if he had jumped yet. Peter ignored the texts, and if he answered the phone he would reply something nonsensical such as "Jim's not here!" and hang up.

As 11:11 am approached, we all went to the circular plinth that Peter called the top. Peter stood on the raised stone platform in the center of the plinth, surrounded by everyone else in a ring around the edge of the plinth. A police helicopter hung in the sky, hovering close to Bell. On either side of Bell, to the south and north that I could see, people sat, some looking up and waiting to see if someone would jump. Peter stood with his arms outstretched, looking up to the sky. The time 11:11 came, and then passed, and nothing happened. Peter climbed down to the saddle and sat on the ground, with his back against the rock outcrop. The police helicopter went away and many of the spectators went home, between 50 and 100, as did a number of the people in our group, including Sally, Summer, and Solomon.

The widely spread story had been that Peter was planning to jump off Bell Rock because it was the end of the world. In his initial YouTube video about the "leap of faith," he says that he will jump off Bell Rock to open a portal. He later recanted this intention, after pressure from his daughter and other family members. He did not want to upset his daughter, and he was afraid his family would put him on a psychiatric hold for the 21st so he would not be able to be on Bell Rock. Instead he said he would go to the top and wait for an extraordinary event to happen, which he believed would be the opening of a portal that he would step through to reach the source code at the center of this simulated reality and remove the virus that threatened our existence. He speculated that this extraordinary event could be something else, though. He suggested it could be the appearance of Jason on the top independently of him, or all of the couchsurfers that came into his life during that period. But crucially, he said he was not going to jump to precipitate the extraordinary event. He would require something to physically happen before he acted and get three independent verifications from other people that they could see it too. There seemed to be a palpable sense of disappointment from onlookers and some people on the top: the hyped event had not happened. However, Peter had been clear in interviews and in person that he was not going to jump unless something extraordinary happened. The police had questioned both Peter and me during the week before the 21st. They asked him directly if he would jump and he said no. We had also taken a member of the Yavapai County Sheriff's Office up to the top of Bell Rock the day before, ostensibly on reconnaissance in case someone got stuck or lost on the 21st so they knew the way, but Peter speculated that this officer was also assessing him and his mental state.

While Peter was clear about his intentions not to jump unless he saw something extraordinary occur, word of his beliefs had spread and was having an effect on others in the local area. While most people reacted with skepticism or curiosity, there was one person on Bell Rock that day who seemed to be taking it more seriously. Eric had come up before 11:11 am, and talked to various people about complicated arbitrary numerical calculations that he claimed indicated that the 21st would be the end of the world. He was a homeless man from Portland, Oregon, who had been sleeping up on Bell Rock for the previous few nights. He said he had read about Peter on the internet. When the film crew was filming interviews with Peter and a few others in the group, this man became increasingly vocal about "what needed to be done" and kept saying he wanted to talk to Peter. It seemed like he was saying he was going to help Peter by jumping and that would reveal what kind of cancer Peter had. Peter had had a malignant tumor in his neck that had been successfully removed in January 2012, but one of the rumors was that he was going to jump because he was dying of cancer. The film crew packed up, saying they thought they were making the situation worse and were going to stop filming. Peter angrily confronted Eric and told him not to jump. He yelled at Eric, "This is my story, not yours! Stay out of my story! Get your own!" There was a tense moment of silence. Then Eric asked if Peter was God, Peter replied that he was not, and Eric asked, "Then how can you tell me what to do?"

Eric then withdrew and lay under his blanket, a practice he called "meditating." Joseph and I went to talk to him, trying to calm him, asking him where he was from, whether he had any family, advising him that no one wanted him to jump. He was angry with Peter after the rejection, and there was some concern he might harm Peter. Every so often he would walk over to the edge and stand there looking down, saying he would take the "Superman route" down. Peter called the police; he was afraid he would be held legally responsible if Eric jumped. Search and rescue came up and spoke to him for about five minutes, concluded he was not going to jump, and went back down. Then a friend of Joseph's came up, carrying a staff with a fuzzy tail attached that he called "Mr. Otter," and he sat down with Eric for several hours and talked to him. After they finished talking, Eric was gradually integrated into the group as the day wore away.

The remaining people steadily left the rock individually or in small groups, when they grew tired and it seemed like nothing was going to happen after all. As the sun set, a large aura formed around the moon in a white perfect circle above us. Eric cried out that it was the portal. Peter agreed jokingly and said it would descend down onto us. Peter's ironic dismissal immediately undermined Eric, and he did not hold on to the idea that it was the portal. It was the reflection of the moon on ice crystals in the clouds, I later found out. It got cold after nightfall. We wrapped up in sleeping bags and several layers of clothing, eating snacks, smoking marijuana, but not really talking anymore. The sense of crisis had passed and it was a very calm and still night. A couple of times Eric said he saw something, but each time it was dismissed as nothing by Peter. Then 11:11 pm approached and Peter played the soundtrack from the movie *Close Encounters of the Third Kind* on his iPad, which created a creepy ambiance, but he stayed where he sat and again nothing happened. It got to 11:50 pm and Peter said we should get ready and go. Eric stayed up on the top, and Peter left him his sleeping bag. He did not want to haul his bag down in the dark, so his stuff was all left up there. We climbed down in the dark quickly with little ceremony. I was relieved to get back on the ground after fourteen hours on top of a rock, but Peter said little. He made a joke about his headlamp being the portal that would move us into the light. We drove back to his apartment, ate Subway sandwiches, and then everyone went home. When I got back to my house, I checked Facebook and Peter had posted a picture of Marvin the depressed robot from the movie *Hitchhiker's Guide to the Galaxy* with the comment "I didn't win."

THE IDIOSYNCRATIC BELIEF SYSTEM OF PETER GERSTEN

The events related above occurred because of a specific prediction Peter made about what would happen on 21st December 2012. This prediction was part of a larger plot, which he called "my story." He explicitly framed what he was doing as narrative while simultaneously narrating it on social media and through media interviews. As such, using social and cognitive psychologist Jerome Bruner's work on how narrative "operates as an instrument of mind in the construction of reality" offers insight into understanding how Peter framed his story and what his purpose was.[7] Bruner outlines ten features of narrative as a guide for the social scientific analysis of this process.[8] Some of these features can be used as tools for helping understand how Peter constructed his life as a story.

Peter Gersten was born in New York City in 1942 to a Jewish family and lived most of his adult life in that city. He was educated at Syracuse University, UC San Diego, and Brooklyn Law School. During my fieldwork, he was a public defender in Navajo County, adjacent to Yavapai and Coconino counties where Sedona is located. He used to work there full-time, then when he reached retirement he was "rehired" in his old position doing part-

FIGURE 12. Peter Gersten and others on the top of Bell Rock on 21st December 2012.
© Brad Gersten

time hours because the economic crisis meant Navajo County could not afford to replace him with another full-time attorney. He said that this role required him to mostly represent members of the Navajo and Hopi tribes for alcohol-related crimes such as driving under the influence (DUI), aggravated DUI, and domestic violence. He worked in the courts in Winslow and Holbrook, which are on the border with the Navajo Nation where alcohol is banned. The border towns attract those who want to buy alcohol, and the result is a slew of public order offenses in those towns involving Native Americans. Peter said he liked this work because it was easy; most of his clients were guilty, so all he had to do was advise them to sign plea deals.[9] It allowed him plenty of time to pursue his real passion, hiking in Sedona.

Before he moved to Arizona, Peter was a criminal prosecutor in New York City, working mostly on murder cases. In the 1980s, he became known as "the UFO lawyer," because he petitioned the government for the release of files about investigations into UFOs and aliens. He had one successful case of this kind. However, he said these cases were pointless because the government did not release anything, they were only required by the Freedom of Information Act to do a "reasonable search." Then they did not find anything because, according to Peter, the people looking did not have the clearance to find anything. He pursued these cases because he found it suspicious that the government said absolutely nothing about sightings. The last case he had of this kind was in 2000. For his part, he did not believe that extraterrestrial beings were visiting the earth. The UFOs that people have talked about in America since the late 1940s were only lights in the sky and triangles. However, they were real because people did see objects that they could not identify, he just did not believe these objects were alien craft. The UFO people, such as the Mutual UFO Network, initially liked him because he gave them credibility, but then they backed away from him when he started talking about 2012 and the simulation, when he apparently became "too crazy" for them. Peter told me that UFOs are planted in the simulation by whoever is running it to cover up their existence as watchers. He called it the perfect cover, creating a phenomenon that most people dismiss as ridiculous to disguise their true purpose.

The stated motivation for his UFO investigations was publicity and attention, and these were his main aims on 21st December 2012 as well. The purpose of his spiritual path was to get attention. However, he did not see what he did as spirituality but as his "story." As he declared on the top of Bell Rock to Eric, this was his story. Yet it seemed to me his story followed a structure common to those involved in spirituality. He gave up a successful career as a New York City prosecutor and worked as a public defender in small-town Arizona just to be comfortable, and creating and publicizing his story became more important than his career. Before coming to Sedona, he had engaged in many practices that fall within the rubric of spirituality, including vision quests, holistic wellness retreats, and UFO investigations.

On a visit to Sedona in 1998, he had an epiphany that reality was a simulation and he had a special mission within it, which precipitated his move to the town. This structure has a degree of what Bruner calls "genericness"; stories in a given context form "recognizable 'kinds' of narrative."[10] In spirituality this pattern occurred in many of my interlocutors' narratives of how they started on their spiritual path: the abandonment of a successful career because it was unsatisfying, followed by a period of seeking, then finding Sedona serendipitously and preferring the comfort and peace of living there over the material rewards of the previous career. As such, Peter's claim that what he did was not "spirituality" is akin to fundamentalist Christians who claim they are not a religion, because from their perspective, what they believe is the truth, not "religion."[11] From an analytical perspective, what Peter calls "his story" is his spiritual path.

The central plot in Peter's story is the premise that this reality we perceive is a simulation. It is a holographic reality; he called it a "cosmic computer program." It is created like any computer program from a source code. Knowing the source code grants the ability to change anything in this reality or travel anywhere in time and space. On 21st December, Peter aimed to reach the source code that lies at the galactic core through a portal so he could change this reality, essentially reprogramming it. This simulated reality was created by an intelligent life-form with advanced technology that could somehow transform energy into matter. Everything in the simulation was an energy pattern that vibrated at a certain frequency. The frequency determined what sort of experience was created in the simulation, and that depended on the being in the simulation. Each person thus created their own reality in the simulation; they had already consented to everything that happened within it. Everyone wrote their own story. Peter thus employed the language of spirituality—energy, frequency, vibration—and the individualist moral imperative that each person is responsible for creating their own reality; as such, his beliefs fit comfortably within the cosmologies of spirituality described in the introduction.

What was distinctive about Peter's framing was the insistence that it was all a story. He told me he wanted to write his story, but he was no good at writing, so he decided to live it instead. And not just live it, publicize it through social media as well so others could hear about it. As such, Peter's spiritual path, his story, can be read as autobiography because he was constructing his version of reality as a narrative about himself. Reading Peter's story as autobiography fits with the primacy of the individual in his beliefs because autobiography is the literary construct that lionizes (however questionably) the autonomous individual.[12] Literary scholar G. Thomas Couser argued that this makes autobiography the most American of literary forms, especially the narrative of the success story based on individual ability.[13] Peter's story is a variant of this well-worn cultural narrative; the individual saving the collective, a familiar tale told about many cultural heroes and religious icons from Jesus to Benjamin Franklin. It was interpreted this way by other participants through mutually understood Christian referents, such as Solomon's comments about Peter's disciples and carrying the cross. Significantly, this cultural narrative was placed in an eschatological frame, enhancing his messianic status.

Individual choice concerning what happens in one's life was in many ways a moral imperative for Peter. He would often comment when bad things happened that he chose this event so there was some lesson to learn from it, and would then spend time musing on what this lesson was that he had programmed for himself. He once asked rhetorically why anyone would choose a "crappy simulation," in reference to a conversation about his clients in Navajo County, many of whom lived lives of abysmal poverty. He concluded that there must be something they thought they needed to learn from that existence. He called his life his ideal reality; residing in a beautiful, sunny place with plentiful hiking, happy and healthy in his seventies, with friends to share his time and pursuits. Morality is in the individual taking care of himself and creating his best life possible. This interpretation of morality allowed Peter to ignore any structural causes of, say, poverty, or his complicity in the criminal justice system that discriminated against Native Americans.[14] Instead, he got to focus on the good things in life and declare his perfect.

Peter created the narrative of his story through denial, a systematic process of ignoring the things that did not fit into his idealized view of his reality or reinterpreting them so they did. Numerous instances of this were evident to me on 21st December, such as why the portal would open at 11:11 am Arizona time and not any other time zone's 11:11, or why 11:11 at all.[15] When Eric saw a circle in the sky and called it a portal but Peter did not. Even to call that plinth the "top" of Bell Rock when it clearly was not, it was just the part that he could reach free-climbing. Peter was upfront about this selectivity, telling me that the simulation was limited to his perception of reality because it only created his present moment. Only what can be sensed by the person within it had to be created by the simulation. As a consequence, if something could not be perceived by Peter, it essentially did not exist. Everything that he experienced fit into the narrative of his story because it was his version of the simulation, and by definition nothing would happen in it that was irrelevant to him. He was the main character in his own story; everything that happened revolved around him. This demonstrated the narrative feature of "hermeneutic composability" where elements were "selected and shaped" according to the requirements of the meaning of the story.[16] While in the cold light of anthropological analysis, it seemed like denial born of social privilege to claim that Navajos living with alcoholism chose a "crappy simulation" in order to learn a lesson, in terms of Peter's story it was part of how he produced the morality of individual responsibility. Each person chose their reality in the simulation, therefore unpleasant realities were lessons to be learned.

Peter was a prolific user of Facebook; this was how he published his story. As well as pictures of people hiking Bell, he often posted stories from various internet sites citing studies performed by physicists and philosophers concluding that we do indeed live in a simulated reality. At the same time, he said proof of this would be suppressed because one of the premises of the simulation was that most people did not realize it was a simulation. Although he had no formal scientific training, Peter's beliefs were in line with certain scientific postulations concerning multiverses made by quantum physicists and philosophers such as Nicholas Bostrom's "simulation argument."[17] In scholar of religion Mary-Jane Rubenstein's analysis, there is a dialectical relationship between science and religion. The Big Bang hypothesis mirrored "orthodox" Christian theology of *ex nihilo* creation. Scientists in the twentieth century attempted to overcome the implication of a supreme being through speculating about multiverses where every possibility of the law of physics is played out.[18] Rubenstein did not mention spirituality; however, it seems to me that it is a religious reflection of the combination of string theory, quantum mechanics, and modern cosmology that she described, where the universe is a self-contained oneness in which God is no longer required to create the universe, God *is* the universe. Peter's innovation was to describe the individual within this self-contained oneness as a simulation, analogous to a computer program or video game, a way of having different experiences. Portals were his way through from this universe to other universes in the infinite multiverse. Science in his belief system is imaginative rather than empirical, using it as a background for the story, employing the narrative feature of "referentiality" where the relation to "truth" is one of "verisimilitude" rather than "verifiability."[19]

As the hero in the story, Peter felt he had a mission. He called it his "assignment." He believed there was a memetic virus in the source code creating this simulation. He described the virus as "memetic" because it downloaded a "techno-meme" into the frequencies that manifest the simulation then continually spread from one mind to another. The source for this term, interestingly, is the scientist and critic of religion Richard Dawkins, who described religion as a virus that spreads from one mind to another and has a specific set of symptoms.[20] For Peter, the virus was a corruption of the source code, located in the galactic center, which he described as not "out there" but within us. It attacked the frequencies of the simulation, thereby affecting our perception of reality. It prevented humanity from coming together, leaving us weak and divided, while simultaneously creating pollution and resource depletion that will eventually undermine our subsistence. He told me that chemicals and "cell phone radiation" were making us infertile, and personalized technology, such as smartphones, was an effective weapon against us through making us dependent on it and the instant gratification it supplied while destroying the planet at the same time. This was a "Trojan horse" attack, where what we depend on for modern society to function was also slowly killing us. He said that if there were aliens, they would not attack with a death ray or invasion. They would poison our water supply, pollute our air, destroy our ability to exist on this planet, and make us impotent so we could no longer reproduce. And that was precisely what he saw as happening in the world around him. The idea of a virus was a metaphor for what he saw as wrong with contemporary society.

Peter's mission was to fix these problems. This virus was introduced into the simulation with silicone-based technology, and after he cleared it there would have to be a moratorium on this kind of technology. Yet it was not only the removal of this technology that was required but also humanity needed to come together, to cooperate rather than compete for survival. What he was suggesting was a death and rebirth of this world. In his words, the simulation needed to be rebooted. There was an element of eternal recurrence to this idea. He said we had done all of this before. He enters the simulation to open the portal, and by successfully doing that he moves on to the next "level," where he enters the source code and removes the virus. The eternal recurrence is similar to a video game; just as a player passes levels to advance to the next stage in a video game, that is how Peter saw his mission. He had done this before and would do it again, on the next level. He once joked that death is just like re-spawning in a video game. What is perhaps ironic is that he used the language of technology: programs, simulations, viruses, levels, while advocating the removal of technology (or at least silicone-based technology) from our reality. This sense of mission created the dramatic tension in the story, the plot line that leads up to the climax of the portal opening. It also placed Peter within the rich tradition of American apocalypticism and millennialism, predicting an end to this world and the beginning of a new one.[21]

The means by which Peter believed he would reach the source code and remove the virus was a portal. The potential for portals opening was not an idea unique to Peter. I found myself listening to talk of portals frequently in Sedona. In the house Peter moved into after 21st December, his new housemate advised him she had closed a portal belonging to the previous owner with crystals. A friend with whom I practiced kung fu told me that his father and he had made a copper pyramid in their garden in Long Island, New York, that created a portal that led to another dimension. There was even a street in Sedona named "Portal Lane" near the central roundabouts. Portals compressed spacetime, allowing for what was temporally or spatially distant to be brought closer. They were routes through planes of existence otherwise sealed from each other. They made the materially impossible, spiritually practical.

Peter believed we went through portals all the time. It was how a different level in the simulation was reached. The portal he wished to open on Bell Rock on the 21st was a powerful one that required him to take people to the top so their frequencies raised the vibration sufficiently that it would open. The first time he went up Bell Rock in 1998, he was with a galactic astrologer who told him it was an intergalactic portal.[22] I asked him if this was the source of his portal theory and he said yes, but also cited the Harmonic Convergence in 1987, when people gathered in Sedona expecting, among other things, a spaceship to come out of Bell.[23] He also mentioned that Bell Rock is in the UFO corridor from Area 51 in Nevada to Tucson in southern Arizona and considered this significant.[24] Peter considered all of these sources clues that helped confirm his belief that Bell Rock was where the portal would open.

Like many millenarians, Peter read reality as permeated with clues.[25] There were no coincidences, only synchronicities that pointed to deeper meanings in the simulation, such as 11:11, 2012, and the Mayan calendar. Peter called 11:11 a "gateway," a symbol that he interpreted as a code in the simulation to help him realize what was going on and remember what he was there to do. Peter started noticing 11:11 in October 1998; the occurrences increased in frequency leading up to 11th November 1998, when he had his epiphany that reality was a simulation and he had to remove the virus. While I was in Sedona, Peter would consistently point out when he saw 11:11 in different contexts. The most significant occurrence for him was on his seventieth birthday when he traveled to the Bahamas with his daughter for a holiday and went swimming with dolphins. The dolphin bit him on his hand, leaving four vertical bite marks. He interpreted this bite mark as significant because the scars looked like the digits 11:11, and concluded that this mark could function like a bar code. He could hold it up to the portal on the 21st so he could gain entry to the source code. Reading reality as a series of clues constructs stories through "narrative accrual," in particular associating things happening at the same time with each other in a meaningful way rather than dismissing them as coincidence.[26] For millenarians, the clues created a story that told them how this world will end and a new one will begin.

Clues came to Peter through television programs and films as well as directly from life events. The motivation behind his most notorious claim, the "leap of faith," came from the episode of the TV show *Lost* called "316."

This was his favorite episode of the show, and in American notation "316" was also his birthday, March 16. This linked to the event with the dolphin that happened on his birthday. *Lost* was a TV show open to interpretation. As a mystery show that unfolded over six seasons, the episodes were peppered with clues to the riddles the show proposed and fans engaged in active detection through repeat viewing.[27] The show ended with the main character getting lowered into the "source" of a mysterious light in order to save the world. Peter read personal relevance into this fictional narrative. It became an inspiration for what his "mission" was, as were other movies and television shows with similar plot points. Media provided him with clues through which he constructed his own narrative of individual messianism.

Nothing that occurred in the simulation was neutral for Peter; everything pointed to something else, a hidden meaning or deeper truth. This included my arrival. I met Peter in September 2012, and we first climbed Bell Rock together on the day that was 101 days before the 21st, a number that to him referred to 11:11. Peter said it was no coincidence for a cultural anthropologist to appear in the story with 101 days to go. I was an alien, one of the watchers in the simulation, sent to monitor his progress. It would be the perfect cover, a galactic anthropologist masquerading as a cultural anthropologist. He sometimes called me Elizabeth, which he guessed must be my name in a previous simulation, otherwise why else would it pop into his head when he was addressing me? It seemed obvious to him and it made him think that he was right about something significant happening. This drew my attention to my role as an anthropologist in my interlocutors' lives; in this context I could not be a neutral observer. Just being present in Sedona at this time meant that I had an effect on Peter's beliefs: I became a character in his story. This raised ethical issues; was I changing what was happening in my interlocutor's life? I think that whether I was there or not, Peter would have been on Bell Rock on 21st December, and he would have found significance in whoever was there and whatever happened. Yet the fact remains that I was there, and this did have an impact.

Scholar of religion Timothy Jenkins argued that in the process of asking people about their beliefs, social scientists can, often unwittingly, help create and develop these beliefs through the rhetorical process of asking about them.[28] Jenkins produced this reflection through rereading psychologist Leon Festinger's classic analysis of an American millenarian group.[29] Festinger placed researchers as observers posing as believers in the group surrounding Marian Keech, who predicted the end of the world on 21st December 1954 and that a UFO would save the believers.[30] When the date came and passed, the observers noted the reactions of the group as they navigated the disappointment of prophecy unfulfilled. Festinger's lasting contribution was the term "cognitive dissonance," which he described as the gap between two opinions or beliefs that do not fit together. This gap creates discomfort and then pressure to reduce the dissonance by changing the beliefs, forgetting or denying the importance of the gap, or obtaining new information to allow beliefs to become consonant with each other.[31] The group around Keech demonstrated a range of these strategies after the prophesied event did not occur.

Jenkins called Festinger's analysis a "psychological description" and offered instead a "rhetorical approach" that emphasized how interrelated parties deployed models of language to construct certain kinds of account.[32] Instead of accounting for how the group was dealing with "reality," Jenkins examined how members of the group produced their interpretations through discussion and analysis with each other, including the members who were secretly observing events for Festinger's study. Festinger also allowed that in a millenarian situation it was impossible for his observers to remain neutral because "any action had consequences"; the observers had to lead meetings, take stands when opinions were divided, and were pressured to quit their jobs.[33] However, Festinger dismissed the influence of the observers, claiming that there was no effect on the continued proselytizing of the Keech group.[34] Jenkins took this situation as the point of departure for his analysis, arguing instead that the words and actions of the social scientists were a crucial part of the dialectical production of millenarian events, particularly in their questions after the disappointing event when they reinforced the idea that that was the reality and it was what the believers should be dealing with.[35] Such "coproduction" is a common trend in apocalypticism.[36] Groups working from what Michael Barkun called a millenarian "script" have their end-time signs confirmed by outsiders' (often hostile) responses to their activities, something to which he attributed the tragic deaths of the Branch Davidians in Waco, Texas.[37] Jenkins's emphasis on rhetorical production and Barkun's concept of a millenarian "script" resonate with Bruner's narrative construction of reality. In millenarianism, a story is constructed through selected references to events read as signs that create a plot that leads to the climax of the end of the world.

During the run-up to his eschatological event, I was afraid that my presence might convince Peter of the veracity of his beliefs to the point where he would jump. It is important not to overstate my own influence, however, since collaborativeness is part of the nature of ethnography, and not only

FIGURE 13. Police helicopter and onlookers on the top of Bell Rock on 21st December 2012.
© Brad Gersten

I but also everyone else present affected his story as well. The playful narration of the self in spirituality located those involved in it as both insiders and
outsiders. They were interested in "new age" practice but they were not "new
agers" in their own estimation, an ambiguously dual position that mirrors
that of the anthropologist.[38] I recognize this ambiguous duality in my relationship with Peter, where we both acted as anthropologist and informant
in our own stories. We both selected certain events from a plural and messy
"reality" to construct coherent narratives. He called his a story that is part of
a simulation, I called mine a book that is part of a career in anthropology. He
put me into his story as an alien, I put him into my book as an interlocutor
and representative of spirituality in Sedona, even though he said he was not
spiritual and I said I was not an alien. Structurally we were these things to
each other even if we did not describe ourselves in those terms.

The interaction between Peter and me became a way for him to reflect
on and even modify his story. I was a sounding board for his ideas because
I was asking about them on a regular basis. It became a reciprocal dialogue
through which we both constructed an understanding of what he was doing.
He would often directly ask me to interpret what was going on or what
things meant. He asked me what I thought of his repeatedly climbing Bell,
and I described it as a ritual. From then on he called it a ritual. I asked why

and he said because I said so and then soon after that conversation he heard a reference to ritual in a movie, so the synchronicity proved it.

It did indeed seem like a ritual to me.[39] There was a consistent structure for each climb. We would meet in the parking lot, then walk down the trail to the base, then we would climb the rock; at the junction between the sheer rock face and the crevice, Peter would stop everyone and explain the two different routes, giving each climber the choice as to which they attempted, then halfway up we would stop on the same boulder and sit and take a rest. When we got to the top Peter would get all the new members to stand on the plinth to the left of the saddle and pose, including a jump that he would endeavor to catch on his camera when they were in midair so it looked like they were levitating. Peter described this as "performance." He said he would bring people to the top and they would just start performing, such as yoga poses, music, juggling, meditations, or ceremonies. Peter would make it sound spontaneous when he described it, but before he took people up he would tell them about what previous people had done and create an expectation for others to continue this, sometimes carrying up props such as guitars or cellos. Peter said on the top people would look "euphoric," as if they had been taken over by a different energy form or even that they were paying "tribute" to whatever kind of intelligence was up there. Then we would climb down. At the bottom he would high-five all the new members, congratulating them for having made it, and he would pay for a meal at a local restaurant. In this way, the people he hosted became "guest stars" in formulaic episodes with a recognizable narrative arc that he subsequently displayed through images and videos posted online.

The recurring characters in the story were his friends in Sedona, but more significantly, Sedona itself and Bell Rock. Peter described himself as having a relationship with this specific rock. He said that to him Bell was a woman, called "Belle," even though typically in Sedona vortex typology Bell was attributed masculine energy. He described Bell Rock and Sedona as life-forms that have their own energy patterns, and he was in some form of contact with them. In doing so, he attributed agency to the rock and the town because he believed these entities to be high-energy life-forms that in the simulation take the appearance of dense matter. Sedona, as mentioned earlier, was the entity that oversaw his program in the simulation, granting him new characters for his story and different plot twists. In doing this, he expanded agency to non-human forms. It must be highlighted that agency is an attribute of energy patterns, so the fact that humans have it as well as rocks is a consequence of both of these forms being composed of energy.

It also allowed Sedona and Bell to feature as characters in his story, which is part of "intentional state entailment"; for entities to act as protagonists, they must be endowed with agency.[40]

Throughout the morning of the 21st, Peter received calls from club members wishing him well, and he was becoming emotional. It was as if they had come back for cameos in his finale. I suggested he had created an event for them to emotionally attach to and find significant. Peter frowned. "Did I just create all this to experience emotion?" Brad said I was like his therapist, leading him to answer his own questions rather than providing answers myself. The point was perhaps not to answer his questions, which were mostly unanswerable, but to have the dialogue, to think through these issues with him. This is what Peter seemed to want from me, perhaps because he saw me as having more knowledge about the simulation because of my role as a watcher. It was impossible for me to even pretend to be an impartial observer. I was a part of this ethnographic situation, helping create what was going on as it was happening in a rhetorical dialectic as outlined by Jenkins. The purpose of our dialogue was on a surface level a search for meaning. Peter wanted to know what it all meant; however, if that was all he wanted, there would be innumerable ways to enrich his life with meaning. Instead, he chose to produce and live a highly specific and elaborate "belief system" that he called a story and publicized through social media. He shaped his reality through telling a story and brought the people around him, family, friends, acquaintances, total strangers, the town he lived in, and the landscape he inhabited, into this story as well.

Stories are worth telling because they relate a breach in cultural norms according to Bruner. A breach means trouble, and "it is Trouble that provides the engine of drama."[41] Peter's story seems idiosyncratic, but the title of this section is ironic. His story is rooted in American cultural motifs: the individual savior of the collective, the multiverse with the door to another reality where space and time are different, sacrificing the self to renew the world. It is normative within the genre of millenarian scripts. He wove these varying strands into his own narrative composition to provide him with a story worth telling to others. The declaration of his leap of faith was his breach, his way of creating trouble. What Peter wanted was drama. By setting a date for the end and declaring his faith in his prediction, he created a narrative arc resulting in a climax, which was anticlimactic as with all millenarian predictions. However, what stopped him from ultimately taking his leap of faith was his family, especially the protests of his daughter. This is the true breach in his narrative construction of reality: his unfettered individu-

alism was restrained by his social relationships. He rewrote his millenarian
script because of his family's protests; family was more important than his
individual path, what he believed was less important than their feelings.
Individualism was as much of a narrative construction as the simulation and
other fantastical elements of his story.

AMERICAN NIGHTMARE: LIVING IN A (HYPER)REALITY SHOW

Peter's narrativization of his own life aimed at dramatizing and publicizing
his experience. This allowed for the constant (over)creation of meaning, as
he read the flow of events and people around him as significant, indicative of
a deeper plot. Peter rendered his story into a structure derived from contemporary American media: that of a reality television show. Using the metaphor of a "game," he said he was in a competition with all the other beings
in the simulation to be the most outrageous, which would then be the most
watched. This would mean he would "win," or get his extraordinary event
and be proven right in his beliefs. He called his reality television show *The
Top of Bell Rock Club*, and everything he experienced was part of the show.
Events were interpreted in episodic format, structured into seasons, with
recurring characters and guest stars, narrated by Peter in his speech and on
his Facebook page. The extraordinary event was the big finale at the end of
the season, with a dramatic climax or possibly a cliffhanger. He described
several different versions of what could happen on the 21st. One suggestion
was that he could go through the portal and then all the club members
around the world would disappear, leaving a mystery to be solved in the next
season. When nothing happened, it was an anti-climax. He did not "win," as
he announced on his Facebook page with the picture of the depressed robot.
This led to a short period of depression, until he decided he had garnered
enough ratings for renewal. Then he constructed a new season of his reality
show, with a new location.

A few weeks after 21st December, Peter announced the next season of his
life-as-reality-show, which he called "The House in Magic Land on Rainbow
Lane." He had not "won," in his terms, but he had been successful enough
to be renewed for another season. He had been evicted from his apartment
facing Bell Rock because of his neighbor's complaints about noise from his
visitors and had to leave at the end of December. This in itself he found

significant. Once the 21st passed, he had no reason to be there, so it then became impossible for him to stay. His new house was near Red Rock Crossing, a popular swimming hole in Sedona, in view of Cathedral Rock, another vortex. The house was on Rainbow Lane, and at the head of the road there was a sign that said "Magic Land Realty," which was the company that leased the house to Peter and his housemate. He continued to take people to the top of Bell Rock, but without any set purpose as to why. He enjoyed it so he continued doing it, and he continued the same ritual and counting the number of people in the *Top of Bell Rock Club*. When this ended after two seasons chronicled on his Facebook page, he moved again to a new residence in the Village of Oak Creek, an apartment above a store called the Bike & Bean, which rented and sold bikes and was also a coffee shop. He called this the second season of the *Top of Bell Rock Club*, which he posted on Facebook under the title "Above the Bike n Bean." He told me just before I left Arizona in April 2014 that he had a new mission, to take 2,222 people to the top of Bell Rock by the winter solstice of 2018 because in that year the winter solstice was at 22:22 UTC, when he would try again to open a portal.

By mid-2018 he had already exceeded his target number of 2,222 people, and by October was at 2,883. He rarely accepted requests through Couchsurfers anymore. Many of his groups were now repeat visitors who had come back to go up with him again, and most of his new members were recommended to him by previous members. His club was growing through word of mouth, and he continued to inspire some level of admiration. There were club members with their numbers or pictures of Bell Rock tattooed on their bodies, and ten returned for his next attempt to enter the portal on 21st December 2018. The group stayed up with Peter for forty hours with a tent and sleeping bags, fasting, and periodically livestreaming on Facebook. After they came down, Peter posted that this was the final episode of the *Top of Bell Rock Club*, and he believed he had been contacted by an entity that night and that he had entered an alternate reality.

Or at least, that was what Peter said. At the same time, he was upfront about the fact that nothing he had a revelation of after his first 11:11 experience in 1998 had yet to come to pass. If anyone, for instance skeptical couchsurfers hiking Bell Rock with him, confronted him on this, he would say that he believed what he believed because of the experiences he had had, and if he was wrong, then that was no big deal. It was all fiction that someone made up, and that was life. He was simply making up a more interesting story for himself than just being an old man who sat by the creek and did paint by numbers, as he sardonically suggested he might do if nothing happened on 21st December 2012. After 21st December, he said he felt empty without his story, so after a short time, he made up a new one. In his own terms, he yelled "plot twist!" and carried on. This was his answer to cognitive dissonance. There was no gap between "reality" and his beliefs because his beliefs created his reality. He did not claim that it was given to him by a divine source, his beliefs were simply what made sense for his story. Since everyone was in their own story, they should make their own decisions and take responsibility for them. This radical individualism is why he never tried to accrue followers.

While Peter did not seek followers, it is clear from what happened on 21st December that a number of people found inspiration in the same sources he did, such as 11:11 recurring in their lives, or from his actions. Peter defined everything he did as the outcome of his individual choices but his story still resonated with others. Jenkins suggested that millenarianism is about the present rather than the future, mapping an experience of uncertainty when "accepted categories" are disrupted.[42] Historian Norman Cohn argued that millenarianism followed social dislocation and anxiety. His theory derived from a historical analysis of the suffering poor during the eleventh to fourteenth centuries in Western Europe who found consolation from oppression in prophecy.[43] Messiahs offered hope, millenarianism "came to serve as vehicles for social aspirations and animosities."[44] Peter's story operated in a similar way to how Cohn described prophecy. It was a narrative that explained his present circumstances, and suggested a way forward.

Peter's social position was very different to the medieval European peasants that Cohn described, however. It is significant in this regard that he did not find a guru or prophet to follow to give him hope, he created his own prophecy. That he was able to do so speaks to his cultural and socioeconomic status; as a middle-class white American male he had ability, opportunity, and validation to create narratives about his life to share with others. Anthropologist Maurice Bloch suggested that narrative is fundamental to a sense of self, personhood, or identity—concepts he clumped together unceremoniously under the term "the blob"—however, not all persons have the same tendency to narrativize to the same extent.[45] Following philosophers Daniel Dennett, Galen Strawson, and others, he positioned "the narrative self" at the higher end of the continuum that constituted the blob, above the core and minimal self. Above this is meta-representation, a capacity of externalizing introspection, which not all humans utilized extensively. Intervening in what he saw as a sterile debate in anthropology about whether there is a "Western" individualized, bounded self and a "non-Western" social, relational self, he argued that some societies reified meta-representation more than others, and therefore more people in those societies engaged in it. Using Strawson's terminology, he called these people "diachronics," and they had a strong sense of meaningful autobiography and narrate this in culturally available ways, talking about internal states, feelings, and their life story. Americans like Peter are taught to construct a seamless integrated life story to present to others, to get jobs, funding, friends, and university places. The middle classes receive economic and social gains from narrating their lives, less so the working classes. However, it is important to heed Bloch's warning not to mistake the story for the self. Class position does not confer different abilities in terms of introspection and narration, just different incentives to perform the self. Peter's narrative concentrated on himself as the focal point of the simulation, and it seemed to be his attempt to find out who was this "self" at the center of the story. More than that, it was about what this self was capable of, and what he could inspire others to do.

There is a certain social experience of powerlessness felt in global capitalism.[46] While each individual American tells their personal story, through words and pictures, especially on social media, significant economic capital and social power remain beyond them. Peter told me that the reason he tried to get attention and publicity, why many people in American society do, is because on some level they know that they are in a simulation. They know that their lives are not meaningful or significant on any greater scale. This existential anxiety leads to a form of acting out, displaying attention-seeking behavior in order to overcome it. They feel more of a sense of realness when others pay attention to them. This is something that philosopher Jean Baudrillard has suggested, that the "uncertainty of existing, and consequently the obsession of proving our existence" matters above all else.[47] Peter's millenarian script of living in a simulated reality created a sense of realness and purpose in a social situation of powerlessness and anonymity.

For Baudrillard, this was a situation of hyperreality created by media, the representation of reality to such an extent that reality was no longer represented, and only the simulation existed.[48] It was a self-referential circularity that echoed Peter's search for experience; he created what he was looking for in the process of searching for it. Yet the fully isolated individual only exists in postmodernist thought experiments and ideological narratives. Bloch made the point that all blobs are socially linked, but those without positive reinforcement for the externalization of their meta-representations focus more on their relationships with others. Peter remained connected to his social relations, inhibited by his daughter's concern, and by the fear of being branded insane by his family. He created a new web of relations with his club members, finding validation through them and reflecting that back onto them through including them in his story.

Peter chose to publicize his story through social media, a forum that approximates hyperreality. It is an endless display of images selected to represent a person's life that for some become more real than life itself.[49] It seemed to me that for Peter, the images he took and posted were in some ways more important than the action of being on the rock itself. The representation of the act was more important than the act itself because that was how he intended to alter the simulation, through changing its programming, rewriting its script. The simulation was part of Peter's narrative construction of reality, it was the landscape in which his story unfolded. In Bruner's terms, it was a "reality" created or constituted by narrative, not concretely "represented" by it, it was a literary convention as much as James Joyce's "Dublin."[50] But on another level the simulation did refer to the material conditions of Peter's life in the same way that Joyce's Dublin referred to a specific place with a material existence. It was not pure hyperreality. There was a breach in cultural norms being explored by Peter's story, a disruption to accepted categories being mapped.

Peter positioned himself as the prophet perceptive enough to realize the simulation and destined to break it down and remake it in his ideal image of a perfected reality. This is the messianic role adopted by Marian Keech and other millenarian leaders, the chosen one who will save the Elect and then go on to remake society according to their ideals. However, Peter rejected the role of hero. He consistently shrugged off followers and demurred to my suggestion that he was the hero in the story. He is better understood as the protagonist of his story than the hero. His story was not some dull tale either, it was a melodrama with strong emotional and moral overtones. It was his way to experience, understand, and reinterpret his emotions and also a way of reinventing the bland, frail, and dependent existence that he perceived as the norm for the elderly in American society. He rejected the role of the marginal old man; he was not going to the creek to paint by numbers. Instead, he went hiking every day, often with people much younger than he was. He invented his story as something other people wanted to engage with and pay attention to, especially young women that he found attractive. This was the breach in cultural norms his story explored, a renegotiation of what an elderly man "should" be doing with his time.

The problem with the analysis of Peter's story as a narrative construction of reality is that when life is seen only as representation, then it is ephemeral, it has no grounding in the material conditions in which the story unfolds. Indeed, as previously mentioned, I think one of the reasons Peter created his story was to ignore parts of his social reality. However, Peter's story also contained a critique of current social conditions. Most obviously in his rhetorical rejection of technology as a virus, but he also, if questioned, disagreed with the prevailing cultural narratives of America. Some couchsurfers that visited him in summer 2014 were traveling the country interviewing people about what they thought of the American dream. They interviewed Peter. He told them that the American dream is really the "American nightmare": a scam, a con, a lie to make us work in a capitalist system that profits someone else, who stores the money but does not reinvest it. They are making us work through the lie that material success will make us happy when it does not. There is no point in working hard: take it easy, be happy, find peace. People who work hard are best experienced vicariously, so you can see what rewards they reap, without having to go through all that effort yourself. His view of capitalism speaks to the sense of anxiety and hopelessness that Cohn considered the root of millenarianism historically. His belief in the simulation and his mission within it provided him with purpose and hope. It also connected him to others, ironically by telling a story in which everything was a simulation revolving around himself. Like Swami Steve in the introduction, Peter was of the postwar generation for whom the American dream was an idea that still held currency. In rejecting its value, Peter still took for granted that it had an existence to refute. Interestingly, those interviewing him were of a younger generation, for whom the idea of the American dream was something to be investigated, like a language being lost as their elders passed away that they were trying to salvage before it disappeared entirely.

In writing his own life as a story, Peter was following the central tenet of spirituality to create your own reality. Significantly given his age, Peter was creating his own ending, going out with a bang, not drifting away forgotten in an old people's home. There are always limits on the ability to determine the terms of one's own existence. The most significant, for Peter, was his family, but there were also competing narratives in the media and around Sedona interpreting what he did differently from how he did. Narrativized social reality is still embedded social reality, and a successful narrative reflects and even critiques the wider context. Peter's creation of a story and casting of himself as the protagonist in a tale serialized through social media was a rejection of the treatment of the elderly as marginal in American soci-

FIGURE 14. Peter sitting on the top of Bell Rock. Visible on his inner arm are his tattoos, which signify "faith" in the Hebrew and Japanese alphabets. Peter suggested they might work as bar codes at the portal, allowing him access to the source code.

ety. He placed himself in the center of his story, not quietly serving others or participating in his family life. As an affluent white male, he was in a social position from which it was possible to rewrite his narrative in this way. Conveniently ignoring this position, he lauded himself as having chosen the best reality possible, connecting his personal choices to a cosmic mission with consequences for the whole universe. He stepped through a portal that connected his own ego to the entirety of the cosmoscape without paying heed to the middle ground, his social reality, that allowed for this leap.

Why do this? If reality is narrative, and he is the writer, he has control. The simulation idea, which I related to the landscape of the story, conveys this sense of control. If reality is a simulation of his choosing, he decides on everything that happens to him. He is responsible and he is in control. How does the individual relate to society? The individual saves society. But in turn he saves himself from the ending he did not want: dying alone forgotten in a nursing home. This tension between his personal need for attention and other people's reinterpretation of his beliefs and actions permeated Peter's story. He consistently tried to act as what Renaissance philosopher Pico della Mirandola called *homo faber*, the man who makes himself, where the creation of one's own reality is the creation of the self.[51] Peter was creating himself, creating his life, through constructing his reality as a story.

AWAKENED ALIENS

Crafting the Self on the Spiritual Path

> Men do change, and change comes like a little wind that ruffles
> the curtains at dawn, and it comes like the stealthy perfume of
> wildflowers hidden in the grass. Change may be announced
> by a small ache, so that you think you're catching cold. Or
> you may feel a faint disgust for something you loved yesterday.
>
> —JOHN STEINBECK, *Sweet Thursday*, 1954, pp. 14–15

WHEN PETER SUED THE US GOVERNMENT under the Freedom of Information Act, he was trying to achieve disclosure. Disclosure is the idea that the US government knows that extraterrestrials (ETs) are real and their ships have been visiting Earth for many years and, sooner or later, they will reveal this to the public. At a 2012 Ascension conference I attended in Sedona about the transformations expected in December, disclosure was described as a necessary part of ascension. The existence of ETs, and their ongoing involvement in human affairs, was essential to spiritual evolution. Disclosure is the revealing of "truth," the moment of certainty over doubt, when questions will be answered, and the seekers will be no longer seeking. It is, in many ways, spirituality's Rapture. It marks the end of the stigmatization of spirituality and the beginning of the new paradigm, when their beliefs change from "conspiracy theory" to "truth." This movement has already happened for those involved in spirituality, at a moment characterized as "awakening." The spiritual path often begins with an awakening when the light of spirituality is perceived and one awakens to the "truth." Yet the truth has always been there, waiting to be uncovered.

When the self is incarnated into the particular physical form of a given lifetime, its true nature is unknown yet predetermined. It must be discovered through awakening, which crafts a sense of self that is at once radically different from the cultural norm but at the same time who one "really is" and "always was." The disjuncture between these senses of self is most acute among those who self-identify as "starseeds." Starseeds are ETs; they are aliens. Specifically, they are human bodies with alien consciousness. Those who self-identify as starseeds reject a sense of self culturally produced from an amalgamation of biogenetic and socioeconomic characteristics and instead embrace a composite self, with both terrestrial and cosmic elements. In cosmologies of spirituality, aliens are beings from different planets or dimensions; however, these beings are not ontologically separate from humans. Reincarnation and multiverses are central cosmological concepts in spirituality that unify human and alien. Both humans and aliens are incarnations of souls in different physical states. My interlocutors would talk about previous incarnations of their soul on Venus, for example, or as a being in the seventh dimension. Aliens are the same as humans, just with different physical manifestations or, to put it in the idiom of spirituality, different levels of density of vibration. Starseeds are a particular subset in that they describe how they were born in a human body, a dense third-dimensional form of corporeality, but then a "seed" was planted inside their consciousness that developed, at different points for different individuals, into an awakened alien.

Starseeds collapse the alienness of aliens, offering revealing insights into the continuities and discontinuities of the spiritual path. Conceptually, aliens are discontinuous with humans; to be alien is to be not human. Since the mid-twentieth century, the term has come to denote extraterrestrials. Following reports of unidentified flying objects in the sky and mysterious crash sites in the New Mexico desert, a florid popular discourse has flowered around stories of abductions, cattle mutilations, and flying saucers.[1] Elements of this discourse combined with older theosophical ideas about ascended masters from other planets offering spiritual insights in a proliferation of what scholars call UFO religions.[2] UFO religions are often brought under the sociological category of "new age" and are also closely related to channeling. Channelers receive messages from a range of non-corporeal entities, including ETs as well as angels, spirits, and ascended masters.[3] For channelers, aliens are another contactable being in their repertoire.[4] In Sedona, I observed Amateo Ra, who defined himself as a starseed, channel his higher self from Sirius in the future. The entity he channeled existed on another planet, in a higher dimension, in the future, but was also a version of himself: "the highest self energy of Amateo, the future essence of Amateo, a Sirian frequency being, transmitting a Sirian energy." This collapses the distinction between alien and human, and moves the discourse of ETs and UFOs from strange beings coming in oddly shaped ships to abduct and harm humans to aliens being a part of humans. Being a starseed involves drawing continuities between human and non-human, present and future, self and other.

At the same time, spiritual awakening as an alien is a profoundly disruptive experience, separating people from kin groups, jobs, and "mainstream" thinking. This chapter is about aliens but also alienation. The basic definition of alienation is a process through which somebody or something becomes alien to something else.[5] The Comaroffs linked fantastical tales of zombies, witches, and alien invaders to discourses of immigration and labor deregulation under neoliberal capitalism in South Africa through the concept of alienation.[6] For my interlocutors in Sedona, the process of awakening was inextricably linked to alienation from the norms, expectations, and ideals that they associated with "mainstream" American society. Awakening is a rupture, a discontinuity, but it is also a realization, a revelation of something that was always there, a continuity. Aliens are stigmatized others, but in calling themselves aliens, my interlocutors were able to realize something they saw as approaching a more "authentic" identity. They became who they "really were," in the sense that the true nature of the self is alien. It is the materialist norms that limit the self to the physical body and the social categories applied to those bodies that were, from the perspective of starseeds, unreal or a lie. They demonstrated a "will to be otherwise," a volitional adoption of a new identity that confers a minority status.[7] It erupted out of their previous life experience creating new possibilities but also new constraints. Becoming aliens meant adopting a stigmatized status; however, this was often a response to a pre-existing feeling of alienation. Awakening was a separation but also an overcoming of separation, a realization of the true nature of the self through crafting a radically discontinuous identity.

FIGURE 15. The Center for the New Age store included a separate UFO Center offering UFO-spotting tours at night.

AWAKENINGS: CONVERSION AND CHANGE

At the age of forty in 2008, Mynzah had what he described as a kundalini awakening.[8] After smoking marijuana for the first time in ten years, he began to feel odd, and listened to the songs "Lateralus" and "Third Eye" by the progressive rock band Tool. He described feeling a burning sensation in his lower back and then saw two snakes going up his spine from the base. As they ascended, areas of his spine lit up. He would later describe this as his chakras activating. This feeling developed into an out-of-body experience, where he experienced himself looking down at his body. He perceived two "blue beings" that cohabited his body with him that he would later acknowledge as part of him, what he called his "Mer Ka Ba."[9] He traveled to another dimension, then came back and saw an arc of energy going out over him and a huge eye, charged with "pure energy."[10] He said it was like a light was turned on inside him, he could "see in the dark."

The next day he looked up the image he had seen on Google and found the exact same thing depicted under the title "kundalini awakening." He looked up kundalini awakening on the internet and it described what had happened to him the previous night. He claimed it was not a conscious choice to be awakened. However, it was intentional on another level, it was prearranged and part of his reason for being in this dimension at this time. Following this awakening, he changed his life completely. He gave up his possessions, left his job at the Department of Education, sold his car, and moved to Sedona. He said he was "called" there, having never heard of the place before his guides told him about it. His guides were spiritual beings that lived on a ship in Earth's upper atmosphere, whose guidance he heard as a voice. One was the soul that animated his physical body before he "walked in," when the starseed consciousness entered his human body at age four, called Jaliel, who had been one of his guides throughout his incarnations. The moment when he entered his physical body and Jaliel left it, he called a "soul exchange," and believed that his skin darkened after this event.[11] Mynzah considered himself "reborn," and he wore ankh rings to symbolize this.

Mynzah described himself as a Pleiadian walk-in and starseed. He explained this by describing the planet as a plant that grows and is harvested. Starseeds are planted on this planet to raise their own consciousness and that of others, to aid ascension to the fifth dimension, and thereby get closer to the divine.[12] He used the word "God" to describe divinity, and said that we are all God, we are all part of the same divine essence. However, we have forgotten this in the third dimension. The experience of the third dimension is separation, but this was a choice made by God to separate for no other reason than "because we could."

Mynzah's soul originated in Maya, the sun in the Pleiades system. When this soul "walked in" when he was four years old, he suddenly became aware of his surroundings and family in a new way. The person whom he called "mom" was not really his mother, she was someone else. She was only the mother to his physical body, not to his soul. He knew he was not from here, he was from somewhere else. He became depressed by this realization. He felt abandoned in a reality he did not like: "There was no one here like me, no one who thought like me, no one who saw what I did, and no one who knew what I knew."[13] He told his cousin about this experience, but no one else in his family, as he did not trust adults, including adults in his own family. He pushed it away as he grew up; comparing himself to a gay person in the closet, he forgot there was a closet, and went back to "sleep" to fit in. His mother raised him in the Baptist church. Even as a child, he thought of what he heard in church as "lies." On some level he felt that hell did not exist, animals had souls, and reincarnation was real even though the pastor said the opposite in church. However, fitting in meant accepting their "lies" rather than holding to his own intuitive "truth."

Mynzah received messages from his Star Family, the other souls he was related to in the universe. He did not call himself a prophet, but a "friend with a message."[14] He told me there were many other starseeds in Sedona; they worked together on a higher level, not physically in the third dimension. He stressed that they were not a club or a "cult." They worked in a city of energy, or a "light city" above Sedona that vibrated on a different frequency invisible to 3D senses. There were also many ships orbiting Earth, and his soul was in one such ship. His physical body was a projection in the 3D while his spiritual essence was in a higher dimension, completing his mission aboard a starship.

Mynzah explicitly called what happened to him, both to me and in his online autobiography, an "awakening." He symbolized this in terms of a light turning on that enabled him to see in the dark, which gave him extra powers of perception he did not have before. Awakening is a central image in the history and narratives of conversion in American religion, particularly evangelical Protestantism. The "Great Awakening" in the 1730s–1740s among Protestant colonialists was just one of the periodic revivals that stimulated religious fervor and dramatic conversions.[15] Mynzah's image of a light turning on to pierce the darkness recalled the final lyrics of the eighteenth-century Christian hymn "Amazing Grace": "Was blind, but now I see." This song drew upon the sudden conversion of its author, John Newton, after near-death in a storm and was featured extensively in the "Second Great Awakening" in the early nineteenth century.[16] Being raised American Baptist, it is highly likely that Mynzah was familiar with this song and related figurations of conversion. In his work on spiritual autobiographies of the evangelical awakening of early modern Methodists in England, D. Bruce Hindmarsh described a "U-shaped pattern of conversion" that replicated in microcosm the biblical cycle of Creation, Fall, Redemption, new Creation.[17] The emphasis in evangelical awakening narratives was on discontinuity. The old was discarded for the sake of the new, the sinner was reborn into a godly life.

Equally, the spiritual awakening was a rupture in Mynzah's life path. It marked a transition from being a person concerned with his material conditions to being one concerned with his spiritual evolution. The epitome of this process was giving up his job and possessions, again something that recalled the revivalists who forsook their old lives to follow or become itinerant preachers.[18] However, the important difference is that the evangelical awakenings occurred within the structure of an organized religion, one that many in the community were equally enthused about. Mynzah's awakening was endogenous, responding not to the words of a preacher but to a casual social occasion where he smoked marijuana. He had to search out a community of like-minded people afterward, which he found through an internet search engine. His spiritual awakening can be likened more to the process of becoming a shaman as described cross-culturally than conversion to an organized religion such as Christianity.[19] It was individual, disruptive of kin relations, economic status, and mental health; an isolating experience that transformed his sense of self from that of an ordinary human to an alien inhabiting a human body.

In the anthropology of Christianity, conversion is often depicted as a Damascene moment; abrupt, disruptive, and transformative.[20] Anthropologist Matthew Engelke warned against overstating the discourse on discontinuity in anthropological studies of conversion. First in his analysis of Masowe apostolic conversion, he used the Comaroffs' idea of a "long conversation" of transitioning to a new religious adherence, one that is always incomplete, a state of becoming.[21] Again in his work on British secular humanism, Engelke attended to the ways that the narrative of a complete break with the past can be a discursive strategy. For humanists it could be a way of setting themselves against what they perceive as their other, organized religion, in particular Christianity.[22] Engelke framed the conversion (if it can indeed be named as such) to secular humanism as a process of realization: his interlocutors read works describing humanism and realized this was how they already thought.[23] Erin F. Johnston used a similar interpretation of the conversion narratives of Pagans in the United States; learning about Paganism was interpreted as a realization that that was the way they had always been themselves, especially the attitude to nature.[24]

This focus on realization as opposed to transformation echoes anthropologist Tanya Luhrmann's discussion of the adoption of ritual magic practices by English middle-class professionals as "interpretive drift," a process she described as slow and steady.[25] Continuity was present in Mynzah's narrative. He spoke about the significance of his childhood experiences as a walk-in, which he then forgot and pushed away as he came to understand their stigmatized status in society and to his family in particular. In his narrative retelling, he was always a walk-in, but only as an adult was he able to realize this fully. It was through his kundalini awakening that he was able to embrace that which he had always been, crafting his awakened self as alien as his "true self." His portrayal of the kundalini awakening as a singularly disruptive event should not be understated, however; as with Engelke's secular humanists, it was a way of framing what he no longer was. Awakening as a starseed involved more than just converting to a different religion. It was a sense of being a totally different type of being, one that was not fully human, nor entirely present on Earth. It was an ontological shift as well as interpretive drift; a realization of what he was already, yet also a radical change in the way he was living his life.

WE ARE ONE: KINSHIP AND FAMILY AFTER AWAKENINGS

The woman introduced as Sierra Neblina was tall, over six feet. Thick wavy brown hair tumbled to her shoulders, and she looked around at the audience with an assured gaze. "The entity known as Sierra is not here," she said. "Commander Ananda is here today, from the Galactic Council." Commander Ananda was an ambassador to Earth aboard a lightship serving the Galactic Federation of Light. He was 1500 years old, but 70 years ago he heeded the call of Gaia and chose to be incarnated as a "conscious soul" in a human body called Sierra Neblina. He described giving his final commands to his crew, entering a small pod, and flying down a chute to Earth, where he transformed into a point of light outside the atmosphere. There he studied the "soul group" or family that he would be born into. Then he was reborn as Sierra Neblina, a woman of Cherokee and Irish descent, who at the time she was speaking at this conference appeared to be in her forties or fifties. In order to keep certain "codes" active, Sierra was conscious of Commander Ananda from the time of her incarnation. This meant the density of the human physical body would not get in the way of their mission, which was to expose the hybridization program of the government that was using humans with Native American blood as hosts to birth human-alien, or "galactic" as they preferred, hybrids. So from incarnation Sierra was part-human and part-galactic.

Sierra's childhood was ruptured by abuse, something she blamed on her mother's repeated abductions by the government. The trauma fractured her mother's psyche and she re-inflicted the suffering onto her children. Sierra was also abducted and carried a hybrid to term that was then taken by the government. The government was in league with a race of aliens called Zetas, who needed the hybrids to rebuild their race. They wanted "Native American bloodlines" because Native Americans were connected to the Pleiades. This program was halted in the 1990s, an effort in which Sierra took part. Now she ran a program called TWIN to help those still struggling with their experiences, other lightworkers, starseeds, and walk-ins. She defined herself as a "braided walk-in," a human body with a galactic consciousness she had been aware of since birth. Sierra and Commander Ananda inhabited the same body, their consciousnesses intertwined; some-times Sierra spoke and sometimes it was Commander Ananda. As a result of this, she had abilities since her youth that had been engineered in the womb. She was a higher vibrational consciousness in dense human form, trained and ready to help wherever she was needed. As part of her mission she had been a sniper in the US Marines, the first woman in frontline combat as part of Operation Desert Storm in the Gulf War.

Sierra was speaking as part of the 2012 Ascension conference, hosted by the internet site and blog radio show the Golden Age of Gaia, mentioned at the beginning of this chapter. Since she therefore had a measure of renown in spirituality-focused internet circles, I googled her and found that a site dedicated to exposing what it called "new age frauds" had taken steps to debunk her identity by adding public records of her military service, as a member of the military police in Colorado, and her birth name, Shannon Marie Hare.[26] Members of the forum denounced her as a con artist, narcis-sist, and fake.

Names grant the power to both fix identity and detach from it.[27] Shan-non Marie Hare became Sierra Neblina, who was an incarnation of Com-mander Ananda. Each of her roles had a different name. Sierra Neblina was the name she used in everyday life; Commander Ananda was part of her consciousness; Shannon Marie Hare was the name on her birth certificate. To debunkers on the internet, the existence of her legal name proved her a fraud; from their perspective, her identity was fixed by legal document. The creation of her new identity as Sierra Neblina was an act of detachment, separating her from her existence as an ordinary human. Renaming herself erased her social history. However, this social history persisted in the form of legal documents, which by some were given more weight; the legal name was the "true" name that revealed the "real" identity of a person.

Commander Ananda was another named entity, one that existed in the same physical body at the same time as Sierra but only sometimes used her voice. He was a change that she announced with an illocutionary speech act.[28] A walk-in is analogous to a spirit that possesses a human host, in that they inhabit the same body but have different identities. Mynzah's was called Jaliel. Naming spirits is an important, if not definitive act, in their realization for the practice of spirit possession cross-culturally, such as in Madagascar as studied by anthropologist Michael Lambek.[29] Since the body is the same, the name becomes crucial in separating the human from the spirit. Lambek questioned whether without a name a spirit can even have an identity. As with awakening, the process is one of realization as well as transformation, a process of continuous becoming that is manifested by naming.

Lambek remarked on how personal names are mostly given by others; indeed, he suggests parenthetically that "If anyone knows of an ethnographic case where people routinely name themselves I would be glad to hear about it."[30] Sedona seems like such a case. New arrivals began to change rapidly, often adopting different styles of dress and a new name. New names were adopted as part of their spiritual path, a new name to reflect the new direction their life had taken. Names were often evocative of the life they now wished to lead, such as Wild Spirit or White Dove. Many people continued to use their given names; it was not necessary or required in any way to think up a new name to "prove" commitment to the spiritual path. It depended on inclination and personal experiences. Some continued to evolve their name with their spiritual path, again depending on how they felt, so Mynzah RavenCrow became Mynzah Atum and then Mynzah Osiris while I knew him, each new name being adopted with no more fanfare than changing it on his Facebook profile. Interestingly, when Facebook changed its policy to require profiles with legal names, Mynzah separated his into a public persona page called "Mynzah" and another under his legal name.

Despite the acceptance of self-naming in Sedona, there was still a certain amount of cynicism about "Sedona names." People who had been there longer would often roll their eyes at the sound of another's fanciful new name and call it a "Sedona name," a name they had just adopted upon moving there. To counter this, they would claim an alternative ancestry to their own unusual name, pointing out that it was not a "Sedona name." Buttercup (see chapter four) explained how her name came from the surname her parents had selected for the family because neither wanted to adopt the other's given surname. ThreeTrees claimed his name was the result of a vision quest. Both emphatically denied that theirs were Sedona names. Rarely were the invented names also their legal names; they were names adopted and used in common speech only. This facet of identity was flexible on the interpersonal level; however, their legal identities remained fixed on a bureaucratic level as part of state surveillance of citizens.[31] I asked Mynzah what name appeared on his military pension check, and he said it was his legal name. Lambek suggested there is no freedom of identity because names are given by others, not the self, and fixed by the state. Self-selected Sedona names faced opposition from other Sedonans, the regulations of social media corporations, and anti–new age "debunking" websites.

The flexibility of identity that many tried to exercise on their spiritual path was tempered by and sometimes in tension with the demands of the market-oriented bureaucratic state in which they lived. They called themselves what they wanted, but the state had a different name for them, unless they took the step of legally changing their name as Sierra Neblina did. This option did not seem popular, perhaps because it was costly, but more importantly it would have again fixed them to a specific name rather than leaving them free to call themselves what they felt like in the moment. The demands of the society they lived in placed constraints on the freedom of their spiritual expression. Anthropologists Barbara Bodenhorn and Gabriele vom Bruck examined the multifarious ways that naming acts to both conceal and reveal identity, operating not simply as assignation but also "discovery, divination, recognition, or inheritance."[32] Names entangle persons in social matrices. In Sedona, this took the particular contour of a spiritual path; a name announced its beginning, but that same name could be used to level accusations of fraud. Granting oneself a new name on the spiritual path was a way of controlling representation of the self, but this was always under negotiation and subject to competing views from peers in Sedona, the wider internet community involved in spirituality, and the state.

Naming is of course central to kinship. In the United States, typically a person's name is given by its biological parents at birth.[33] Changing one's birth name and family name is a way to "decenter" biological kin.[34] Spiritual awakenings often distanced people from their biological kin and drew them closer to a new formulation of family. Sierra Neblina talked about viewing her new family from space, calling them a "soul group." Unbeknownst to me at the time I saw Sierra speak, I had met others in Sedona who identified as being part of her soul group. I met Alan through the Arizona Conscious Communications email list, on which he had advertised himself as a shaman, life coach, death coach, lightworker, and web designer. A white man in his late fifties, with short black hair, he had moved to Sedona in January

2012. He told me he started on the spiritual path when he met his "sister," Rebecca, at a Landmark education conference he was running for a private firm, where he was responsible for organizing seminars teaching work effectiveness.[35] Rebecca was his sister by choice. His blood relations, his sister, brother, and two children, had not spoken to him for between five and ten years. He described Rebecca and he as coming from the same "soul pod," which meant the same as what Sierra called "soul group." Another term was "soul family," a group of souls who are reincarnated together and have deep karmic connections. Alan and Rebecca ran a business together and lived together in Sedona; indeed, his reason for coming to Sedona was because she moved there.

Prior to his awakening, he was a multi-millionaire business consultant in Portland, Oregon. Originally from Seattle, he had attended college in Portland and stayed there to develop his career. A self-described "hatchet man," he was responsible for firing staff from companies in trouble and fixing their problems. He had an expansive $6 million house, his wife was a member of the country club, and their two kids got everything they wanted. He had a list of things he wanted and when he would get them by. Then he got it all by the age of forty-four and thought, what now? He was not happy or satisfied with having everything he had thought he wanted. He needed to change. First he admitted he was gay. This led to a messy divorce where his wife got everything, and some things were even burned and destroyed. His children no longer spoke to him because they blamed him for taking their comfortable life away from them. Leaving with only a duffel bag and his baby book, he started again as a publisher of a gay-friendly business directory in Colorado, where he met Rebecca. They ran a business together in Sedona helping souls transition to their next incarnation, a practice they called "death coaching."

Rebecca was a registered nurse and had worked for many years in care homes and hospices. She referred to Alan as her "brother." Rebecca had been married to Sierra Neblina. She described Sierra as a student of hers, but she had stopped teaching her because Sierra stopped following her truth. Sierra had since broken up with her, but Rebecca told me that she knew they were still together when she listened to Sierra's spirit rather than her conscious being. Her conscious being spoke from ego, whereas her spirit spoke from source. Sierra had "a lot to work through" in this lifetime, according to Rebecca, but they had had many lifetimes together. They were "soul mates," and in each incarnation they had lessons to learn through their relationship. So they both were and were not married, she told me with a smile. They were married in the sense that they were soul mates, partners through many incarnations who would always find each other in each new lifetime and go through what they had to learn this time. But they were not married in the legal, third-dimensional sense, nor were they, at the time of the interview, in a romantic relationship.

After a period of several months without seeing any of them, I bumped into Rebecca at one of the grocery stores in Sedona, and she told me Alan had moved out and would no longer speak to her. She did not know why. Resignedly, she said it was time, though; he was meant to stay with her for two weeks and ended up staying fourteen months. The business was her sole responsibility at the moment; she was still trying to set everything up, and doing her job as a registered nurse at the same time. So Alan was no longer Rebecca's "brother"; he had left Sedona and moved on. According to his Facebook page, he next became a life coach in San Diego. He did not reply to any of my messages asking why he had left Sedona. Sierra left the Golden Age of Gaia and started her own endeavor, an internet radio station called Galactic U. Later she returned to Colorado to continue working in the medical marijuana industry.

When I asked people I knew in Sedona systematically about their "soul family," the common answer was that this referred to people on the same spiritual path as they were. Sometimes they referred to this as their "Sedona family," meaning specifically the other spiritual people living in Sedona, or their "galactic family," if the interlocutor focused their spiritual path on aliens. What became clear to me was that those involved in spirituality figured their relations with others on a spiritual path in kinship terms, as family. This was perhaps simply because they felt closer to people who had the spiritual path in common. It was a way of recognizing common beliefs and group membership. However, there was more to it, as it was often the case that going on the spiritual path involved rejection by or of their biological family. On the one hand, they were seen as weird, strange, ridiculous, even mentally ill by their families. On the other hand, there was a sense from some of my interlocutors that they did not want to associate with people who were not on a spiritual path because that lowered their vibration. Sometimes, leaving their family was formulated as a necessary part of being on the spiritual path. Others found that their families eventually came to terms with the change.

Spiritual brothers and sisters, soul family, are types of elective kin, who are chosen rather than biologically related. The classic work on American kinship by anthropologist David Schneider formulated kin relations as organized by symbols of "blood" and "law."[36] Blood relations had primacy in kinship networks because they were supposed to be the ties that bind for life, whereas relations by law were significant but based on codes of conduct and therefore lacking the same permanence. Numerous studies have subsequently revised the applicability of Schneider's formulation to the whole of "American kinship."[37] Kath Weston analyzed the kin networks of people who self-identify as gay or lesbian in San Francisco, looking at the way kin terms are reorganized in response to coming out, which can distance or break down relations with biological family.[38] Close friends, partners, and ex-partners became kin, often using the terms "brother" and "sister" to denote intimate bonds of interdependence and solidarity. Kin terms were also used to signify membership in a community, although Weston questioned the uniformity of "the gay community."[39] Soul family can be seen in a similar way, signifying close relations that have sprung up in place of strong connections with biological kin and symbolizing spiritual like-mindedness and identity that are still framed on a structure of biological kinship.

Soul family can also be likened to membership of religious communities; for example, Puritans called each other "brother" and "sister."[40] This is perhaps more of a general feature of closely bonded communities that oppose their intimate interconnections to those with outsiders; for example, Mynzah also referred to his fellow Marines as his "brothers." There was a further cosmological implication in the term "soul family," though. Fenella Cannell discussed how Mormons believe their families chose each other before birth, challenging Schneider's characterization of the "American family" as based on "blood" and "law" as a Protestant majority idea that ignored the historical contingency of the terms and how different religious groups constructed them differently.[41] For Mormons, all families existed before birth in the prior world, even adopted families, and chose each other on the Great Tree. Similarly, the soul family was a group of souls born into this incarnation together. They existed prior to this life together and chose each other. Sierra Neblina used the image of being a light hovering above Earth and viewing her soul family. "Soul pod" extended the plant metaphor of a group of seeds growing separately from a single source.

Sometimes the image of a contract was used. Alan talked about signing a contract with Rebecca prior to incarnation that they would be together throughout their lifetimes. The soul family could include other souls who were incarnated as humans, such as Alan and Rebecca, or souls incarnated as human and their guides, such as Mynzah and Jaliel, or humans and aliens, such as Sierra and Commander Ananda. These relationships were figured as kin relations, but they were not so much chosen as preordained. Sometimes these relationships could be biologically connected as well, such as Mynzah's twin daughters whom he identified as fellow starseeds from Venus. The changes that occurred with a spiritual awakening had extensive ramifications for kinship. Biological kin were distanced, and new kin relations were established, figured as spiritual. Kin relations could be between humans, aliens, and other entities with different vibrational frequencies. The symbols of "soul" and "seeds" were as significant as "blood" and "law."

Although ideally "soul family" was an inclusive term and seemed to offer the opportunity for any who also followed the spiritual path to have the closeness of kin relations, there were limitations to the concept of soul family in practice. This can be seen in the case of Alan, who left Sedona and stopped talking to Rebecca, just as his relations with his biological family had once broken down. Although Rebecca considered herself "married" to Sierra on a soul level, on a personal level their relationship had broken down because Sierra was not "living her truth." This suggests that in practice soul families were predicated on social codes of conduct rather than bonds that would last many incarnations. There were gaps between the daily experience of family and the ideological construction of what the ideal family should look like.[42] Margaret K. Nelson argued that family is not simply a structure that exists *sui generis* but a performative act: people "do" family. In the case of soul families, what is figured as a preordained and even transcendent kinship relation is in practice dependent on the performative actions of the persons involved.

People involved in spirituality are often cast as "seekers."[43] My interlocutors in Sedona did seem to fit this characterization, as they moved frequently between groups, workshops, conferences, trainings, channelings, and classes. But it seems that perhaps what they were searching for, more than God, was family. They did not fit with their natal families anymore, particularly the starseeds, or they had rejected their family for other, personal reasons. The "nuclear family" as described by Schneider has been radically altered in the United States by broader social shifts including economic mobility, changing gender norms, and increasing life expectancy, to the extent that Janet Carsten suggests that the ideal of a stable, traditional family unit was a "minor historical blip" in the mid-twentieth century.[44] Within a more mobile economy the family unit can be a negatively valenced form of dependency; however, its dispersal can mean the loss of a crucial support network.[45] Seekers in spirituality searched for an alternative that was more accepting than their biological families, but that still offered a loving, protective force. However, soul families seemed to rest on fragile ground, and things fell apart: the groups splintered, friends fell out, your sister was no longer your sister, was she ever so? Soul family provided a weak replacement for a kinship system undergoing extensive reorganization caused by social forces much broader than the particular lives caught up in it. The result of this reorganization was often a sense of belonging nowhere, a loneliness, seeking for someone like them but finding no one, a feeling of alienation.

ALIEN NATION: RACE AND CLASS

Ethnically mixed, Mynzah's father was Blackfeet, white, and black, and his mother was Cherokee, French, and Spanish. On his birth certificate, it was written "Native American" for his mother and "Negro" for his father. I asked him if he described himself as Native American and he said no, since he was only part Native American and he did not want to mislead people into thinking he grew up on a reservation. During his childhood, his father had been a heroin addict and alcoholic, who was frequently in trouble with the police. His parents divorced when he was nine, which prompted a move from East Palo Alto in the San Francisco Bay area to Exeter, in Central California. On his first day of school in Exeter, the other students called him a racial slur. Exeter was a predominantly white community, in which he was one of only a handful of black residents. Later on he did make friends at that school. He emphasized to me that he wanted to be seen for who he was, not his skin color. The two were, by implication, separated for him. On visits back to East Palo Alto, a predominantly black community, he found he was no longer accepted there because he spoke in a way that was identified as "white."

Personally, he did not identify as black or mixed race or even as a person; he said he was from another planet entirely. Being human was a matter of playing a certain role to him, and difference was a performance, as if people were merely characters in a play or a reality television show.[46] In his essence, which he labeled his soul, he was neither black nor white, nor even a boy as opposed to a girl, he was a "walk-in," something else entirely. Yet over time he understood himself as a boy and that that was said to be different from girls. Gender equality continued to be an important principle for him. He told me that women needed to be empowered and stand up to men, whereas men needed to embrace the feminine and "get off the throne." As a child, he witnessed the physical abuse of his mother by her then-boyfriend, which upset him so much that during one incident he turned a garden hose on them. The domestic violence was not limited to that relationship. His mother beat him after her divorce from his father, at one point accidentally breaking his arm. His grandmother and his great-aunt also periodically hit him as a form of physical punishment. The lesson he learned from this experience was that those who say they love you hurt you. He described himself as a feminine child, very sensitive, who cried at everything, particularly fighting. However, he changed as an adolescent; he began to get into trouble himself, trying heroin and crack cocaine.

After leaving high school, he joined the US Marine Corps in order to get his life back on track. Looking back, he was critical of the institution, commenting that the Marines trained young men to kill, which was not their natural disposition. However, at the time he was an enthusiastic recruit. When he was discharged over an administrative error at the start of the Gulf War, he felt guilty because he was "deserting his brothers." Now he felt sorry for them because it was bad for the soul to be in the military. Following his discharge, he became a police officer in a sheriff's department in central California. Later he became a school counselor, helping kids before they got into jail, and then a bureaucrat in the Department of Education, helping poor families with claims. He had a BA in management and organization development, and an unfinished MA in business and education, with an emphasis on school counseling from Fresno Pacific University. During this period of his life, he was trying to be a "good American citizen."[47] He was committed to supporting and working for "the system," until his awakening abruptly broke him out. It is relevant that both Mynzah and Sierra Neblina had military connections. The US military figures widely in alien mythology as participating in, benefiting from, and covering up contact with ETs.[48] The highly complex technological apparatus of the US military filled American skies with strangely shaped crafts, spurring tales of UFOs, especially in the Southwest, which has been used as a vast proving ground for military equipment from the 1940s atomic tests onward. It is not incidental that Mynzah followed participation in the military with a spiritual path centered on being an alien.

Mynzah told me that when he was in the Marines, and his subsequent careers, he was following what he called "the American dream." He defined this dream as going to college, getting a job, owning a house, getting married, having children, then the children achieving all those things but better, in a constant cycle of the same material things getting bigger and more expensive each time. But then he realized it was only a program to keep us in line and controlled, to stop us thinking for ourselves. He called it free-dom *from* choice, just following what we had been told to do and to want. He preferred Timothy Leary's dictum instead: "think for yourself; question authority."

Spirituality is not an anti-capitalist or anti-modernity political "move-ment" in any sense of the term. It does, however, seem to involve a reorien-tation in relation to certain organizing social constructions. Race and class, even gender, were seen as third-dimensional concepts. The true self, which was a frequency of energy and not a form of physical mass, did not have these characteristics. Following the spiritual path granted the opportunity to overcome or discard race and class. Mynzah explicitly rejected identify-ing his true self as a black man, or a person of color, or as middle class. He sought to transcend these categories. Unlike Amelia in chapter one, rather than finding spirituality after losing everything, Mynzah gave up his hard-earned middle-class life in order to go on his spiritual path. He inverted the meaning of the American dream from what he had been taught; it was not a route to freedom but a means of control.

There is a difficulty talking about race and class in America because of the widespread denial that a rigid structure of socioeconomic class exists.[49] Class structures are meant to belong to the hierarchical Old World; in Amer-ica, meritocratic individualism reigns, and so class is no longer relevant. Anyone who works hard can "bootstrap" themselves to success. This does not mean that there is not an awareness of social and economic inequalities in America, it means that those inequalities tend to be framed as the result of personal choice or failure, or the result of racial disparities. An interest-ing recent change in class discourse in the United States is the emergence of a reified "white working class," most often referenced in relation to the outcome of the 2016 election.[50]

Echoing these discursive notes, Mynzah mentioned that his mother's boyfriend was a farmworker and that his family was poor in relation to the white families in the community; however, he focused on this as a racial issue rather than a class dynamic. Class was only mentioned explicitly by two people in the two years I was in the field. Donna, a black woman writer and probiotics salesperson, described three "cultures" in Sedona: the upper class who could live where they wanted, the middle class who were glad to be living there, and those who were "just happy to be here, and wouldn't be anywhere else." Significantly, she did not label this group lower or working class. The other was a white male spiritual tour guide who styled himself

"Mr. Sedona," who told me that there was a marked wealth polarization in Sedona, people were either very rich or very poor, and that I was sitting with Sedona's "middle class"—him and his business partner. In suggesting this structure, "Mr. Sedona" was reproducing a discourse of the squeezed middle class in America. Economic inequalities were becoming so extreme under neoliberal policies, especially after the financial crisis, that the middle class was disappearing.[51]

In her history of the English working class, Selina Todd indexes class in two ways: as a relationship "based on inequalities of power" and as a self-identification.[52] Class is a relative marker of identity constructed through perceptions of self and other. In Donna's scheme there was a clear gradation based on inequality; the upper class could do what they wanted, and the middle class was grateful if they got it. The lower or working class remained unnamed, identified only through a platitude, an empty space filled with the discursive silence on American class. This silence is magnified by a spatial absence. The working class was isolated and separated from the middle class and upper class in "urban villages" of ethnic enclaves in the United States.[53] Sedona was an enclave compared to the surrounding towns. The higher rents and house prices meant service workers, many of whom were Latina/o, lived in Cottonwood, Cornville, or Camp Verde, and commuted to Sedona for work.[54] This situation has been exacerbated by the lifting of regulations limiting short-term rentals, freeing up landlords to participate in websites such as Airbnb for a higher profit than renting to lower-income tenants.[55] As a result, many of my interlocutors have subsequently moved out of Sedona to the surrounding towns or moved out of the area altogether due to the lack of affordable housing. Class was harder to see in Sedona because the price of the land, inflated due to the tourist industry, created a homogeneity in terms of race and class, and most of the long-term residents were white and middle or upper class. The value of owning land in Sedona was so high that some of the "super rich" owned property there, including the late Arizona senator John McCain, actor Sharon Stone, and the estate of Walt Disney.[56]

The poor moved on; as "Mr. Sedona" explained to me, they came with dreams of following their spiritual path in Sedona and could not make it so had to leave. There were very few services available to support lower-income people, particularly those who struggled to find housing. I met Vincent, a starseed from Sirius, in a coffee shop one day, when he interrupted a conversation I was having with a well-known local musician. Vincent was homeless, and I took him to breakfast once every week or so. He had previously worked for the federal government and the Peace Corps but had contracted

HIV, developed AIDS, and by the time I knew him, suffered from AIDS-related cognitive dementia. He bounced from cheap rentals to motels to shelters run in Cottonwood by Catholic Charities and other groups. He did not stay in Sedona often, as the police there quickly moved him on if they found him. He told me he manifested an invisibility cloak to protect himself from them, but it did not always work. As "Mr. Sedona" said, there was a polarization of wealth in Sedona. Those at the bottom end simply vanished from view.

However, poverty was often framed as a choice. Vincent consistently spoke of himself as manifesting exactly what he wanted. When his invisibility cloak did not work, it was because he really wanted the police to find him and give him a warm shelter for the night in a jail cell. When I asked if he wouldn't rather have a house, he would often say that would mean he would not have been where he was, and wherever he was, that was where he was meant to be. The ideology of providence in spirituality masked social inequalities, and everything that happened was what was meant to happen. Those who had to leave were "spit out" by the energy. This combined with individualism to create a double bind. The individual created reality as they wanted, so everything that happened to them was both preordained and their choice. If you were homeless, suffering, and dying on the street, then that was exactly what you had chosen to happen in this incarnation. There was little sense of class consciousness or joining together to address widespread socioeconomic inequalities and advocate for change. Personal suffering was instead a direct route to cosmic alignment with the energy of the universe.

Class remains difficult to acknowledge; it runs against strong beliefs in "meritocratic individualism."[57] Class is also subsumed by discourses on race and ethnicity.[58] Race is seen as self-evident and natural. It holds a much more potent historical visibility in the United States than class, due to the legacy of slavery.[59] However, Sherry Ortner argues that race is intimately intertwined with class. White Americans who might be seen as working class due to income or employment status define themselves as middle class because to be lower class is to be an ethnic minority.[60] Issues of race and class are then assumed to be significant only to those groups marked as part of the "underclass." Being white and middle class is "normal" and therefore unremarkable. This relegates poverty to being an issue for racial others and blinds white Americans in particular to their own privileged status.

Mynzah dwelled upon how his ethnicity marked him out as different and the effects this had upon his life. He used alien mythology as an alternative to the racial discourse of America. He was not black or white, he was not even human but Pleiadian. This is literal alienation; he recreated his identity as that of an alien. He did not fit in with black people or white people, and so instead saw himself as from another planet, and interpreted the darkening of his skin at age four as a sign of soul exchange. Alienation has a complicated genealogy as a term, but to return to the basic definition given at the outset of this chapter, of the process through which somebody or something becomes alien to something else, Mynzah's awakening can be seen through this lens. He was excluded from the white community in Exeter for being black, he was excluded from the black community in East Palo Alto for talking white. He became alienated along racial lines from both groups. He was also in a family situation of pervasive domestic violence. He then described his experience of having an alien consciousness "walk in" at age four and realizing that his mom was not really his mother. He became alienated from his mother. His career as a Marine, police officer, and bureaucrat was his attempt to "fit in" and be a "good American citizen." This ended with his awakening when he perceived this system as controlling and authoritarian. He became alienated from the state.

Sociologist Richard Sennett suggested alienation could be a sane response to social conditions of inequality.[61] Reflecting on Mynzah's narrative, his realization of alienness comes in progressive stages, capped off by a transformative awakening that responded to processes of social and political alienation. The philosophical literature on alienation is rich, so any selection naturally excludes many productive alternatives, but to make sense of this process of alienation I turn to Hegel, who used two German terms for alienation: Entäußerung and Entfremdung.[62] In Marx's work on alienation, these two terms were used interchangeably and with substantively the same meaning, but in Hegel's the meaning was different and, in this case, illustrative.[63] Entäußerung is a giving up, externalization, or realization. For Hegel, alienation was inevitable because of the self-externalization of labor, where a concept within the head is made external and therefore separate from its producer. This realizes the product of labor but also necessitates a separation from its creator. Entfremdung is alienation, disaffection, estrangement. Hegel also talked about alienation in political terms, in which the citizen is alienated from the state through assigning their natural rights to it in exchange for its protection. In Mynzah's narrative of becoming an alien, these two processes of alienation were at work. The first of Entfremdung, estrangement from his family, his race, and the state, that is, becoming alien. The second of Entäußerung, realization and externalization of what he always was, that is, making himself alien.

Seeing himself as an alien, or starseed, therefore became an act of lib-eration, of defiance. If there was no one here like him, if he did not belong, then he could find himself elsewhere, beyond the confines of this planet and its social and economic inequalities. If people were racist to him, he transcended race. If his job controlled him, he gave it up. Being an alien therefore meant being more than human. It meant being able to free himself from the restrictive structures in which he was caught. Vincent's reimagin-ing of homelessness as what he was meant to be doing can also be seen as liberating in this way. Rather than as some form of false consciousness, he was transcending the idea that he should feel bad because of the situation he was in. His soul was from Sirius, and his mission on this planet was to live the life of Vincent and experience all that entailed, raising the vibration of everyone he met. He was not in a subjugated socioeconomic position; on the contrary, he was on a mission of a higher order. Mynzah too reframed his life to that of a higher calling. The act of declaring oneself an alien can be a powerful way of overcoming social and economic alienation.

However, Sennett follows his suggestion that alienation could be a sign of sanity with the reflection that American workers' feelings of alienation often resulted in individuation and internalization of blame for the struc-tural forces they suffered.[64] It was a way of dividing the self that created calm by separating the work-self from the "real self" and thereby obviating the inequalities of class from affecting who they "really" were. Mynzah's shift from good American citizen to awakened alien likewise resulted in a divided self, locating the solution to the problems he suffered in his perception of himself, not in the conditions that caused the problems in the first place. Yet I argue that the sense of self he crafted was more than divided; it was compos-ite, because he fused the separated parts together to allow for a feeling of tran-scendence beyond the social conditions that limited him. The overcoming of social constructions of race and class is a central aim of the spiritual path, allowing for culture to be discarded and left behind as third-dimensional, as the path leads beyond the self through a portal to the universe.

DO WHAT YOU LOVE: WORK AND
JOBS ON THE SPIRITUAL PATH

In early March 2013, I attended a starseed conference at the Sedona Public Library. Its featured speakers I mostly knew already from numerous events, conferences, and workshops in Sedona. It began with what Randell Standswithbear, an aging white musician who claimed Cherokee ancestry, called a "hug it out" session with your "star family." To the sounds of Sister Sledge's disco hit "We Are Family," the audience of around thirty people got up and embraced each other joyfully. I stayed in my seat writing on my iPad, and most people ignored me. A middle-aged white woman with glitter lightly dusted over her face and a sickly sweet tone of voice came over to me, saying her name was Tina. She said I was hiding my light, but I could let it shine, I did not have to be small anymore. Holding my shoulder and arm, she said I was among family here.

This framing as family seemed odd to me. I had paid $90 to sit in the public library, listening to music, channelings, and speeches, and the room was surrounded with tables where the speakers offered their wares for sale. It seemed closer to a corporate conference than a gathering of kin. But one of the speakers came from a very specific community that I was also a part of; she had completed a PhD in social anthropology at the London School of Economics.[65] Elizabeth had been a diplomat with a career in the State Department, but now she was speaking at this conference about "starseed diplomacy" in the Sedona Public Library. Having been forced out of the foreign service on account of her age, although she complained bitterly that there was no legal age limit for the civil service, she looked for ways to continue diplomacy despite the forces that tried to stop her from being a diplomat. She found this through starseed radio, where she could spread the messages she felt were important. Her awareness that she was a starseed came through a gradual process of reflecting on visions she had had while in the field and the feeling that she had had "something on [her] shoulder" looking after her when she was in war zones. We are all citizen-diplomats and starseed diplomats, she claimed, and we could all send out the messages we felt were important through the internet and social media, and that is diplomacy.

Being a starseed granted Elizabeth a new way of framing her career as a diplomat following what had clearly been an acrimonious ending with the civil service. Others speaking at the conference had also found ways to develop their self-identity as aliens into a means of supporting themselves financially. Krista Raisa channeled the Orion Council during the conference. I had met and interviewed her previously in Sedona. She ran a You-Tube channel, Instagram feed, and Etsy store, where she uploaded videos of her channeling, sold products she made, promoted products that she got paid to market online, and gave advice and feedback to her subscribers.[66]

Many of her videos were psychological and relationship advice coupled with talk about aliens.[67] She had also published nine e-books of her channeled messages, and with her partner, Ra Arcturus, sold a metal necklace called a Sa-Ra key for $155 that aligned the chakras and raised vibrations.[68] Krista identified as a Pleiadian, whereas Ra identified as an Arcturan. They were "good aliens," meaning they were here to help Earth in the war between dark and light, surrounding Earth in their ships. Ra described the *Star Wars* movies and the *Star Trek* television series as "downloaded" or channeled messages. The key they sold helped people who were "blocked" from awareness of the good aliens open up and receive their messages. They described the physical body as separate from the soul. The soul was in another part of the galaxy, but it was connected to and controlling the body. Interestingly, Krista and Ra both identified as biracial or mixed race, and their backgrounds involved living outside the United States. Krista self-defined as Finnish American and lived in Finland during her adolescence, while Ra said only that he grew up in Germany. Both were in their mid-twenties. Krista also had an apparently harmonious relationship with her parents, who both feature on her YouTube videos, offering spiritual insights of their own. There seemed to be less problem for Krista identifying as a starseed than for Mynzah or Sierra; perhaps because of her age, it caused less disruption in her family. She also did not leave an established career to follow her spiritual path but incorporated it into her working life from the outset.

When asked his occupation, Mynzah called himself a "server of the collective or the divine"; he was here to serve. More concretely, he was an artist and he performed readings and healings. His income came from these activities and his military pension, and he said he did not need much to live on. He did not own a car; he considered it too expensive, dangerous, and damaging to the earth, and he did not want to pay for gas and give money to oil companies. He performed readings with cards—tarot, oracle, and Mayan zodiac. The latter was done online with a program. He mainly did distance readings, using a person's full name and date of birth. He then emailed them a reading. The primary mode of contact with his clients was online: he had a website, a Facebook page, a Pinterest page, and a YouTube channel. Generally, he would only work with a person once; he would try to help them, but he did not want them dependent on him, nor did he want to keep taking their money. He did not have a schedule of fees for services as many readers did in Sedona; he would only ask for a "love offering," which could be anything they wanted to give, from nothing to cash or trade of goods or services.

Many of my interlocutors expressed a desire to live without money so

Who are we really is the important question and is only answered by the experience of Self Realization...the Revelation of Love incarnate, a singular Being eternally manifest...One. ~ Mynzah

FIGURE 16. Digital art by Mynzah, turned into a meme, shared on his website and Facebook pages. © Mynzah

they could pursue their spiritual path without distraction. However, in America you must have a job. Social welfare is limited. There are fewer relief programs for the poor in the United States as a result of neoliberal policies shrinking the welfare state.[69] More than this, having a job is central to the construction of identity for most Americans: it is an organizing principle of the normative valuation of self.[70] A job means independence and financial security. Having a job is closely tied to notions of self-worth, and losing a job can subvert this because work has a moral value. Within this context, intentionally giving up a job to follow a spiritual path is a rebellious act. Mynzah rejected his career of working in "the system," where he made sufficient money to support himself and held positions of social authority, and instead got rid of his possessions and moved to Sedona. Krista and Ra tried from the start of their working lives to earn money in a way consonant with their spiritual paths. Like many others who came to Sedona, they were drawn by the community of like-minded people and what was termed the energy of the place. But they still had to earn a living. Economic instability was a factor in many of my interlocutors' lives. They mostly lived on low incomes; earning between a few hundred and two thousand dollars a month was the norm. They tended to rent rooms in the houses of wealthier Sedona residents; people involved in spirituality were very rarely homeowners. It was common for new arrivals in Sedona to live in their car or camp in the forest or beside the creek until they found somewhere to live. Those who did have economic stability were ones who maintained their employment outside their spiritual path, such as Peter in the previous chapter, who worked as an attorney. Making a living as a starseed involved pursuing multiple different revenue sources, including offering readings, running a YouTube channel or hosting an internet radio show, and selling products online and as a vendor at the frequent spirituality-focused conferences held in Sedona.

Running a YouTube channel earns money by becoming what's called a "partner," regularly uploading videos that receive thousands of views and hosting advertising for which they earn a proportion of the advertising revenue.[71] The business model based on sharing content appealed to starseeds because they could work from home while the wider community of people interested in UFOs and starseeds online provided a large and growing audience for their videos, far beyond the size of following they could attract in their physical surroundings. Making money as a starseed thus was part of the larger "gig economy" that enshrined the principle of short-termism in labor relations.[72] The gig economy grew particularly after the financial crisis of 2008, when workers were "contractors" rather than "employees" and performed temporary, fixed-term, contract-based service tasks with little more connection to their employer than a consumer had with a brand.[73] In this new economic form, labor protections are minimal, payment oscillates, and work is increasingly commodified. It is a direct result of the withdrawal of labor regulation in neoliberalism. Younger people are more likely to be involved in the gig economy than older people. On this point it is significant that Mynzah had a military pension and Elizabeth had a work-related pension to provide reliable financial support. The new economy also allowed for a greater degree of religious individuation than in congregational religions; as practitioners, starseeds were not dependent on a local community, nor did they need to maintain a physical building. Since they found their audience online, they could remain disconnected from others involved in spirituality in Sedona because they interacted with and received financial support from a much larger, dispersed network on the internet.

Economic instability was rarely framed as a problem, however. Many phrased their instability as an asset. They were free to follow their path, unfettered by responsibilities. There was a sense that it was better being against the system and embracing the instability that ensued than being trapped in a nine-to-five that did not allow time for their spiritual exploration. It was framed as a choice. Instead of being restricted to a specific career path as a means for survival, they were free to create their life as they chose, a choice that was at the same time preordained by the soul contract they had worked out before this incarnation. Mynzah turned against his previous jobs in authoritarian institutions, something he explicitly called a rejection of the American dream. Krista and Ra did not mention this ideal; they had little expectation of continuing and increasing economic security or prosperity. For them, work was temporary and instrumental, each piece part of a larger composite that provided support. However fragile patchwork income was, they interpreted it as freedom from institutional control. The digital platforms that made this possible created a space for new social imaginaries, potentially offering a way to transcend alienation.

In the works of both Hegel and Marx, alienation was thought through primarily in terms of labor.[74] For Hegel, all labor was alienated, and this was a necessary principle of its existence due to self-externalization; the product of labor cannot exist without separation from its creator. However, for Marx this was a historical condition of capitalism and as such not inevitable. The specific configurations of the market system and commodity production in capitalism, particularly in terms of private property and the division of labor, resulted in the alienation of the worker from both the products of labor and the means of production, which were controlled by the capitalists.[75] This meant that transforming the political economic system can end alienation, and of course in Marx's theory this meant the revolutionary overthrow of capitalism and the establishment of communism. Marx's formulation of alienation was taken up by Frankfurt School philosophers Theodor Adorno and Max Horkheimer, who extended the theory of alienation beyond the division of labor to the whole of modern society, particularly manifested in mass media, the "culture industry," and political leadership, in which they saw alienation as increasing the risk of authoritarianism. The constant search for work and pleasure by consumers, who were no longer producers, buffeted by the manipulations of media, dominated by technology, was a sign of "the compulsive character of a society alienated from itself."[76]

Do the forms of work employed by starseeds following their spiritual paths offer a route beyond the alienation of labor? Mynzah's employment was self-directed and he retained control over its products. He sold his own art, readings, and writings online. His diversity of occupations echoed what

Marx was proposing as the ideal in pure communism when the division of labor had ended and individuals were no longer subjected to a single task. However, Mynzah still had to alienate his products from himself by selling them in a market system in order to earn money to survive. More importantly, his earnings from these endeavors varied greatly, and his stable means of support was still his military pension. He was therefore primarily supported by the remittance he gained from "the system" he deplored as authoritarian and controlling.

Hosting a YouTube channel seems to be the embodiment of Horkheimer and Adorno's culture industry, representing everyday life as entertainment, making life indistinguishable from its media representation, and earning a precarious living from this commodification of life itself. Living everyday life as an alien may seem a far cry from the flat, reduplicative media representations Adorno and Horkheimer decried, but this ignores how banal much of the starseed material is. Beyond the seeming sensationalism of claiming to be from the Pleiades or Sirius, the average video uploaded by my starseed interlocutors was tediously mundane: how to tell your "true" friends from your "fake" friends, "giveaways" of products, how to deal with people who dislike you or lower your vibration. This is not to judge the content of those videos so much as to say their purpose seemed to be to give people advice on how to live their daily lives as starseeds. And of course, the revenue from these videos came from hosting advertising for a range of entirely third-dimensional products. Being an alien was not so much a transcendent action but yet another form of lifestyle branding, another product to sell by workers who not only consume but were consumed.

All of which goes to suggest that rather than liberating themselves from labor alienation, my starseed interlocutors were caught between dependence on state welfare or employment-related benefits and the precarious unregulated short-term gig economy, which offered little economic security and few labor rights. In Marxist terms, they did not own the means of production, which still belonged to Google and the other online platforms they used. In Adorno and Horkheimer's terms, they were engaging in the meaningless facsimile reproduction of culture for the sake of consumption, all the while creating more benefits for the corporations that hosted their endeavors than for themselves. While following their spiritual path meant rejecting traditional employment, such jobs were in increasingly short supply in the new economy. They were perhaps rejecting something that was not on offer in the first place. They were also taking the self-transformation that has always been at the heart of spirituality beyond an emotional, psychological process into an economic process. The reified self that transcends dimensions and exists simultaneously on Earth and in ships in orbit is also monetizable. Who they are and how they earn money have fused so that the real self and the worker self are no longer separable, they are one.

DISCLOSURE: REALIZATION/TRANSFORMATION

Starseeds believed themselves in possession of a truth most others could not see, the existence of extraterrestrials and their ongoing involvement in this planet's affairs. Awakening opened their eyes; they could see the light. It was a personal journey of transformation but also a realization; this is how things always were, they just did not see it before. Someday, soon, my interlocutors hoped, disclosure would occur. Awakening on a mass scale would follow. The light would come on for everyone; all eyes open, everyone awakens. Disclosure provides a frame for thinking through continuities and discontinuities on the spiritual path. It was a new revelation of something that was already the case. A transformative disjuncture that comes through a realization of something already existing. It is both continuous, a reality that already existed, and discontinuous, radically different from what was assumed to be reality prior to disclosure.

Awakening as an alien prior to disclosure is a personal journey that led my interlocutors into a stigmatized identity; separating from their kin, quitting their jobs, feeling out of place in the third-dimensional world. Mynzah felt out of place during a childhood in which he experienced racial exclusion, domestic violence, and family breakdown. If being human meant enduring such things, better to be an alien. In these circumstances, alienation could seem like the sane response to social inequality. But does calling oneself an alien really offer liberation from alienation? To take just the example of race in Mynzah's case, while for him being an alien from the Pleiades meant being neither black nor white, the wider discourse of "races" of aliens reproduced American discourses of race as a natural, biogenetic "fact." The most common alien races mentioned by my interlocutors were Nordics, Greys, Zetas, and Reptilians. Nordics were fair skinned, with blue eyes, beautiful, tall, and strong, a replication of the Aryan fantasies of white supremacists. Reptilians were the "evil" aliens, dark skinned, serpentine, aggressive, and acquisitive, a mixture of Christian demonology with stereotypes of malicious dark-skinned others.[77] The Zetas and Greys were said to create "hybrids" by searching for specific "bloodlines"; in Sierra Neblina's story it was Cherokee, a reinforcement of material-semiotics of "blood" as an immutable biogenetic substance that determined identity and attributes much as in racist fears of miscegenation. Native Americans reappear throughout the tales of starseeds, such as Sierra Neblina, as a romanticized other used to endow spirituality. To what extent is liberation from alienating social constructions of race really possible in this frame?

Moreover, equating seeing oneself as an alien with social and economic alienation glosses over an important point: in spirituality, aliens and humans are in fact the same. Both are entities in the universe of equivalent essence—they are both composed of energy—but with different vibrational frequencies. Starseeds are human bodies with alien, or as they would say galactic, souls. The human body exists in the third dimension while the soul is somewhere else, in a different galaxy or onboard a ship. The soul is akin to a drone operator, maneuvering the physical form at a distance. This is called bilocation and has a rich history in esotericism as part of astral projection beliefs and practices.[78] The difference between humans and aliens is one of spiritual development: aliens are more advanced spiritually (except Reptilians) and starseeds are more advanced spiritually than third-dimensionally bound humans. It is a difference in degree, not of substance. Humans become aliens and aliens become human, depending on the view taken. Difference is therefore an illusion of perspective. Disclosure reveals this universally. Alien and human are simply different energetic frequencies of the universe, but they are both part of the universe and as such the same. There is no difference, no separation, no alienation, only oneness. The difference between alien and human is therefore collapsed, and what seems at first to be a radical discontinuity is in fact a seamless continuity.

This collapsing of distinctions into a continuous energetic flow undermines much of the potential critique of the American political system. In 2017, I got in touch with Mynzah because he had been very quiet online for the past year and this seemed strange for someone who made a portion of his earnings through internet marketplaces. He let me know he had recently returned from Boulder, Colorado, to Sedona with his musician/conservationist girlfriend, but they were living in Cottonwood, as they could no longer afford Sedona rental prices. I asked directly if his diminished online presence was a result of the increasingly poisonous discourse on social media since the 2016 presidential election. He denied it and told me that he did not get involved in politics, and it did not matter to him who was president. Reality is controlled, not by the government, but by

Divine Order, which included Donald Trump. There were no coincidences
or mistakes; everything that occurred was all part of our evolution: "I don't
see this reality as 'real,' it is a dream state . . . a micro within the macro." His
only concern was to keep his self healthy, happy, and balanced. He did not
take on negativity by getting involved in politics, religion, or anything that
divides instead of unites. He did not have a problem with Trump or current
politics in the United States. While he said he would like to see more unit-
ing on Earth instead of dividing, what was happening was part of the plan
as well as part of the illusion. I found it surprising coming from someone
who so strongly rejected authoritarianism in American state institutions
that he would shrug off what seemed to me like a dangerous and dramatic
lurch toward authoritarianism in the presidency. But his position recalled
Vincent's on being homeless: whatever happened was meant to be, it was all
preordained, as we had chosen it to be. The only thing to do, therefore, was
take care of the self.

4

TO YOUR HIGHEST VIBRATION

Hierarchies of Food,
Boundaries of the Self

A polluting person is always in the wrong. He has developed
some wrong condition or simply crossed over some line which
should not have been crossed and this displacement unleashes
danger for someone.

—MARY DOUGLAS, *Purity and Danger*, 1984, p. 114

A SAD DIET FOR A SICK NATION

THE FIRST THANKSGIVING I SPENT IN Sedona, my yoga teacher invited me
to join her family for a meal at her brother's home in Glendale, a suburb of
Phoenix. A sprawling Mexican American brood of siblings, their spouses
and children, and a stern Spanish-speaking matriarch, they invited me into
their home without fanfare, and I arrived with a pumpkin pie that my land-
lady had made. She had made three, and insisted I take one, telling me that
was the norm for arriving at a Thanksgiving dinner. When I got there, I saw
there was a table of eight or nine similar dessert pies and two cakes, so I
added my pie to the table. The NFL game played on the big-screen TV. Beers
were drunk and chips were dunked in a selection of dips. The food for the
main meal was served on a side table. Before we ate, we all held hands in a
circle and everyone said what they were thankful for: friends, family, and
food. Then we formed a queue behind Rosa, the matriarch, and filled up
paper plates with turkey, mashed potatoes, candied yams, sweet potatoes,
corn on the cob, and rolls. I ate so much I was thoroughly stuffed. After din-

ner, I sat out in the garden pregnant with digesting food, watching the kids play with a football, unable to move.

The Thanksgiving meal is in many ways the archetypal American meal, a tradition that recalls the founding of the nation by European Protestants.[1] My hosts invoked this history during the giving of thanks preceding the meal, and one person specifically singled out "the English" for their role in creating modern America. Of course, Thanksgiving commemorates the giving of food by Native Americans to the early Pilgrim settlers. Setting aside for a moment the imperialist history obscured by this mythic narrative, what I find significant is that this event commemorates the inability of Europeans to feed themselves sufficiently in their new land. The foods present in this meal are the traditional Thanksgiving foods: corn, potatoes, and turkey. Foods that have taken on potent symbolism from this history. The abundance is also stereotypically American. There was so much of it, more than the people present could ever eat in one sitting, so many pies that I ended up taking the one I brought home again untouched. The way it was cooked maximized the salt, sugar, and fat content: yams were boiled in sugar to become candied; potatoes were removed of their skins and pulped with milk and butter to become mashed. There was a semiotic continuation of simultaneous profusion and deprivation; eating a lot of food, but food that was not very healthy.

These twin themes of abundance and nutritional impoverishment dominate public policy and medical discourses of the "standard American diet." Lauren Berlant characterized this diet as a "high-fat, high-fructose world of cheap pleasure food."[2] Obesity is framed as an epidemic within these discourses, a costly failure of will by individuals too lazy to maintain the healthy, productive body required of liberal subjects. Behind the discursive isolation of obesity as a symptom of personal failure, Berlant identified an old story of "the destruction of bodies by capitalism in spaces of production and the rest of life."[3] The food system in capitalism simultaneously overfeeds and undernourishes, resulting in the "mirror symptoms" of obesity and emaciation.[4] Both of these symptoms are wrought on the bodies of the poor, as food producers in the global South remain malnourished while the working poor in the United States suffer the highest rates of obesity. The built environment and employment conditions in America exacerbate this; fast food and vending machines make food of poor nutritional quality easily available, during a working day too long and exhausting to leave time to cook at home or get much in the way of exercise, and driving is often made mandatory by distances, lack of public transportation, and dearth of sidewalks. The government further encourages poor health in low-income neighborhoods through zoning laws mandating space for fast food franchises and rewarding schools' partnerships with soda companies. American workers' true four food groups are sugar, fat, salt, and caffeine, according to Berlant, because this is what is available to them and what enables them to get through the day.[5] This imperils public health at the same time as responsibility for personal health is rhetorically situated almost exclusively on an individual level. When obesity is cast as the result of lack of will and poor food choices, then the structural conditions of the capitalist food system are obscured. Survival becomes a matter of "slow death," where people live but not very well.[6]

My interlocutors in Sedona positioned themselves within this discourse, and those involved in spirituality invariably rejected the "standard American diet." It was viewed with disgust and suspicion. Still, they reproduced the individualism of the discourse by asserting that Americans often made "bad" food choices. However, the available choices were viewed through a conspiratorial lens. Despite the hand-wringing efforts of politicians and health professionals to encourage good diet, "unhealthy" food was much easier, cheaper, and more immediately obtainable than "healthy" food. Why would this be if someone wasn't also benefiting from it? The state was, in my interlocutors' view, complicit with corporations in creating a food environment marked by abundance and scarcity, overproduction and wastage. Poor-quality foods produced diseased, disordered bodies. They saw what Berlant called slow death occurring to those with poor diets and blamed the state, yet the solution lay with the individual choosing a better diet, purifying the self.

In her account of Malay kinship on Langkawi, Janet Carsten related how the sharing of food was part of the process of becoming kin through incorporation; sharing food made people more similar.[7] Commensality is an act of relatedness, a way of creating ties between persons. In Langkawi this was enacted in particular in the sharing of full rice meals among kin and of wedding feasts among the wider community.[8] Food prepared by the community could be eaten without fear of witchcraft or poisoning.[9] Anthropologists attend to multivariate ways that food can operate to symbolically separate and/or connect persons. The sense of safety through commensality is lacking in the attitude of those involved in spirituality toward food. Inverting Carsten's formula, the foodways in spirituality are an act of nonincorporation, sealing off the self as separate from the polluted environment through ascetic practice. Maurice Bloch reminds us that commensality is the foundation of social life; sharing food means sharing substance, creating bonds between those who share, implying trust that one will not be poisoned.[10] The fear for Bloch's Zafimaniry interlocutors was of a sorcerer adding poison to the food; for my interlocutors in Sedona, the fear was that the food itself was poison. The food provided by the industrial system was suspect, contaminated, and impure. In rejecting it, they were rejecting commensality with the industrial system through their food choices, refusing to consume the food it provided. They were rejecting the legitimacy and authority of the state that authorized and legitimated this food system.

The industrial food system was a misuse of land. It produced foods that were plentiful but undernourishing, creating poor diet that undermined personal health. Returning to the Thanksgiving meal, the history that this celebration conceals is one of appropriation. The foods that became symbolic of the birth of America were foods grown on stolen land. The products of this corrupt genesis were polluted, for my interlocutors. And while they seldom named this history of genocide in their reasoning, they rejected its outcome, the inadequate diet composed of nutritionally depleted food grown on abused land.

A QUEST FOR SPIRITUAL PURITY

The garden at the ChocolaTree was decorated with fairy lights. Serving a menu of "fresh pure ingredients" that were 100 percent organic and completely free of grain, gluten, and GMOs, the vegetarian restaurant had a contrived ethereality reflected in the twinkling multitude of colored plastic-encased electric bulbs. I sat with two friends at one of the large round wooden tables on stools fashioned in the shape of tree stumps. Hungry and thirsty, I ordered an "adaptogenic tea" brewed from chaga, reishi, and red belted polypore mushrooms and goji and schizandra berries, and a dish called "Sedona 2012" that was a spicy tomato wrap filled with quinoa, stewed potato and carrot, wild rice, mushroom sauce, pico de gallo, onion, garlic, guacamole, hot sauce, creamy vegan cheddar, and honey mustard. It was a squat one-level building with a wooden exterior, housing a restaurant and artisanal raw chocolate production. As well as the food service, it sold products such as kombucha, ormus, nutritional supplements, herbs, seeds, crystals, oracle cards, sage bundles, essential oils, and decorated blue glass bottles. Works by local artists adorned the walls, nestling next to statues of Indian deities and a large lingam stone. There were oracle cards on the tables, as well as laminated flip charts explaining foods like tepache, a "traditional exotic pineapple elixir" that is organic, raw, and fermented, a supplement that aids weight control and digestion, boosts the immune system, supports metabolic activity, and enhances cell and liver health. When I placed my order, the server called "love in" rather than "order in." They deducted 10 percent of the bill since I was a "local," meaning that I had been there often enough for the server to remember my face. The food was, as always, served at a languid and leisurely pace. We waited enjoying the ambiance of the garden, the air suffused with the rich smell of mint plants and the sound of live didgeridoo music. As we ate, we tasted each other's dishes to delight in the variety of foods on offer. After we finished eating, we sampled some raw chocolate. I had a "bee pollen cube" and "magic healing bar," $2.22 for the half-inch-square piece and $3.33 for the two-inch bar. As we left, I felt the familiar, ominous rumble in my guts that let me know I had eaten enough healthy food that I would soon experience a rapid and uncomfortable digestive cleansing.

The ChocolaTree restaurant displayed many of the facets of what may be heuristically labeled "the spiritual diet." This is a constellation of foodways gravitating around a core principle of eliminating the aspects of the standard American diet considered polluting, poisonous, or generally undesirable. These foodways included preferences for organic produce, locally sourced food, vegetarianism or veganism, home-cooked or "artisanal" products, raw food, and the exclusion of substances such as gluten, soy, or "processed" food. Like the raw chocolate sold at the ChocolaTree, such foodways often had a high price tag attached. There was a diversity of approaches to these foodways, and the way these principles were interpreted was neither uniform nor straightforward. In order to unpack the complexity of the spiritual diet, a closer focus on specific foodways is required.

Findal and Buttercup ran an "artisanal alchemy" company whose products were sold in the ChocolaTree, and they were also friends with the owners of the ChocolaTree and central figures in the social group associated with that restaurant. Buttercup met Findal at a kundalini yoga retreat. Originally from Ohio, Findal already lived in Sedona at the time and she moved there to be with him. Buttercup previously had lived in Paris, Switzerland, Brazil, and Africa. She used to be into political activism and completed a degree in development studies at a university in Massachusetts; however, she said she gave up on politics in favor of spirituality because change had to come from the individual, which would then be the catalyst for change in society.

They were both very thin, tall with long angular faces, and they both wore similar kundalini white and last-elf-in-the-forest-style clothing. Others in Sedona commented that they shared "the same energy." They self-identified as "lightworkers" rather than new agers, which Buttercup defined for me as "someone who intends and focuses on bringing more light to this world through their embodiment (presence) and actions" while adding the caveat that that was her answer of the moment, which could of course change in their constantly evolving spiritual journey to a higher state of consciousness. They both peppered their speech with happy little audible sighs. They artificially contrived their language to portray a more positive state of consciousness, saying "as you love" in place of "as you like," addressing people as "dear," and referring to everyone as "friends." They slept under a copper pyramid, which they said had a high vibration so anyone sleeping under it had their vibration raised. They also had copper pyramids above their water cooler and sofa; the one above the sofa was "activating," according to Findal, because it was designed according to the dimensions of the Great Pyramid in Giza and built on the Fibonacci sequence, which he claimed reflected the "precise math of nature." Everything for them was "light and love," "your highest truth," "blessed," "amazing," or "beautiful." Nothing was just OK, fine, or acceptable. Their lives were directed toward spiritual evolution achieved by raising the frequency of their energy to the highest vibration through how they spoke, where they slept, how they earned their money, and the food they ate.

Buttercup described their diet as organic, gluten-free, raw food vegan. Gluten was eliminated because it functioned "like glue" in the colon, removing the nutrients out of food as it was digested, which created disharmony in the body.[11] Soy was also excluded from their diet because it was "genetically modified" and "full of additives." Buttercup recommended I drink homemade almond milk instead of soy milk.[12] No "processed" or genetically modified food was any good. These were poisoned with pesticides, adulterated with vaguely defined "toxins" and "chemicals," and corrupted by "artificial" human methods. These were the lowest-vibration foods. Findal and Buttercup were advocates of "living food," such as sprouts, which had the highest vibration because they were still alive when eaten. Foods found in the wild were preferable to cultivated foods, so it was better to eat a blackberry found growing outside on a bush than one bought in a store. Fermented foods and drinks were also advocated as containing the most beneficial bacteria and nutrients to help boost the immune system, but moreover because they were still living and growing in the form of yeast. The highest vibrations were found in foods that were either still alive in some sense and/or had the least influence from humans. Foods with an alkaline pH built a strong immune system and in particular prevented cancer, and so were preferable over foods with an acidic pH. An interesting exception to this particular rule was kombucha, which they produced and sold through their company. Kombucha, in terms of pH, is acidic; however, Findal claimed that it "alkalizes" once consumed and was therefore very beneficial to health.

Findal and Buttercup's diet was based on a series of eliminations of specific substances: gluten, soy, animal products; preferences in preparation: raw over cooked, organic over non-organic, handmade over industrial production; and preferences in sourcing: found in the wild over bought in a store, locally derived over imported from a greater distance. This constructs a hierarchy of foods expressed through the spiritual idiom of vibration. At the top of the hierarchy, with the highest vibration, are foods found in the wild, living, raw, with an alkaline pH. These foods are vegetables or fruits; eating live animals or fish was excluded due to the principle of veganism, and non-gluten grains were excluded because they required cooking. Foods that are made at home by one's own hand have a higher vibration than foods bought at the store, although if purchasing from a store it is better if that store is local, in this case in the Sedona area, or if that is not possible, then organized as a small business rather than a large corporation. The purpose of this hierarchy is to achieve spiritual evolution through consumption.

The foodways with the highest vibration exhibit the least amount of cultivation, which is to say, the least amount of change by humans. These foodways are the closest to "nature" and have the least intervention by human "culture," in the form of cooking, transportation, packaging, or processing. A higher vibration is associated with less human intervention; as discussed in the first chapter, nature is at its most natural without humans, so food is most beneficial to human health when humans themselves have affected it the least. Leaving aside the other axes of this hierarchy for a moment, this association becomes clearer through a focus on the opposition of raw and cooked. In his structuralist analysis of myth, Claude Lévi-Strauss observed that in a selection of different cultures raw is analogous to an uncultivated state and that cooking is a process of transformation akin to socialization. From this he made the proposition that in terms of structural relations of categories, raw is to cooked as nature is to culture.[13] Lévi-Strauss further elaborated a "culinary triangle" that is marked by three poles of raw, cooked, and rotted, where "the cooked is a cultural transformation of the raw, whereas the rotted is a natural transformation."[14] The raw is associated with nature, the cooked with culture. In terms of the hierarchy presented here, wild/raw/uncultivated/vegetable are most closely associated with nature and domesticated/cooked/cultivated/animal are most closely associated with culture. Closer to nature means a higher vibration, which in turn means it is the best for personal health and spiritual evolution. A diet consisting of raw food is a rejection of culture in favor of nature.

However, nature and culture are not unproblematic labels, in the same way that organic and processed are not unproblematic labels. The concept of nature in use here, as in the first chapter, is culturally constructed. Findal and Buttercup's foodways portray nature as uniformly positive; food that is "closer to nature" is better nutritionally and spiritually. Nature has a higher vibration than culture; it is closer to source, the very highest vibration. By leaving food raw, culture is cleansed from the diet, bringing the body in closer alignment with nature. Spiritual evolution is the journey toward unification with source, and foodways that have a higher vibration contribute to this endeavor through a system of eliminations and avoidances.

Their diet is in many ways a form of asceticism. It is a way of creating and maintaining spiritual purity. Eating high-vibration foods allowed Findal and Buttercup to embody the qualities associated with having a high vibration. Consumption was therefore an "act of incorporation" for them, and eating the food granted the symbolic associations of that food.[15] For Findal and Buttercup, wild food was good because its source was pure, unaffected by humans, uncultivated, and therefore more natural. This in turn suggested that they themselves were "more natural," they were distancing themselves from culture. Red-meat eating is central in American culture as a sign of virility and masculinity, particularly in cattle-ranching states like Arizona. Not eating meat is a way to signal a distance from these values; it is an act of non-incorporation.[16] Through their veganism, they were not participating in mainstream American culture; instead, they were purifying themselves of its deleterious effects.

The foodways of Findal and Buttercup formed a system of rules of avoidance aimed at purification through excluding or minimizing exposure to impurity. According to Mary Douglas, purity rules reveal social boundaries; they make them public and visible through what is avoided as impure.[17] Impurities threaten the social order. The boundaries revealed by Findal and Buttercup's food rules suggest who is or is not, or is more or less, spiritual. A person on the spiritual path should be eating foods with the highest vibration. This was closely associated with physical health and well-being. The boundaries are constructed on both a social and corporeal level. In rejecting the "standard American diet" as polluting, my interlocutors reaffirmed their corporeal boundaries in an act of self-mastery that simultaneously closed them off from mainstream American society. They do not eat what most Americans eat, and they therefore will not suffer from the illnesses that are most prevalent among Americans: obesity, heart disease, and cancer. The food environment of secular America is considered harmful by certain sects of evangelical Christianity who also follow a raw food diet justified as more healthy.[18] The evangelicals of Hallelujah Acres rejected the secular diet on medical, scientific grounds, but following it maintained a spiritual boundary of purity, isolating them from mainstream, secular America, and elevating them as Elect. The foodways of the spiritual diet created a similar boundary demarcation. Indeed, the parallel was made explicit by Findal when he told me that the biblical Essenes followed an "amazing raw food diet" that allowed them to birth a "pure spiritual being" in the form of Jesus Christ. Maintaining health was a way of securing and controlling the boundaries of the body against hostile or uncontrollable elements in the environment.

There is then equivalence between the social order and the corporeal order: both are maintained through adherence to purity rules. Amit Desai's Adivasi interlocutors joined the Hindu sect Mahanubhav as a means of ensuring purity and virtuousness.[19] They believed the teetotalism and vegetarianism required by this sect would protect them from witchcraft and magical attacks. Purity maintained a corporeal boundary, keeping out the physical pain inflicted through such attacks. Similarly, the spiritual diet was most often described as a way of maintaining personal physical and mental health, in the face of pain inflicted through metabolic diseases, cancers, and mental illness. Buttercup asserted that adherence to her diet rules helped her recover from cancer and post-traumatic stress disorder brought on by an abusive relationship. Desai suggested that the Mahanubhav diet rules solve "being in the world" problems.[20] In the case of his interlocutors, witchcraft; for mine, it meant to keep out "toxins" introduced to their diets through human processes of modification. Renouncing foods is a way of purifying and cleansing the body, which makes the body a better instrument for purifying the soul. The ascetic Jains studied by James Laidlaw progressively renounced various categories of food until they subsisted only on water for periods, some going as far as fasting to death.[21] The renunciation of various categories of food in the spiritual diet is similarly a religious act of purification. It is a way of keeping out the harmful aspects of the environment.

These food rules create boundaries between order and disorder. The order that is being maintained by the spiritual diet is a corporeal order;

disorder is the fat, diseased body brought on by the standard American diet. Corporeality is therefore unstable; it needs to be stabilized through adherence to specific rules of consumption. The instability of the body is also suggested in the cosmologies of spirituality. Bodies can move through dimensions and jump through portals; they are not fixed in the third dimension. The third dimension is dense, fleshy, and heavy; higher vibrations are lighter. Findal told me that "our bodies are light," meaning composed of light. It is only incarnation in the third dimension that gives them the illusion of mass. Following the spiritual diet makes the body lighter; it loses bulk, becomes less earthy, less fleshy. It makes the body less like a body, transforming from flesh to pure energy, from form to formlessness. Ultimately, the body dissolves and dissipates into pure light, pure energy. Like the Jain renouncers, the logical consequence of this diet is death, a process of purification into non-existence.[22]

For the Jains, any existence involved violence, therefore fasting to death made sense, in religious terms, by reducing the violence caused through everyday living and ensuring a better reincarnation. In spirituality, the higher you raised your vibration in one lifetime, the closer you came to unifying with source and therefore finished with incarnation. In a similar way to the Jains, it brought you closer to the soteriological endpoint. For the holy women in medieval Europe described by Catherine Bynum, fasting was one of the few socially acceptable forms of asceticism and opportunities for religious vocation, and controlling food intake made sense because food was one of the few forms of social control women had.[23] This is different to the Jains, who fasted at the end of their lives, indeed were primarily men, and were giving up control, giving up on the inherent violence of everyday life. Medieval women ascetics were taking control. In spirituality, the environment was seen as poisoned through human social action, and renunciation of food groups was a way to cleanse the body of this poison and enhance spiritual purity. They were controlling their foodways, their bodies, because they could not control the environment, which was framed as attacking the body. Asceticism is a way of managing the relationship of the religious, pure body to the secular, polluted environment.

This dynamic is made explicit by the example of breatharians, who were said to consume no food at all, only water and sunlight. However, unlike the Jain renouncers, they were expected to live rather than fast to death.[24] It is significant that I did not meet any practicing breatharians in Sedona. They were an ideal, a fiction, a utopian dream used to illustrate the highest level of the hierarchy of the spiritual diet that was at the same time unattainable. They were the ultimate symbol of non-attachment to the food system, of separating the body from the environment. Douglas highlights how the linguistic root of "holy" in Hebrew is linked to separation.[25] The Jain renouncers, the Medieval European holy women, the Mahanubhav sect, the Hallelujah Acres raw vegans all used food restrictions as a form of separation from the environment, a way of inculcating holiness through symbolically separating themselves from the impure world. Asceticism operates similarly in spirituality, separating practitioners from the environment, the food system, and non-spiritual, "mainstream" society through food restriction. The result was life, rather than death, and perhaps even eternal life through reunification with source. Ultimate purity meant total separation from third-dimensional reality.

The highest level of this food hierarchy is to not eat food at all. This did not have to be achieved through starvation, it could also be achieved through the consumption and use of "elixirs." Together Findal and Buttercup manufactured and sold what they called elixirs: kombucha, ormus, and misting sprays composed of essential oils. I went to a course on kombucha, ormus, and essential-oil fabrication at their "alchemy temple," which is what they called their house. All of their concoctions were designed to have the "very highest vibration," which was purported to be "in harmony with earth." Kombucha is tea fermented with fruit, herbs, vegetables, or flower essences added as flavorings. It was spoken about as a living entity. Buttercup told us that it would like what we like, so we should play music we like, keep it away from electronics or wireless routers so it was not affected by the radiation emitted, and create a sacred space for our kombucha to grow in. She advised us to give it "love and sweet pure intention" through music, meditation, singing, yoga, and copper pyramids. The brews under their copper pyramid were ready faster, they claimed, and were thicker and "happier." The benefit of drinking kombucha was that it helped detoxify the body; in particular, it did "miraculous things" for the liver. Again we see the association of purity with life here. The intention of the brewer must be pure to help the kombucha grow because it is fermented, it is still living, so it has a high vibration. It is pure, it is alive, but it is not food, it is a drink, indeed a marginally alcoholic drink.[26]

Similarly, the elixir called "ormus" was not a food but a fabricated substance, invented in 1975 by an Arizona farmer named David Hudson. The name is derived from the description "orbitally rearranged monoatomic elements," sometimes also called ORMEs or M-state materials. It is a combination of the caustic powder lye, salt, and seawater.[27] Findal and Buttercup

equated it to the "first matter" of the alchemists.[28] They used it as anointing
oil and ingested it in small quantities. An essential part of fabrication was
to "charge" the ormus in a spiritual as well as chemical sense. The intention
used during preparation was integral to this charging process because the
substance vibrated at the frequency of one's state of consciousness at the
time. They used Dead Sea salt to aid third-eye activation, as it was a pure
source of salt. The seawater they used was purchased online from a group
who dived into the deep to procure water that had not been affected by
pollution and contained no sulfur. This emphasis on purity of ingredients
and purity of the intention of the maker made it an "amazing substance"
that was full of light and minerals. It was a superconductor that amplified
whatever intention was charged into it once it was ingested. Ormus that had
been charged with a suitably positive intention made whoever ingested it a
"better cosmic antenna," which meant that energy would flow through them
more, thus raising their vibration and bringing them closer to source. Findal
half-joked that the main benefit of ormus was levitation; it made the body
lighter to the point that it would leave the earth entirely. Here again we see
the connections between a high vibration, lightness, and purity on both a
physical and spiritual level.

The holism central to spirituality means that the body and spirit are not
separate. The aim of ingesting these substances is to both improve physical
health and evolve spiritually because these two processes are inextricably
intertwined. By not understanding this connection, biomedical doctors did
not understand the true causes of health and disease. "Health" in this context is the alignment of the mind and the body with spirit or source. This
meant orienting beliefs, language, and thoughts as well as diet toward the
highest vibration. Findal and Buttercup described as "alchemy" this practice of improving the holistic combination of mind, body, and spirit, which
they called a "metaphysical" practice because it was "beyond physical." The
medieval alchemists attempted to turn lead into gold. Findal and Buttercup
understood this process symbolically. The heavy, dense substance of lead
represented a lack of caring, a lack of consciousness, and the heavy, dense
third dimension. The alchemist added the *prima materia*, which for them
was ormus, representing compassion, and thus produced gold. Gold cor-
responded with the sun or light, which according to their interpretation of
alchemical language meant a higher state of consciousness; in their spiritual
idiom, it was the highest vibration. The physical process of making potions
reflected a deeper, inner alchemy. It was a way of bringing more light into
one's being and then spreading that out into the world.

This kind of "spiritual alchemy" continues a historical trajectory of esotericism that follows the interpretations of C. G. Jung and other twentieth-century psychologists. The medieval alchemists literally believed they were turning lead into gold and finding the secret of immortality; later on with the ascendancy of chemistry, alchemy fell into disrepute, and serious scholars such as Jung who found interest in it tended to try to rationalize it by calling it a metaphor for spiritual improvement and enlightenment.[29] The common theme of alchemy is a quest for purity, with the chemical purity of substances acting as a model for spiritual purity.[30] Findal and Buttercup placed themselves in this longer history of esotericism by calling themselves "alchemists" and the process of fermenting tea "alchemy." The term was closely aligned with the term "lightworker," which Findal and Buttercup also used; both evoke the importance of raising vibration through association with pure substances of gold and light. Ultimately, they claimed, the need to physically make potions would recede and they would become that gold or light, it would shine from their being. The goal, therefore, is a spiritual purification of the self that then spreads out to others.

There was another level through which this process of alchemy was understood. Findal also called it a "metaphor" in a capitalist money-centered society of how to support oneself. Making money was the "lead," a dense, third-dimensional process. However, they made money through spiritual practice, thus turning the "lead" of the necessity of making money into "gold," or spiritual practice, a purer substance with a higher vibration. Findal and Buttercup ran a small business, marketed as "artisanal," with Findal as the "chief alchemist" and Buttercup as the CEO. They were an example of a curious breed in Sedona, "conscious entrepreneurs," people who tried to combine their spiritual path with making money through business. Spirituality and business have many complex intersections, particularly between corporate positive thinking and spiritual groups promoting New Thought self-help techniques like est.[31]

This was a controversial combination, as a common complaint against Findal and Buttercup was that they were "just trying to make money" and therefore not doing "real" spirituality. Given this background, it is significant that they defined their company as "artisanal." Heather Paxson explored the way artisanal cheese makers elaborate what they do as a traditional craft opposed to industrial mass production through the use of the term.[32] The Vermont cheese makers used distinctions between "handmade" and "industrial" in a similar way to separations between "organic" and "non-organic," as a way of connoting the hierarchical difference between their product and regular cheese.[33] Artisanal cheese production maintained the variation that they associated with nature, while industrial production created standardization. Findal and Buttercup were self-consciously placing themselves in this lineage as a way to combat associations between making money from business and corporate, industrial systems. They were closer to "nature" because their production was artisanal, they were not part of a system that abused the land and produced toxic food. They were turning the "lead" of commodity exchange into the "gold" of spiritually pure consumption through artisanal production.

The spiritual food rules of Findal and Buttercup constitute a hierarchical social order, where the highest level is not eating at all, surviving on air, light, and elixirs that purify the body, maintaining the boundaries of the corporeal body and the social body. This creates a body that is the inversion of the caricature of the "fat American" supposed to result from the "standard American diet." It was not incidental that Findal and Buttercup were both very thin. They were also tall, white, and as small business owners, economically middle class. In broader American culture, eating sparingly and excluding foods is a demarcation of upper-middle-class behavior; the higher-class body is a thin body.[34] Findal and Buttercup's diet was "high class" in the social hierarchy of spirituality; they could see themselves as more spiritual than others because of their diet. They were also higher class socio-economically. Their artisanal company was successful, unlike many others in Sedona. This meant that Findal and Buttercup did have more resources than others, and they had easier access to a wider range of foods through which to construct their high-class diet. They acted superior but they were also superior in terms of economic capital. They had a successful business, social capital, and a cohesive social group around them.

This assumption of superiority did not pass without comment in Sedona. Others I spoke to expressed opinions that Findal and Buttercup were absurd, cultlike, and self-aggrandizing. Theresa, who lived in Sedona to recover from a brain tumor, regularly remarked on what she called the "right-wing spirituality" of the "spiritual drag queens" in Sedona. People who thought they were right about everything and everyone who disagreed with them was wrong. They wore sundresses and no makeup, they used their appearance to put on a performance of being spiritual. This kind of spirituality was like religion in her opinion. She found their actions contrived. Theresa would often comment in our conversations on the "spiritual drag queens," whom I subconsciously associated with Findal and Buttercup, when after about a year of knowing each other she explicitly identified the type of person she

meant as Findal. Another acquaintance I asked directly if she knew Buttercup and she made a negative noise, indicating she knew her and did not like
her. She called Buttercup a "blisstard." Previously she had been involved in a
community space called the Greenhouse that was run by Buttercup and the
ChocolaTree owner. There was a long list of banned things at the entrance:
"no meat, no smoking, no drinking, no drugs . . ." The negativity turned a
lot of people off, I was told; it was not a democracy, but a dictatorship of
Buttercup. The Greenhouse ceased to be a community space soon before
I arrived, when it was turned into a grow space for sprouts run by a couple
of guys who worked at the ChocolaTree. The "ChocolaTree crowd" was a
social group explicitly identified by others with Findal and Buttercup, a raw
food diet, and a sense of superiority and exclusiveness.

Trying to achieve purity means expelling the impure, socially and cor-
poreally. It is important to analyze what is meant by purity in this context,
since it is an ideologically loaded term. Purity can mean natural, unspoiled,
simple, and earthy but also aseptic, scientifically clean, free of germs, and
hygienic.[35] The contrast comes from two culturally constructed definitions of nature, one that is based in religion, the other in science. Purity in
spirituality contained elements of both. It was an association with nature,
simplicity, and lack of spoliation and also with being clean and not leading to sickness. The foodways of spirituality were justified with reference
to science, but also built on a structure of religious myth. They relied upon
a constellation of terms delineating a Manichean dichotomy of food that is
not easily mapped onto reality. "Organic," "raw," "natural" were all equated
with "good," whereas "processed," "genetically modified," "corporate" were
equated with evil. This is the mythic structure of spiritual foodways. As
suggested above, a structuralist analysis of these myths reveals an opposition between nature and culture, where nature is the absence of human
intervention.

Even a brief examination of the concepts used in this structure reveals
their ideological construction. "Processed" food was often used as the example of "bad" food, referring to food that was bought in packages from
stores created by agribusiness corporations, something like cheese-in-a-can.
However, a lot of food is processed. Kombucha is processed, since fermenta-
tion is a process done to the raw materials by humans. Cheese is processed
even when it is "artisanal"; such cheese makers use less mechanization, not
none.[36] Processed food is not necessarily unhealthy, it depends on what the
process is and what the foodstuff is changing from and to. For example, raw
milk is often less healthy than pasteurized because of the presence of food-

borne pathogens.[37] "Organic" is similarly a complex ideological construct. "Organic" in chemistry means containing carbon. The USDA regulation on organic food mandates production without the addition of synthetic substances such as chemical fertilizer or artificial food additives.[38] It is marketed and legally defined as more "natural."[39] What this means in actuality is not obvious, however. The organic label is allowed on products that have ingredients that are 95 percent organic; 75 percent organic ingredients gets the label "made with organic products." In nutritional terms, not all organic food is healthy, just as not all processed food is unhealthy. "Natural" pesticides can be more harmful than "chemical." Organic food is now made through the same mass production methods as non-organic, and the industry is also dominated by a few large companies geared toward maximizing profit.[40] Even a term as seemingly self-evident as "raw" is a construction; certain types of chocolate were considered "raw" so long as they were not heated above 115 °F/42 °C.[41]

Underlying this structure of interrelated ideologically constructed concepts is a specific meaning of nature, one associated not just with human activity but with the specific kind of human activity found in industrial capitalism and the food system that supports it. Industrial cuisine is based on processing, specifically freezing and canning.[42] Colonialism was made possible by it.[43] Cheap, calorie-dense food is important in capitalism as a fuel for workers and a profitable commodity for corporations.[44] The ideological distinction between processed/not processed or organic/non-organic refers to an underlying structural difference in the relations of capitalist industrial production. By trying to eat foods that are found in the wild, or made by artisans, or not packaged and sold in a store, my interlocutors were trying to eat foods that were not created in the capitalist industrial food system. In the narrative of progress, machines replace humans because they are more efficient. The food toward the top of the hierarchy in Findal and Buttercup's diet is less efficient, made by humans, or even better, eaten as it is found. It is an inversion of "progress." Progress has not made food better; it has degraded it, contaminated it. It has misused the land to bear spoiled fruits. By valuing purity, they are valuing human labor. Even more valued is that which is taken directly from nature, with no human corruption at all. At the top of the hierarchy is light, and the most pure is that which is the most "natural." Completely removed from human culture, the third-dimensional, the corporeal, and the mechanical, it is the negation of corporeal existence altogether. It is not-food. This mythic system is a rejection of industrial cuisine, the narrative of teleological progress, of settler colonialism, of capitalism itself. It is a rejection of "the standard American diet" and the food system that produces it. Their food choices are part of cosmologies of spirituality that mirror an ideal construction of the social order.

INSECURITIES OF SELF AND SOCIETY

On a trip back to Sedona in 2015, I visited my friend Saanvi, who had recently stopped living in her van and rented a manufactured home behind a pizza place in West Sedona with our mutual friend Kate. Since I was heavily pregnant at the time, Saanvi and I decided to indulge in hot fudge brownies and ice cream, followed by a large pizza and chicken wings shared between us. When she came in that evening, Kate saw what we were eating and joked that we would die of sugar poisoning. Saanvi and I laughed about how much we ate. She said normally she did not have this type of food out of respect for Kate and because it was no fun to pig out on junk food by yourself. Kate was a raw food gluten-free vegan, with a desire to train as a raw gourmet chef. On their fridge was a list of foods she had banned from her diet, including tomatoes, potatoes, and kale, many vegetables and fruit often thought of as healthy, and other consumption restrictions, such as only eating fruit on its own and not eating melon with any other kind of fruit. The list surprised me. When I asked her what the problem with kale was, she told me it had a substance in it that she believed made it unhealthy but that she could not remember the name of it. Kate spoke about "chemicals" being bad for you. All processed food was also bad, although she could not remember why when I asked. Saanvi said Kate was always into the next faddy diet, changing regularly, trying to be as healthy and pure as possible. Later, Saanvi told me that Kate ate fish, not realizing veganism excluded fish.

The next day on a trip up to the creek, I asked Kate about her diet. She told me that all she ate was bananas and protein powder. She was 80 percent raw, with an exception for coffee. On our way out of West Sedona we stopped at Natural Grocers, where we were given a free bar of (non-raw) chocolate as a promotion for Mother's Day. Kate ate the whole bar. She said when she got near chocolate it was hard not to eat it all at once because she usually denied herself things like that, so it was very difficult to resist. She also got seaweed snacks and zucchini that she ate in the car. She said being raw was hard, especially when eating out. She had been vegetarian for about a year, since she had been driving back from Milwaukee with a hitchhiker, and she got stoned and started talking about the goat's cheese he had given her: did the goats want to give up their milk? Did it hurt them? So she became vegetarian. Then she met two raw food vegans through her job at Natural Grocers, who taught her that eating meat released ammonia in the body, which caused sickness. So she became a raw food vegan. Her diet was based on restriction, refusing certain foods as she learned their harmful effects from people she knew that she trusted about food. It worked, she said, because she felt healthier than ever before, she had "more energy."

When I asked, she agreed that she would call herself spiritual, definitely, but not "new age" because she did not really know what that meant. Spirituality for her was working on herself, having a relationship with herself, being conscious of the way she spoke to herself. It was also related to the way she lived her life: her food choices were related to spirituality because it was part of feeling better in her self. To take care of herself physically was part of her spirituality. Spirituality for her was about care of the spirit and soul. Growing up in Phoenix, she learned about spirituality after she moved to Sedona for drug rehabilitation. She had been a heroin addict for three and a half years. After the premature death of her father, she started taking oxycodone in eighth grade, and by ninth grade she was on heroin. Working part-time in the modeling industry, she dropped out of school by tenth grade, never completing her general educational diploma.[45] With the support of her mother, by late adolescence she was clean after attending an in-patient rehab facility in West Sedona that promoted diet over medication as a means to deal with the physical side effects of withdrawal. The treatment gave her a new model for taking care of herself through diet. While she was there, they kept her on a non-dairy, no-sugar diet, with a little meat and eggs.

Given her prior career as a model, I wondered how much of her diet was about maintaining her physical appearance. When I asked if she avoided dairy to aid weight loss, she denied it, saying only "Dairy is gross."[46] Her diet was based on similar binary associations as Buttercup and Findal's: natural was good, organic was good; human-made or processed was bad. Similar accommodations and compromises ensued; for example, she mentioned eating tofu and I said that was processed, and she shrugged. Kate's diet regulations focused exclusively on personal well-being; there was no notion of the politics of industrial agriculture or land use or indeed much talk of vibration. "Regulation" is also possibly too strong a term, since her food choices were in a constant state of flux. The last time I checked in with her, after she posted a picture on Facebook of her boyfriend and her enjoying fresh-caught grilled octopus, she said she tried to be 70 percent raw vegan

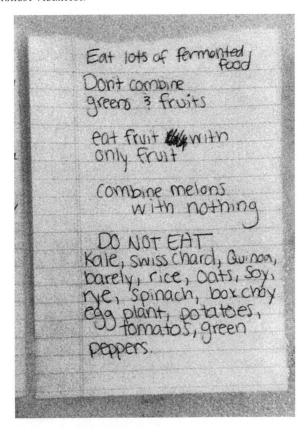

FIGURE 17. The note on Kate's fridge detailing what not to eat.

while remaining open to new food types. It seemed as though the fixation on purifying her body through diet was a response to drug addiction, an attempt to physically and emotionally cleanse herself of a toxic experience.

Kate's flexible approach to diet did not mean she was not serious about spirituality, however. In general, she was a fairly changeable person. Her ambition to be a gourmet raw food chef was replaced with an attempt to return to modeling, all the while actually working as a server who brought drinks to guests at the pool at one of Sedona's many upscale resorts. This kind of mutability was typical of people in Sedona. Indeed, one of the things that differentiated Findal and Buttercup was their rigidity, especially in social aspects. In contrast to their policing of the boundaries of their social group, Kate happily lived alongside Saanvi, who ate what she wanted to, including junk food, and focused on exercise as a way to maintain her physical and mental health. They would negotiate the difference in diets through jokes.

For example, there was a chart on their fridge of Saanvi's butter consumption. Kate had commented about it and so they kept a record of how many sticks of butter Saanvi had eaten, roughly a stick of butter a day. Kate's quest for purity was therefore maintained on a personal, corporeal level, but not on a social level as with Buttercup and Findal.

Kate's diet also gives a clearer picture of how categories of food are mediated on a personal level. The way she navigated a raw food vegan diet was different to the way Buttercup did, who told me she was strictly 100 percent raw vegan yet she ate raw chocolate, which as mentioned above is technically not literally raw. Kate's foodways also bring into sharper relief how the intersection of spirituality and diet is contingently negotiated through everyday life. It was common for my interlocutors to rely on broad-stroke dichotomies of food and its sources as either "good" or "bad" with imprecise notions of how this connected to health or social effects. Underlying these foodways is a subtext of wealth and class. A focus on "good" nutrition is a class issue, a marker of taste or what Pierre Bourdieu called distinction.[47] It is a marker of higher-class status and better access to resources, particularly since "fast food" and "junk food" are often cheaper and easier to procure in America.[48] As mentioned above, there is also an association with the fat body and unhealthy food and lower-class status. Eating healthy and being thinner often equates with cultural assumptions about how much money one has to spend on food that reflects a social reality where it is more expensive to buy food marketed as "healthy" even if this does not have a direct relationship with being beneficial for human health. This was a problem I found my interlocutors with lower incomes negotiating on a daily basis through their foodways.

During a shopping trip at the local organic grocery store, New Frontiers (subsequently taken over by Whole Foods Market, now part of the Amazon conglomerate),[49] with a member of my kung fu group, Greg, he wondered what would be best for him to eat for lunch. Then he shrugged and said that since it was New Frontiers, it was all "good" anyway. Whether this meant good for his health or good for him spiritually was not explicated. He wanted to eat well, and shopping at New Frontiers was to him an easy way of doing so, since it was dedicated to selling foods that were "healthy." It was a shortcut, in other words, to a beneficial quality that he desired to incorporate into his body and his notion of self. However, it was more expensive to shop there, and since Greg worked as a restaurant server in a cowboy-themed restaurant in Uptown, his income fluctuated. He relied on tips, and the minimum wage for tipped employees in Arizona was so low ($4.25 per hour in

2013) that his weekly wage was often entirely deducted as tax. Tipping was generous in a tourist town like Sedona, and the restaurant charged a 20–25 percent gratuity as standard, yet it was not stable. Some nights he could come home with hundreds of dollars, others he would not make enough to cover his gas to drive to work. Despite this precarity, it was important to him to spend a large proportion of his income on food from the organic grocery store, in order to partake of the quality he associated with it.

There is a specific notion of quality at work here. Food was considered of a higher quality if it was of a type or from a source that correlated with the higher levels of the hierarchy outlined above, even if this correlation was only superficial. Thus food that came from a source that was seen in some way as more natural, meaning with less human intervention, was better quality. However, this did not necessarily mean it was more nutritious. The sourcing of water can perhaps make this distinction clearer. I heard many times that the tap water in America was no good, principally because the government added fluoride, which was considered poisonous or toxic.[50] Fluoride was purposefully put in water by "the man," who was "trying to keep us down," according to Greg, because it calcified the pineal gland and obstructed the connection to source. The pineal gland was the physical root of "your spiritual connection," in Greg's words, the part of the brain that connected the physical body to the soul or higher self. The reason the American government might want to inhibit the spiritual development of its citizens will be explored further in the next chapter.

To avoid this danger, Greg purchased non-fluoride toothpaste from New Frontiers. His shower was fitted with a filter so he would not be sprayed with fluoridated water. At restaurants, he ordered bottled water rather than tap water. At home, he drank only water from the spring in Oak Creek Canyon that he collected in glass or BPA-free plastic containers. This water came directly from the earth and had no fluoride added. That meant it was better for him physically and spiritually because it was better for his health and would not calcify his pineal gland. However, the creek water was later analyzed by a local resident who claimed it had high levels of naturally occurring arsenic, over three times the Environmental Protection Agency's recommended limit. It is problematic to assume that "natural" is the same as "good for human health." Arsenic even in low quantities is associated with increased risk of cancer, and in high quantities it is poisonous. It is also naturally occurring in the soil and water in this area of Arizona without human intervention. Arsenic is natural, but that does not mean it is beneficial for human health.

Buying food that is organic, shopping only at Whole Foods and its sub-sidiaries, driving up to the canyon once a week to collect water from a spring; these are all more costly in terms of time and money than the alternatives that were considered less healthy, less beneficial, and of a poorer quality by my interlocutors. It would be much cheaper and easier to eat at Burger King, shop at Safeway, and drink the tap water. Organic food is expensive, and people feel compelled to buy it despite the higher price because of its alleged health benefits.[51] Consequently, my interlocutors found ways around paying a premium for food they considered healthy. One weekend I spent with Kate and Saanvi, Kate had brought home a box of free organic bananas from Natural Grocers (the other organic grocery store in Sedona at the time), and exclusively ate that fruit all weekend. It may be more expensive to buy organic, but if less is consumed, this can compensate for the higher price. Similarly, Saanvi procured much of the produce they ate from the local Sedona food bank; a friend of hers ran it and kept the best organic and gluten-free items for them to choose before they were made publicly avail-able. The restrictive diets some of my interlocutors followed helped save them money. Cleansing or fasting can be a cheap way to live. It adds an extra dimension to eliminating a food group, such as meat, if that also saves sig-nificant expenditure on food. Economics played an important role in food choices. Indeed, the decision to eat "healthy" along spiritual lines led to a diet that could be described as "food insecure."[52] Food is a spiritual issue in Sedona, but it is also an economic issue.

That food insecurity exists in a country that overproduces food is testa-ment to the inequalities in access to and distribution of food.[53] Through-out America there are "food deserts," areas where there is no grocery store within ten miles by foot or thirty miles by car.[54] Valle, where I spent the last few months of my fieldwork, is a food desert. The nearest grocery store was forty miles by car in Williams; there was a general store at the South Rim of the Grand Canyon that was thirty miles away, and a gas station selling only snacks and packaged foods at the central intersection of Valle that was seven miles away from where I was based. The aim of Thom and Benito when they moved out there was to live off the acre of land they had bought, growing vegetables organically and raising chickens for eggs and meat. Benito told me that the American economy was failing and more people would have to turn to living as they did, growing their own food and being self-sufficient. It would become a necessity. He said this would lead to a "homesteading renaissance," the spiritual and economic regeneration of America. Their aspirations for self-sufficiency tapped into a long history in the United States. During the Revolutionary period, the colonies provided all the food for the people there without relying on imports, working the land and producing their own food was an important part of the emerging national identity and Revolutionary politics, and indeed the Revolution was partly a response to British taxes on foodstuffs.[55]

However, it was difficult to produce enough food to feed everyone who lived on the land in Valle. The soil was poor and the climate was difficult. The first greenhouse they built was destroyed in a storm when winds reached 35 miles per hour. Wild jackrabbits then ate the exposed plants. More than once the dogs broke free and mauled the chickens. Open-range cattle trampled through the gardens regularly and ate all the plants they could access. The growing season was only three months long; in the summer the sun was too hot, and in the winter the ground was too cold. A food diary I kept for a week revealed the limits of their self-sufficiency. Most of the produce was bought from a grocery store in Flagstaff or given by Benito's father, who maintained a garden more successfully in Williams. Their diet contained numerous items bought from the gas station in Valle, such as chocolate bars and cans of Coca-Cola and Budweiser. In the seven-day period I kept the diary, they only ate two items from their own land: tomatoes and a duck. The difficulty of growing their own food there, and their inability to consistently buy produce because of the distance, meant they often ate food bought from the gas station or Taco Bell, where the cheapest taco cost only $1.

Thom and Benito were in many ways trying to achieve the diet most esteemed in spirituality. Food produced directly from the earth, by one's own effort, without any "artificial" interventions in the form of pesticides, fertilizers, or genetic modification. It remained an elusive goal, however, because of the lack of resources available to them. The only land they could afford lacked a fresh water source and had poor soil and a harsh climate. They could not afford to cultivate it easily, so they grew very little. They found themselves relying on food sources such as the gas station and Taco Bell that did not provide the quality of food they desired.

Access to food reifies the existing class structure. Those with fewer resources find they only have the money and time to procure food that is less beneficial for their health and creates bodies that are marked as lower class, which compounds their lower-class status. Time is an important factor here. Many of the foodways esteemed in spirituality take more time, such as cooking and growing one's own food, growing food without pesticides, or getting water from a spring rather than a tap. In many ways it reflects the concerns of the international "slow food" movement.[56] This movement advocates the

FIGURE 18. A garden on Thom and Benito's land, with green onions and sunchokes growing.

value and pleasure in eating and living in a way that is more deliberative and processual than the pace of life in industrial capitalism allows. However, the difference between fast food and slow food parallels the difference between lower class and upper class. It is easier for those with more resources, in terms of both time and money, such as Findal and Buttercup, to achieve a "slow food" diet than Benito and Thom, who despite their efforts still relied on various forms of "fast food." The foodways in spirituality were therefore still mediated by variable access to resources, that is, by the structure of socio-economic class.

THEY MAKE YOU SICK

Peter's cancer came back in late summer 2014. The tumor in his neck returned with friends. Five at the back of his throat and mouth. He said he did not want to do the radiotherapy; instead, he would just go up to Bell Rock with some morphine, as he did not want to lose his quality of life. That was before I went to Burning Man; by the time I came back on Labor Day, he was booked in for an eight-week treatment, starting in the last week of September. Peter's son was an oncologist, who informed him he had a 100 percent success rate with radiation therapy on this kind of tumor. Peter had wanted to delay by two months to try to heal his cancer with diet, but his son and daughter had both objected. His son sent pictures of people who had waited, with huge tumors bulging out of their necks. His daughter wrote a long email saying he was afraid, and that since he was always telling people to get over their fear in climbing Bell, he should follow his own advice. Their interventions changed his mind. He still adopted a raw vegan, gluten-free, organic diet alongside having radiotherapy treatment administered by an oncologist. His insurance covered it, so he only had to pay $30 per week as a co-pay. There was only one drug he needed to get that would be very expensive. He said all his friends on Facebook had been giving him advice on what to eat, what not to eat, what to think about, suggesting that the tumor was caused by emotional blockage. Peter was adamant that he did not have any emotional blocks. He still thought his life was great and that he chose everything that happened to him, although he was having a harder time explaining to himself why. He was worried about the radiotherapy sapping his strength and fitness, so he was planning to work out every morning before the treatment. His son said he would be fine after popping an OxyContin.

Peter's cancer went into remission, and he is still alive as of the time of writing. His approach exemplifies the interwoven network of conventional and alternative therapies, issues of insurance and cost, and considerations of quality of life versus likelihood of remission that go into individual responses to cancer.[57] Cancer was in many ways an emblem of the problems many of my interlocutors identified in American diet and society. Much as Peter related, I was told that poor diet, negative thinking, and low vibrations caused cancer. It was an effect of living in the third dimension. The body became so corrupted by pollution that it destroyed itself, and the density of the third dimension metastasized in the body. Cancer was also described as an "industry." Chemotherapy and radiotherapy were not real cures, but moneymaking scams sold by the pharmaceutical industry, whose real intent was to profit from the problems caused by the diet peddled by agribusiness. The real cure was right diet; certain high-vibrational foods were claimed to cure cancer, just as the wrong diet of low-vibrational foods caused cancer. This connection was obscured by the government through agencies such as the American Medical Association so that "Big Pharma" could continue to make money with false cures; they were all in cahoots, of course. This was evidenced by the fact that legally doctors were not allowed to prescribe diet as a cure for cancer, nor were non-medical professionals allowed to make such claims, even if they believed that was what cured their cancer.[58] It was a total system of corruption: bad food sold in bad faith caused disease, bad medicine was sold to perpetuate rather than cure the disease, enriching the corporations that made both the food and the medicine. The pharmaceutical industry, agribusiness, and the medical profession were little more than snake-oil salesmen in this view.

Cancer was the state of sickness in the body that low-vibrational food caused. The hierarchy of food in spirituality, spoken of through the idiom of vibration, produced certain types of bodies. Findal, Buttercup, and Kate all followed raw food vegan diets and all had young, lean, and light bodies. They physically embodied the highest vibration. The cancerous body is heavy, dense, and old. In adopting the raw food organic diet, Peter was trying to change his body, rid it of disease, perhaps even reverse the aging process. The cancerous body is the flesh corrupted by the impurity of the third dimension. The highest-vibration diet was meant to purify it, cleanse it, purging the body of cancer. The bodies with the highest vibration were thin, young, and free of disease. These are also the ideal characteristics of the body in American society more widely.[59] Despite the rejection of the "standard American diet," the spiritual diet produced what could be termed standard American bodies.[60]

Alongside a certain type of body, there is a certain notion of self being constructed through these diet choices. It is an autonomous self, one that does not require the support of corporations, governments, or doctors to sustain it. In other words, it does not rely on the state, given that both private

and public institutions were seen conspiratorially as part of the same corrupt system. Both food and medicine could be derived from the immediate
environment, without the corrupting influence of the industrial food system. As Findal said at the alchemy workshop, what our body needs grows
in our environs, we are a part of our environment, a part of nature. Human
culture is what separates us from our true nature, which is to be a part of
nature. Nature is the least human intervention. Thus, the autonomous self
is also the natural self. The hierarchy of foodstuffs and sources separates the
self from reliance on the state, from the action of other humans. It creates a
sense of self that is in a state of nature, wild and uncivilized. The process of
spiritual evolution separates the self from culture, in the sense of civilization.
The highest vibration possible is light, which is stateless. The self sustained
on air and light has no need for the political-economic state machinery;
it is also without form or matter, it has no density. The aim of the spiritual
diet is to liberate the self, ascend beyond the third dimension, both in the
sense of political authority and of form or matter.

Spiritual evolution is conceived of as a process of healing. The true
essence of being is spirit. We are separated from it in the third dimension,
and this separation is experienced as sickness in our fleshy, dense bodies.
The symptoms of this sickness are illnesses such as cancer, heart disease, dia-
betes, the morally valenced twin failings of obesity and anorexic-spectrum
eating disorders, and pathological personality disorders such as drug addiction and PTSD. The cause is neoliberal capitalism: its diet, its food system,
its corporations, their greed in selling us the cause and the cure by controlling access to medicine and healthcare, their influence in government.
This sickness breaks the connection with spirit, sometimes symbolized as
a calcification of the pineal gland. Part of the spiritual awakening, often
the impetus for it, is getting rid of this sickness. The cure for this sickness
is found in changing foodways to increase vibration, and raising the vibration decreases separation. It is a portal to unification with source. The more
people that heal, that raise their vibration and elevate themselves closer to
source or spirit, that purify themselves through diet, the greater the benefit
to the planet and all humans. Fix the self to fix society.

There is in this aspect of the cosmology of spirituality an esoteric idea,
that of correspondences.[61] The self is a microcosm of the cosmos, which is
the macrocosm. That is why spiritual evolution is seen as more effective
than political activism, because it achieves the aims of political activism on
a spiritual level, which is the "real" existence upon which this material reality
is epiphenomenal. The middle level of society is skipped over; it is only an

illusion. The result of this idea of correspondence was that my interlocutors focused primarily on their personal needs, especially their physical health, as a means to following their spiritual path. Yet the pure self, separated from society, with hermetically sealed corporeal boundaries, purified from all corruption, was always an ideal that they never fully achieved. As related throughout this chapter, they never completely separated from the food system, they never existed purely on light. The raw food diet was too difficult to maintain consistently for Kate; Thom and Benito's land did not produce enough food to sustain them; Findal and Buttercup needed to engage in commerce to support themselves economically. The requirements of their dense, fleshy bodies persistently held back their aspirations to a spiritually pure state. The third dimension could never be ascended out of completely.

The hierarchy of foodstuffs is outlined here as an ideological construct. How it played out on an everyday basis in Sedona was always murkier, riddled with contradictions and accommodations. It did point toward political economic inequalities in American society, where profits often do take priority over human needs. However, by resorting to individual solutions to social problems, the existing political order is reified, not rejected. The rejection is only ideological, it is a symbolic rejection; at the level of collective action, nothing is achieved. The hierarchical order of the spiritual diet reproduces the class structure. The body produced by this diet is still the young, thin body idealized in American society. The responsibility for well-being is still placed upon the individual, and health is still associated with higher-priced foods and time- and effort-intensive labor. Despite the symbolic rejection of industrial neoliberal capitalism, the effects of the spiritual diet reify rather than challenge its contradictions. Yet there was still clear concern about the political economic system, a suspicion that all was not as it was meant to be.

5

WHAT IS WRONG WITH AMERICA?

Conspiracy Theories as Counter-Narrative

> The main thing that I learned about conspiracy theory, is that conspiracy theorists believe in a conspiracy because that is more comforting. The truth of the world is that it is actually chaotic. The truth is that it is not The Illuminati, or The Jewish Banking Conspiracy, or the Gray Alien Theory. The truth is far more frightening—Nobody is in control. The world is rudderless.
>
> —ALAN MOORE, *The Mindscape of Alan Moore* (film), 2003

THE IDEAS ABOUT CANCER AND ITS exploitation by "Big Pharma" for profit point to a deeper narrative in spirituality. One that described bodies as under attack from the environment they lived in, an environment controlled by secretive cabals composed of corporations, scientific institutions, and government agencies. The mistrust of these agencies was so extensive that it seemed to constitute an elaborate conspiracy theory. At first, I found this surprising; it seemed a very negative view for people so concerned with positivity to hold. On reflection, however, it seemed as though conspiracy theories formed the obverse of spirituality. The darkness to its light, a theodicy in a system otherwise constructed around a notion of divinity, the universe, geared toward the highest good. The feeling of strangeness that both spirituality and conspiracy theories arouse points to a deeper connection. Both express a profound distrust of scientific and political authorities. While perhaps it may be tempting to dismiss my interlocutors as marginal people rejecting authority structures from which they are prima facie excluded, it is telling that their voices of dissent emerge from a position embedded in the

racialized history of colonialism in the Americas. Within this history, rationality exerts considerable ideological leverage. The overlap of conspiracy
theories and spirituality speaks to a deep epistemological rupture fissuring
contemporary American society.

Conspiracy theory is a loaded term. It was often deployed by my interlocutors as a boundary marker: "I don't believe in conspiracy theories,
but . . ." The phrase was used to suggest an awareness of how their words
may be interpreted while trying to bracket themselves off from this. To call
something a conspiracy theory is to take a stance on its rationality, which
points toward the genealogy of the term. It was introduced by Karl Popper
in the second edition of *The Open Society and Its Enemies* as a form of mistaken thinking.[1] For Popper, a conspiracy theory was a form of false belief,
akin to religious superstition, something that arose specifically in response
to secularization. People could no longer blame God for misfortune, so
they created vast interlinked conspiracies of evil men tinkering behind the
scenes of society causing bad things to happen, mistaking complex socio-
political causation for individual agency. Popper's work was very influential
on subsequent interpretations of conspiracy theories by political scientists
who use it to describe theories about vast intricate networks of secret plots
and concealed instigators behind world events that are motivated by nefarious ambitions for money and power, theories that they are then at pains to
declare false.[2] It is a pejoratively evaluative label, and in calling something
a conspiracy theory, an author is taking a position on the veracity of that
theory. Political scientist Alfred Moore called this the "positive" approach to
conspiracy theories that views conspiracies as atavistic threats to the proper
functioning of liberal democracies that need to be dispelled.[3]

The other main approach, according to Moore, is the "critical" approach,
which is to examine the term "conspiracy theory" itself and how it constitutes the boundary between legitimate and illegitimate knowledge.[4]
Anthropologists routinely take this approach, suggesting that conspiracy
theories are simply theories wallowing in the shallow end of the power-
relations pool.[5] In this view, theories are given credibility by whoever has
the power to do so, rather than the abundance or lack of evidence in their
favor. Anthropologists focus more on what conspiracy theories tell us about
society, a concern that cleaves to anthropological work on rumor and occult
cosmologies.[6] Rather than determining whether conspiracy theories are
true or false, this approach examines the political conditions that produced
them.[7] Following E. E. Evans-Pritchard on witchcraft among the Azande,
anthropologists try to show how conspiracy theories, like rumors and occult

cosmologies, are internally, logically coherent in a relativistic sense.[8] There is, however, a "lingering functionalism" behind this approach that suggests that conspiracy theories are doing something of social value, specifically for subaltern peoples struggling against subjugating relations of power.[9] They are a coded way of "speaking truth to power." It is then the maneuver of the powerful to dismiss them as conspiracy theories. The anthropological approaches edge toward conspiracy theories cautiously, speaking of them as just theories, without supporting or dismissing them, while the political science approaches stridently dismiss them as both patently false and a threat to the health of the body politic.

In approaching conspiracy theories as simply theories, their similarity to religious beliefs becomes apparent.[10] Both are non-falsifiable claims about social reality that grant agency to causation in a way that challenges assumptions of rationality. The strangeness of certain beliefs is often apparent to the believer as much as the non-believer. It is not that they are confused by or unaware of this strangeness, rather they believe that in certain circumstances there are occulted dimensions to reality that only the initiated are aware of.[11] Understanding is granted by initiation; the believer believes themself to have access to knowledge that the unbeliever does not.

Yet initiation hinges on the acceptance of authority. Being granted access to special or secret forms of knowledge relies on believing that those passing on that knowledge are trustworthy. Who is accepted as an authority is socially constructed. Science constitutes part of the network of authority in America because of its methodology of empirical investigation, what Popper would call falsifiability. Incorrect assumptions can be discarded when empirically demonstrated to be false. When political scientists argue that Americans "ought to know better" than to believe conspiracy theories, they are employing the ideology of science as authority.[12] This ideology supports the veneration of rationality as a cultural norm and social good. Yet the very idea of rationality is part of the racialized history of colonialism in the Americas, a package of ideas and norms that support white colonialist supremacy. The other side of conspiracy is therefore transparency, the ideal developed, liberal societies are transparent and rational and have no place for conspiracy. Those societies that call themselves developed and liberal are those that benefited from the expansion of colonialism around the globe and perpetrated the extraction of resources and bodies that followed.

Anthropologist Michael Taussig's work on the history of colonialism in Colombia reveals how brutally that rationality was imposed. The reluctance of Amerindians to labor in rubber plantations was met with enslavement, torture, and genocide by the colonial authorities.[13] Yet they justified these atrocities through the frame of rationality. Raw materials could be exploited for profit, this required labor, the closest and easiest available was the Amerindians, therefore in the logic of colonial economics, it was rational to force them to work. This conceptualization of rationality comes from the intellectual tradition that defines it as "the application of logic, of pure thought untempered by emotions," which then forms the basis of scientific inquiry.[14] However, David Graeber argued that such thought is simply not possible. The assertion of rationality then becomes a political position; it is a way of saying whoever disagrees is clearly insane. It is an expression of power. There is a clear parallel here with asserting that something is a conspiracy theory. It is aligning that claim with irrationality, and then dismissing it. This maneuver has been used repeatedly throughout history to justify the violent expropriation of land, resources, and human bodies by white colonial powers, the most recent and currently most powerful example of which is the United States of America.

Rationality as a concept was cultivated historically as part of a package of distinctions through which Europeans and white Americans came to understand themselves as different and better, part of what made them human as opposed to the not-fully-human black and brown persons they subjugated.[15] Esotericism was part of the epistemological exclusion that undergirds the historical constitution of rationality, and more so, certain persons and societies as rational. When my interlocutors push back against the notion of rationality dominant in their society and the authority structures that support this notion, they are not descending into madness but renegotiating what is taken as authority. They are elevating their "heart wisdom" over "head logic" because logic and rationality are implicated in the abuses of the "old paradigm." That this should come from a group of people embedded in an esoteric religious form is not so surprising when considering the role of esotericism in the historical production of what is constituted as legitimate knowledge. In his history of the emergence of probability in the 1660s, Ian Hacking related how knowledge became a matter of the evidence of things rather than the acceptance of ancient authorities or witness testimony.[16] The evidence of things came from reading the signs of nature, a process that emerged through the "low sciences" of alchemy, geology, astrology, and especially medicine. The emergence of what is now considered empirical natural science from what is now derided as "the occult" is well attested by historians.[17] The latter was gradually pruned from the tree of knowledge to become the stigmatized debris. In the process, what colonial

Euro-American authorities sanctified as objective, rational, and therefore legitimate knowledge was constituted.

Spirituality is a context in which the occult's existence is already accepted. Invisible forces are at work in reality, according to my interlocutors, some are benign and some are malevolent, and as with conspiracy theories, everything is connected. The hidden interconnections they perceived evoked a feeling that the world did not work in their favor, expressing a helplessness to control the conditions of their lives. The larger structures of society, such as the government, the media, and mainstream science, were generally seen as hostile. Their theories and beliefs constitute a counter-narrative that stands in a dialectical relationship with the "mainstream" narrative of American society, a counter-narrative that continues the long historical relationship between the occult and science, between stigmatized knowledge and legitimate knowledge, between irrationality and rationality. These binaries are mutually dependent and constituted through the dialectical relationship of narrative and counter-narrative that creates a social space for what is knowable, thinkable, and sayable. What constitutes knowledge in the "mainstream" narrative is denied by my interlocutors, often for the reason that it is part of this narrative, and they are more likely to hold positions that are contrary to this knowledge. Spirituality and conspiracy theory thus form part of a counter-narrative, one that is part of a longer historical trajectory in the United States that views whoever holds power with suspicion. The visibility of this counter-narrative increased after the 2016 presidential election, when the social prevalence of suspicion of authority became more widely reported on in the traditional media. The alarm sounded in those reports echoes the warnings of political scientists that the existence of conspiracy theories is detrimental to liberal democracy because it undermines faith in institutional authorities. The counter-narrative of conspiracy is not new, however; what has shifted is rather the boundaries between the margins and the mainstream. The political center has shifted to occupy ground once ignored as the social fringe.

EVERYTHING IS NOT AS IT SEEMS: THE COUNTER-NARRATIVE OF CONSPIRACIES

At the end of a grueling kung fu session, I said I felt spacey, that sometimes all the qigong meditation made me floaty. Roger agreed, he said he felt

FIGURE 19. Chemtrails on a clear day above Valle.

the same, it was probably because "they were spraying a lot this morning." I asked if he meant chemtrails, and he said yes. Then he pointed to the sky and said the long lines of cirrus cloud crisscrossing the sky were chemtrails. I had never heard of chemtrails before, but in Sedona they were accepted as everyday knowledge. Chemtrails were said to be the result of spraying aerosols into the atmosphere, usually claimed to be made up of microfibers or "nanofibers" consisting of aluminum, barium, magnesium, strontium, and other elements. These concoctions are sprayed into the air from canisters in the wings of commercial and military aircraft or as additives in jet fuel. They appear as thick streams of white cloud across the sky. The government is responsible, possibly with the collusion of Monsanto or other corporations, various benevolent or nefarious reasons are attributed, and usually the claimed effect is to alter the climate. However, even when benevolent reasons are attributed, there are damaging side effects to human health. For example, it was said to cause "chemtrail flu," a flu-like sickness with the symptoms of fatigue and upper respiratory illness without fever. Chemtrails, or "aerial spraying" as it is also called, are also linked to cancers, Alzheimer's disease, heavy metal poisoning, and autism. It is said to "toxify" the soil and

FIGURE 20. Chemtrails or contrails? The cross of trails in the center is not expanding, implying contrails. Whereas the trails to the right are expanding, suggesting chemtrails.

plants, making it impossible to grow food without purchasing Monsanto-patented, aluminum-resistant, genetically modified seeds. The practice is called "geoengineering," and what they mean by this is purposeful climatic modification that is happening without the consent of the people.

Skeptics say the trails they are pointing to are harmless, ordinary contrails, caused by condensation from jet engines at high altitudes. However, my interlocutors claimed they lasted longer and looked different to contrails; they spread out over a greater area, which ordinary contrails did not. Once on the top of Bell Rock, Peter pointed to a series of chemtrails that looked like a double helix in the sky above. He called it "aerial spraying," so as to avoid arguments about contrails versus chemtrails. There were many aircraft trails in the sky that day. I pointed to a plane and asked if that was a contrail and the wider plume hanging in the air beside it was a chemtrail, and Peter confirmed they were. So there was a visual difference claimed to be discernible between contrails and chemtrails. This theory is not limited to Sedona. There is a huge amount of speculation and accusation on the internet about chemtrails. When asking about the subject, I was often referred to two documentaries on YouTube, *What in The World Are They Spraying?* and the sequel, *Why in The World Are They Spraying?* Both had over a million views. There are thousands of websites, social media threads, and internet forums dedicated to uncovering the truth of chemtrails.[18] There is so much speculation surrounding this issue that governments and scientific organizations have been forced to respond and declare chemtrails fictitious.[19]

I met Bobby at the Sedona branch of Unity Church, a New Thought–aligned non-denominational nationwide religious organization. He had only recently moved to Sedona and was living in a tent on Forest Service land. He had grown up on a self-sustaining farm in Kansas, and now worked as a landscaper, psychic, and shaman. Previously he trained as a radiographer, but stopped because he felt the medical industry was run by pharmaceutical and insurance companies and was aimed at making money rather than helping people. He told me he believed chemtrails were real and were polluting the soil with fire accelerants, which were increasing the number and intensity of forest fires. The other purposes were weather control and mind control. He claimed all soil was polluted and toxic because it contained aluminum, barium, and magnesium from spraying; even organic farms were contaminated, but less so. As a consequence, everyone had toxins and parasites contaminating their bodies. He told me a biannual cleanse was necessary to combat it. He blamed the government for chemtrails, and said they wanted to keep the truth from us. The aim was always making money; just as the medical industry did not want to cure cancer, it wanted to make money off it by selling expensive chemotherapy and radiotherapy treatments. The government was using chemtrails to pollute the soil to prevent us from growing our own healthy food. With sufficient nutrients from food, the body could heal itself, even from terminal illness; without it, we were dependent on expensive drugs and supplements from the pharmaceutical industry.

While the acceptance of chemtrails was commonplace in Sedona, not everyone saw such negative motivations behind them. Amateo Ra was a trance channeler and conscious entrepreneur, who had developed his ability to receive messages from other dimensions while working as a court stenographer. When I met him in Sedona, he was running the Ascension Academy with a partner, which was a "Magical Mystery School," aimed at helping people with their spiritual evolution. I attended an event of theirs at the Hampton Inn, during which Amateo channeled his higher self from Sirius from the future. Among other messages, it was claimed that chemtrails were being sprayed as a preventative measure from "solar systemic space weather influence." The government was afraid of this influence and was trying to decrease global warming by reflecting the sun with aluminum released via chemtrails. However, this whole process was the reflection of our own desire to block out things in our consciousness, which resulted in them becoming toxic. Therefore, even though the chemtrails were sprayed out of good intentions, the impact was negative. There was no separation between the government and the people, however, because these were all part of the same thing, oneness, which Amateo called the singularity. It was a sign of our lack of spiritual evolution; chemtrails were a physical substantiation of this attempt to try to block things out and remain separate, when instead we should let everything in and embrace the oneness. Chemtrails were thus part of the illusion of the third-dimensional reality that there was separation, and the way to overcome them was to evolve spiritually ourselves because we were the same as the government and the chemtrails were really part of us. Amateo thus offered an explanatory model for chemtrails that assimilated them into a cosmology of spirituality. His explanation defused the negative aspects by reinforcing the principle of oneness.

Chemtrails were not only discussed in conversation and at events, they were the frequent subject of Facebook status updates. Jill lived in her camp trailer parked in the driveway of a friend of mine; she taught Reiki and Nia (a dance style combined with martial arts), and performed a version of the *Nutcracker* using LED circus toys rather than ballet. Soon after this show, she announced on Facebook that she was leaving Sedona, after a sojourn of some three months. She declared she was returning to Minnesota, where her family lived, because the chemtrails in Sedona were blocking her spiritual evolution.[20] Jill went on to comment on this post, saying there were more chemtrails over Sedona because "they" were trying to block the spiritual energy of the place. Since the airport in Sedona was not a "real" airport, there should not be any commercial planes flying over the town.[21] She then posted pictures of the chemtrails, as did another commenter. Other comments circulated about using the power of thought to clean the skies and getting educated on the government's attempts to poison us.

Jill then posted a link to an article about chemtrails, claiming she knew they were real because she had previously worked in aerospace engineering. The article cited high levels of aluminum and barium in Phoenix and linked them to aerial spraying. The report was unsourced and contained data on high levels of certain metals in the atmosphere, then claimed these were the elements common in chemtrails. There was no evidence presented to support this connection, nor were any alternative sources for the elements considered. It was a fairly typical report on chemtrails compared to others I have read on the internet and had emailed to me by my interlocutors. They

generally included unsubstantiated claims, large tables of data without citing methodology for how that data was collected, followed by conclusions
that this must be the result of aerial spraying. They lacked methodological
rigor and were not published in peer-reviewed journals. They constituted
their own genre of amateur scientific research, yet they were held to be
authoritative based on their conclusions rather than their methods. What
was different from Amateo's explanation, which assimilated chemtrails into
a cosmology of spirituality, was that Jill's relied on her authority as someone
with knowledge of science backed up with evidence in the form of scientific
papers. Jill felt that science and spirituality confirmed each other, and as
someone with knowledge of both she could stand as an authority. Her interpretation reinforced that chemtrails were damaging, as Bobby's did; unlike
Amateo, she did not impute a positive intention behind them.

Each of these theories about chemtrails was founded on a different source
of authority: personal experience in industry, amateur scientific reports,
and direct revelation from a non-human source. Explanatory models were
improvisational, and what constituted knowledge and evidence varied.
Interestingly, no one told me they had read official reports by the EPA or
US Air Force and therefore considered chemtrails false. When greeted with
skepticism, they would advocate testing the air personally on a day with lots
of spraying, to see firsthand the levels of chemicals. This is also what is done
in YouTube documentaries like *What in The World Are They Spraying?*, in
which they get a small child with a mason jar to collect a sample to show that
the levels of aluminum can be found that easily. This recourse to amateur
research, direct revelation, and personal testimony is how conspiracy theories construct a counter-narrative about the world. It is a way of describing
what is going on and why, in opposition to officially sanctioned authorities, such as government agencies or tenured scientists. In spirituality, this
counter-narrative focuses in particular on the environment, technology, and
health, what Lawrence Quill called "technological conspiracy," where scientific and technical elites are portrayed as using their skill sets to undermine
and exploit the rest of society.[22] It is a discourse that questions and attacks
the authority of those elites while simultaneously employing the methods
and techniques on which those elites base their authority.

In terms of chemtrails, the counter-narrative expresses fears of being
poisoned by vaguely defined "toxins" that are also reflected in concerns
about food discussed in the previous chapter. These "toxins" represent an
attack on the body. The most commonly cited "toxin" is aluminum, often
incorrectly identified as a heavy metal, which operates as the smoking gun

of chemtrails. Aluminum is a naturally occurring element in soil, it is very easy to get samples contaminated with trace amounts of aluminum, but it can be harmful in high concentrations. Its prevalence and harmfulness are conflated in chemtrail discourse as proof of unnatural additives in the air and soil that cause health problems. This created a lot of anxiety among my interlocutors because it could not be avoided, unlike certain foods. The only way to combat it was to eat certain supplements, for example chlorella (a type of algae), perform regular cleanses, or think positively so as to manifest good health despite the pollution. This anxiety feeds on a truth: the average person is unable to control their environment, particularly in terms of what is in the air and water. Airplanes do spray harmful gases into the atmosphere, principally carbon dioxide. Jet fuel is a pollutant, a leading cause of anthropogenic climate change. Chemtrails can be read as a commentary on what is happening to the environment, one in which climate change becomes a purposeful attack on the people. Contrails may not be chemtrails, but they are pollution and they are affecting the climate in ways that are proving disastrous for the well-being of human societies.[23] The attack on the body of citizens by fossil fuel emissions sanctioned, promoted, and even subsidized by the state is quite real.[24]

What is occurring in chemtrail theories is perhaps less irrational and more "rational in excess."[25] As Didier Fassin suggested about conspiracy theories concerning the spread of AIDS in South Africa, they address directly the enormous power that state-sponsored science and medicine have over the bodies of citizens, particularly poor and marginal groups. Equally, chemtrail theories spread in Greece in response to the economic crisis in 2009 and the loss of financial control over the economy that ensued, with corresponding fears of a pervasive New World Order taking over.[26] Conspiracy theories extend the truth of these power relations over the limits of what is accepted and fall into the realm of the absurd. It is reported in mainstream news media that geoengineering to combat climate change is suggested by some scientists as possible, but it has not yet been tested at scale because of concerns about long-term effects to the environment and human health.[27] In chemtrail theories, geoengineering to alter the climate is already happening, and reports by scientists proposing potential tests are read as proof that this is what is being done.[28] What this suggests is a fear that people have no control over corporate and government use of the earth, which affects their personal health.

These concerns stem from a particular distrust of the US military. Chemtrail fears started in the mid-1990s, with the publication of an air force report describing fictional representations of future scenarios, including one in which the weather was weaponized by 2025.[29] The advanced technology and lack of oversight in the US military feeds into conspiracy theories. The 2025 report is often linked on chemtrail sites as evidence that chemtrails are real and caused by the military's weather control schemes. Historically, the US military did spray harmful chemicals on unsuspecting populations and even their own forces, for example the use of Agent Orange in Vietnam.[30] Government, the military, and corporations are linked in fears about the "military-industrial complex," the aims of which are felt to support elites at the expense of the masses. The past misdeeds of the military and the government add credence to the counter-narrative.

In Sedona, theories about chemtrails joined with related suspicions about the harmful effects of fluoride and vaccinations to form a counter-narrative to authorized explanations of scientific progress, health provision, and environmental change. It is a systematic contradiction of official explanations, homogenizing such explanations to a "them" evilly manipulating and colluding against "us." The counter-narrative is a collection of linked theories, some of which posit specific conspirators, others that merely cast aspersions about the power structures in American society. The overall effect is the suggestion that what appears is not what is; there are invisible forces at work. Reality, especially as depicted in the mainstream media, is illusory because it is being consciously manipulated by those who hold power for their own gain. Empirical facts cannot be relied on because these are presented by contingent actors who have motive and bias, who want something, usually money and power. The recurrent question posed is *cui bono*? Who benefits from the way things are being presented? There is a long history of anti-government and anti-elite sentiment dating back to the colonial period that feeds into the counter-narrative, a general feeling that whoever holds power should be regarded with suspicion.[31] Conspiracy theories are part of this long history of American populism; indeed, the Constitution itself includes conspiracy theories about King George III.[32] The existence of elites has been regarded with suspicion in the United States since the founding of the nation.

POWER AND ITS DISCONTENTS: THE DARK CABAL

In order for there to be a conspiracy, there need to be conspirators. The clearest personification of the malevolent force behind the counter-narrative was the "dark cabal." Dennis, a musician and businessman, described the dark cabal as "Reptilian," the name for the evil aliens popularized by author David Icke.[33] The dark cabal was a group of around fourteen families, including the British Royal Family and the Rothschilds, who control all the finance and banking in the world. Dennis claimed the freemasonry pyramid on American currency is evidence of their existence, which he described as "not a secret." They are open about what they are doing, which is keeping the majority in servitude. These families inbreed and control bloodlines so as to remain pure; they are the 1 percent. This guarantees their children will continue their control of resources. Dennis advised me that they were not "evil," however; they were just a part of the experience we have created and, since we created reality with our thoughts and actions, we could get rid of them anytime we wanted. Other entities in the universe find it ridiculous that we pay to live on our own planet. We could end it very easily, by not paying tax, paying off debts, or paying rents, and the financial system would quickly collapse. We consent to our servitude, and this had to change or the world would not continue. Some people thought the solution was in building bunkers and stockpiling resources, they thought they could live on the planet without seven billion others, but Dennis called this "playing into fear." He aimed to work to help build the community and support between people instead. For him this was the link between conspiracy theories and spirituality: spirituality offered the solution to the problems conspiracy theories diagnosed.

The dark cabal was, however, one label among many. In Sedona, there were a number of different terms used. I would sometimes hear talk of the Illuminati, the New World Order, or, to combine the two, the Illuminati-controlled NWO. The first person I stayed with in Sedona, Vixen du Lac, gave me a complicated diagram of the New World Order showing the many intricate connections between groups and events in recent history. This idea of everything being connected resulted most often in an amorphous, unpersonified "them" or "the system" as the ones behind everything. Often it was simply "the government" that was at fault. There were so many different aspects that to single out any one group seemed pointless. It was a "group-personality" of conspirators.[34] The aim of this byzantine collective was to gain power, sometimes termed as setting up a New World Order, where they would have total control of the economy, remove civil rights, and commit genocide of certain populations. They were effectively playing God, or perhaps more accurately, the Devil. Ideas about the dark cabal operated as a theodicy in spirituality, explaining the origin of evil in a universe that was

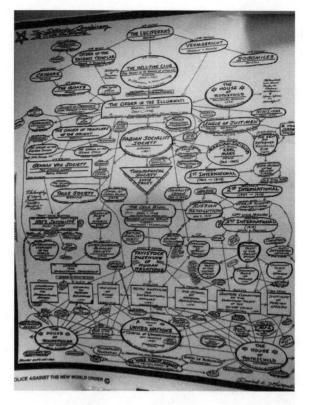

FIGURE 21. Diagram of the New World Order; note the copyright to "Police Against the New World Order," a right-wing militia organization in the Pacific Northwest.

fundamentally good.[35] While referring to them as "the government" or "the system" may seem to refer to an earthly evil, these were manifestations of third-dimensional reality. Evil exists because we are still in the third dimension, and whether it is called the dark cabal, the government, the system, Reptilians, or the NWO, the end result is still the same. Things are not as they seem, and the way to "truth" is through spiritual development of the individual.

There is an important social class dynamic to these framings because the dark cabal is the elite. Whether they referred to wealthy powerful families in finance or politics, such as the Rothschilds, the Rockefellers, or the Bush family, or to corporations, such as Standard Oil, BP, or Monsanto, or to vague conglomerations such as "Big Pharma" or the "military-industrial complex," what my interlocutors meant was the groups who had power.

These groups were perceived as not caring about the average person. They wanted to control everything, and in particular they wanted to make people dependent on their products to increase profits, for example genetically modified aluminum-resistant seeds that could still grow in the soil after aerial spraying. This can be seen as a way of describing the inequality of American society in a way that vilifies it and holds specific people responsible. The powerful American families and corporations are made the cartoonish bad guys behind complex political-economic problems, with influence and resources that vastly overwhelm ordinary citizens. The emphasis shifts away from collective political action to individual spiritual action. Dennis was rare in proposing direct political action to oppose the dark cabal; most of my interlocutors said only a shift in consciousness, ascension to a higher dimension, could solve the problems brought about by their machinations. The existence of social inequality is part of living in the third dimension; overcoming it is a matter of spiritual evolution.

Not everyone in Sedona eschewed political action completely, however. Anne was seventy years old and a self-described activist. At the time we spoke, her latest campaign was against the installation of smart meters, which she said were part of an electromagnetic grid used for mind control by the government. It was this mind control that she believed was used to make James Holmes, the mass shooter in the cinema in Aurora, Colorado, snap and go on a rampage in 2012.[36] The government also controlled food, through genetic modification, and communications, through monitoring calls and emails, and the weather, through chemtrails. The plan was to control people through technology, placing Anne's fears in the realm of technological conspiracies. To prevent the installation of smart meters, which read the electricity meter automatically and sent the reading back to the Arizona Public Service Electricity Company (APS) electronically, she was campaigning in local council meetings to have them banned, launching petitions that she lodged with APS directly, and spreading information so people knew they could opt out of the proposed installation program.

Anne had also actively campaigned against the streetlights that were installed along the central highway bisecting Sedona, the 89A. By the time I spoke to her, the 106 lamps were already set to be installed. She attributed this failure to the fact that Sedona politics was corrupted by cronyism and corporatism. There was a group called the Sedona 30, she told me, people who have been in Sedona over thirty years, fifty-seven of them in total, who were the local power brokers, predominantly businessmen and property owners. They got rid of the Arizona Department of Transportation (ADOT) offer of ceding the 89A to the city council along with $16 million and instead kept the highway in state control and ensured that the streetlights were installed. They did this through illegally sending it to a ballot and turning people against the deal. It was an administrative measure, not a legislative one, so it should never have been sent to the ballot, in Anne's opinion. But the city attorney was corrupt, and no one "calls him on his shit." Through this collusion, vested interests in Sedona got the streetlights installed against the wishes of the majority of residents. Anne accused the Sedona 30 of wanting to turn Sedona into the Las Vegas strip.

The Sedona 30 is a real group of people who have been in Sedona over thirty years. It was founded in 1982 with the purpose of working toward the "betterment of the Sedona community."[37] They called themselves community leaders, and were the kind of old white men found in positions of power throughout America. Anne was pointing to local power structures and how they worked in favor of the older, wealthier residents of Sedona, and against the interests of the spiritual community, who were generally younger, had been there for less time, and had less economic leverage. Angela LeFevre, who unsuccessfully ran for Congress in northern Arizona in 2012 for the Democrats and subsequently was elected to the Sedona city council, told me that the main concern of the local council and other community leaders was to preserve Sedona the way it was, limiting development while still attracting tourists, which were seen as a necessary evil for the economy. She said the spiritual community was seen as "fringe" and their opinions were not normally solicited on local matters. The streetlights and smart meters were both controversial local issues in Sedona for the people I knew involved in spirituality. Most of my interlocutors that I asked about it were opposed to the installation of the streetlights on the grounds of aesthetics and light pollution, although once they were actually installed many said they were not as ugly as they had feared. Smart meters continued to be an issue in Sedona, with many claiming they had adverse health effects. When APS rolled out installation of the new meters, residents were able to opt out if they wanted, for a monthly $5 charge and a $50 fee.[38]

These Sedona conspiracy theories indicate that the counter-narrative can be found on the local level as well as large-scale overarching plots about government and corporations. Small-town politics fuel conspiracy theories as much as the oblique workings of the federal government. Anne was one of the few involved in spirituality who took an active role in campaigning against issues she cared about on a local level. It is telling that her efforts were nearly always unsuccessful, as with the streetlights, or only partially successful, as with the smart meters. There is a powerlessness of the single person who lacks political or economic position in large complex societies, even at the local level. This powerlessness often finds fruitful expression in the counter-narrative of conspiracy theories that alleges that everything those in power do is corrupt, self-serving, and dangerous. The social class dimension of conspiracies is highlighted again. The working class suspect that the middle class and upper class always conspire, having meetings they are not invited to about things not to their benefit. In Sedona, the spiritual community was not respected or included in politics or public life; as a group they can be seen as a "lower class" even if some who followed a spiritual path could be wealthy (although this too was very rare). Their social and political exclusion spurred the counter-narrative; they looked to other sources of authority and knowledge. People in power are often assumed to have "higher knowledge" that justifies and legitimizes what they do, in a mystification of class relations.[39] The marginalization of the spiritual community encouraged them to doubt the higher knowledge of those in power, especially when coupled with their own framework for receiving knowledge from alternative media, amateur research, and the internet, as well as divine revelation in the form of "downloads," which they tested against their own intuition, or "heart wisdom." They did not believe in the mystifications of the powerful that granted them authority. Spiritual authority came from within the self.

WHO DO YOU BELIEVE?

There were many theories in Sedona about how the government was harming its citizens; what I rarely heard was a committed affirmation that they would never do such a thing. Cynicism about the intentions of the government seemed to be characteristic of my interlocutors involved in spirituality, with corporations, the media, and science also coming under skeptical view. This characteristic seems to be common among Americans who are marginalized based on their race, income level, or political affiliations.[40] It was not necessary for a person to believe in the dark cabal to be doubtful about what "they" were "really" doing. Among my interlocutors, believing official accounts was often taken as a sign of gullibility. You believed "the man," which meant you were duped by the system, one of the "sheeple" who was still "asleep." The internet played a significant role as a forum for the discussion of different viewpoints and dissemination of theories. Websites such as worldtruth.tv and naturalnews.com were trusted more than established scientific journals or the mainstream media. The internet was often seen as freer and more democratic than traditional information services.[41] Watching YouTube videos was a major source of information for my interlocutors, and to a lesser extent talk radio and internet radio shows, such as Alex Jones's *Infowars*. Such outlets called themselves the alternative media and claimed to reveal the truth, based on the assertion that unlike the traditional or mainstream media, they were not controlled by vested interests. As mentioned earlier, many of the videos and articles from such websites were shared widely on social media or found via Google searches, which were perceived as impartial listings of information. However, as was widely reported after the 2016 presidential election, the algorithms of search engines and social media were skewed to produce results based on users' previous preferences, creating an echo chamber effect where results were reinforced by user biases. In the aftermath of the election, this effect came under scrutiny as it was reported that "fake news" articles slandering Democratic candidate Hillary Clinton in particular were being shared widely because they agreed with users' prior opinions.[42]

The two most shared websites by my interlocutors on Facebook during my time in the field were worldtruth.tv and naturalnews.com. They were fairly representative of the massive proliferation of alternative media sites that infested the internet at that time. They both published articles that could be deemed "fake news" or conspiracy theories. Both had around a million likes on Facebook and claimed a global audience. The articles were mostly posted by the founder on worldtruth.tv, whereas naturalnews.com had a small group of regular contributors, the most prolific again being the founder.[43] Articles on these sites made bold claims to reveal the "100% undeniable truth" on issues, but then were poorly sourced and referenced if at all, referencing sources that either did not support the claim made or came from other conspiracy theory websites with the same claims. Interestingly, they frequently referred to authorities on issues, for example well-known whistleblowers such as Edward Snowden, unnamed officials at the UN, non-US government ministers, or medical doctors or scientists who had turned against the mainstream. They were using the same types of authority figures to produce the counter-narrative as were used in the traditional media—politicians, scientists, and doctors. The counter-narrative was still based on the same types of sources for truth claims: insiders, people with position, power, training, prestige. However, they were trusted because, crucially, they had turned against the mainstream.

The evidence presented on such sites was claimed to be empirical, in that it was based on observations; for example, an oft-made claim was that anyone can see the chemtrails in the sky. This approach was coupled with suggestions of scientific tests; for example, naturalnews.com claimed to have its own mass spectrometry instrument to performs tests in the public interest, although complete data sets and methodology were not included with the assertion of what had been tested with this device. They were using the scientific method, or some version of it, to combat the mainstream narrative issued from scientific authorities, corporations, and government. Rather than eschewing science, they were using its methods to get to the truth, which was obscured by the deceit of the traditional media and scientific institutions rather than a failure of the scientific method itself. Another favorite tactic was to take studies that have been done and extrapolate the results to make them seem more wide-ranging than the original study intended.[44] Such websites were not using faith-based statements to argue against science; although they were called quacks, they in turn called mainstream science quackery.[45] What is interesting about this is how it is not the method of science that lacks legitimacy in the counter-narrative, it is the mouthpieces.

Science therefore has legitimacy in spirituality. Indeed, spirituality used scientific theories, especially those found in quantum physics, as the basis for religious elaboration.[46] As mentioned above with Jill, personal knowledge of and professional experience in science was not necessarily felt to be incompatible with spirituality. Indeed, Jill was not alone among my interlocutors in suggesting that scientific discoveries "proved" the claims of spirituality. Historian of esotericism Olav Hammer called this "scientism," which he argued was the mistaken interpretation of scientific theory used for religious purposes.[47] It was constructed explicitly in opposition to mainstream science; only those with spiritual insight could truly understand what science revealed because they were not bound by limiting materialist determinism. By understanding spirituality and combining it with science, they could reveal the truth. This strategy was reproduced in the counter-narrative by using the same methodology as scientists. Websites like worldtruth.tv and naturalnews.com claimed to reveal more because they were not bound by the "cover-up" to which all mainstream authorities were committed.

A feature of conspiracy theories generally, according to political scientists, is this rhetorical strategy that employs a "quasi-academic style" as a way of distracting from the gaps in the argument.[48] Similarly, Uscinski and Parent point to the use of errant data and unfalsifiable claims as markers of a conspiracy theory as opposed to a credible theory.[49] But what is a theory here? Data is only errant if one particular account is accepted; the data that do not fit into that account then become errant; however, theories gain their credibility from power and social status.[50] Many of the works by political scientists and anthropologists address specifically political conspiracy theories, and an important caveat is that it is much harder to falsify political conspiracies than scientific conspiracy theories. Chemtrails and anti-vaccination theories are easier to discredit than suggestions of government involvement in false flag attacks. The two feed into each other, however, because distrusting politically sanctioned authorities affects the credibility of medical and scientific authorities. As such, although chemtrails and anti-vaccination theories have been repeatedly and exhaustively debunked by scientific authorities, they continue to have a receptive audience. The problem is not lack of information or education, it is skepticism about the authorities providing this information. In the counter-narrative, there are no impartial observers, everyone has a position, and the one to believe is the one that confirms what is already believed. Definitions of conspiracy theories as false and separate from proper investigations into (often political) conspiracies hinge upon how much "properly constituted epistemic authorities" are believed.[51] If they are, then Watergate can be sanctioned because the *Washington Post*, the *New York Times*, and Congress have investigated it and found it true and that is accepted, whereas chemtrails are not because the EPA and other scientific and aviation authorities say they are not. However, if properly constituted epistemic authorities are not accepted, then any number of conspiracy theories can be entertained and believed. The line between theory and conspiracy theory is blurred when social institutions are not found credible.

The issue is who is considered as an authority, and it goes directly to the processes through which knowledge is socially constructed. In cognitive anthropologist Dan Sperber's "naturalist approach" to "apparently irrational beliefs," he takes it as rational to believe propositions when the source is a credible authority.[52] In his field site in Ethiopia among the Druze, this meant the tribal elders. The United States is a very different kind of society, and what the recent fake news debate has highlighted is the extent to which there is no single accepted source of authority for Americans. Conspiracy theories about Hillary Clinton proliferated because those opposed to her politically portrayed her as criminal. This effort came to a head in the Pizzagate conspiracy theory, which alleged that Clinton and her campaign manager were running a child sex ring in the basement of a Washington, DC, pizzeria, a pizzeria that did not even have a basement. The rumors were circulated based on leaked emails that mentioned pizza frequently, and resulted in a man opening fire in the pizzeria because he wanted to "self-investigate" them.[53] Denials of this conspiracy theory in the media and by the politicians implicated have not abated it. Articles and videos shared on the internet are given more credence because politicians and the mainstream media are viewed as liars. Indeed, the term "fake news" has been adopted by President Donald Trump to dismiss any news reports he dislikes. It has since been used in a similar way to how "conspiracy theory" itself is used, as a way of undermining and dismissing dissent, often by those in power, not those outside of it. What this suggests is the fractured nature of authority in American society, one that has serious implications for a consensus agreement on what is valid knowledge, what is "true," even what constitutes "reality." Theories such as Pizzagate do not really explain anything; they seem to arise out of a poisonous air in a society riven with mistrust.[54] Rather than expressing suppressed anxieties, such theories seem to undermine the notion of truth itself; everything becomes a matter of perspective, of whose side you are on, leading to a potentially dangerous breakdown of societal consensus.

The truth is a political issue in the counter-narrative. Official denials are dismissed and taken as evidence of a cover-up. It becomes impossible to deny the assertions made in the counter-narrative because denial is inverted, disconfirmation becomes confirmation. It is easy to see the counter-narrative as simply wrong, and if those engaged in it knew good science and critical thinking, they would know better. However, the counter-narrative is more a response to the nature of authority in the United States. Authority is inextricably linked to power; having authority is having the power to decide, define, order, influence, make things happen. The strong vein of individualism in the United States claims that authority is properly the right of the individual citizen. Social institutions, especially the federal government, have been treated with suspicion since the inception of the nation because they are seen as infringing on individual rights.[55] In spirituality, this is given a religious rendering. Only the individual has authority to decide legitimate knowledge, because each person creates their own reality. My interlocutors used the alternative media in conjunction with intuition to decide which theories they found credible. They would read something, and if it seemed right to them, often put in terms of "feeling" it was right, then it would be accepted. This followed the practice in spirituality of putting feelings, or heart wisdom, above logic, or head knowledge. In cosmologies of spirituality, head knowledge relates to mind, which is third-dimensional thinking and as such to be treated with suspicion. Heart wisdom relates to intuition, which is closer to source or spirit, and listening to intuition is a way of aligning with the energy of the universe. Arguments based on logic were therefore treated with skepticism, especially if they went against a person's intuition. The cosmologies of spirituality demoted logic, and consequently rationality, as inferior to the higher knowledge that could be gained through aligning oneself with the energy of the universe. Logic and rationality were third-dimensional; they supported the materialist old paradigm way of thinking and acting that put money and profits before people and spiritual development. Spirituality contained a radical rejection of rationality, inverting the values of modernity. If logic dictated that the world should be the way it is, if it was rational to accumulate profits through poisoning the environment and endangering the health of the people, then logic and rationality were part of the problem that spirituality aimed to address.

CONSPIRACY THEORIES AND SPIRITUALITY

Conspiracy theories and spirituality have a shared territory to the extent that the term "conspirituality" has been suggested to theorize this conjunction.[56] In terms of content, both are stigmatized discourses, covering contested topics such as astrology, UFOs, and naturopathic medicine.[57] These topics are popularly believed but dismissed by epistemic authorities in society.[58] This does not mean they cannot be found meaningful, relevant, or even beneficial by people. When the mainstream rejects what they are interested in, they may be prompted to reconsider other rejected issues, creating a domino effect where stigmatized discourses are accepted one after another until one is fully committed to the counter-narrative. However, I found that few of my interlocutors were simply contrarian, accepting things merely because they had been excluded from the mainstream. Both conspiracy theories and spirituality are premised on worldviews that everything is connected, and make a similar use of science to try to prove matters that are ultimately unverifiable.[59]

There is a more direct connection between the two, however. My interlocutors would often tell me that it was necessary to change the current system or the world would not survive. Conspiracy theories provided a narrative about what was wrong with the world, and spirituality was how to fix it. The dark cabal had made the world toxic. They could be defeated by detoxifying, which meant changing diet and lifestyle along spiritual lines, such as eating organic food, decreasing stress, and cleansing. The counter-narrative of conspiracy theories suggests that modern life is poisonous on purpose, and spirituality is the antidote.

The connection between spirituality and conspiracy theories is not obvi-ous, however, and may even seem contradictory. If reality is manifested through thoughts and words, why does evil exist? Why would anyone think chemtrails into existence? This is where the idea of the dark cabal comes in. There are groups of people so tied to the current third-dimensional reality of greed, materialism, and anger that they create ripples of negativity throughout the dimension. It is then the responsibility of spiritually awak-ened people to defeat this negativity with positivity. As already mentioned, conspiracy theories offer a theodicy in cosmologies of spirituality, explain-ing why evil exists, why the new age has not yet happened.[60] A number of the popular conspiracy theories in Sedona were figured around forces directly impinging on spirituality, such as chemtrails and fluoride calcify-ing the pineal gland. The machinations of the dark cabal were targeted at them because spirituality was a threat to its plans for world domination. The more general aims attributed to the dark cabal—depopulation, fear, chaos—increased the overall level of negativity, which would lower the dimensional vibration. Raising the vibration through spiritual development would help stop them.

Roger told me that focusing on paranoid conspiracies, as his father did, did not really help anyone. What if all the soldiers just stopped fighting? What if we all stopped paying our taxes? The system would crumble. The way to get there was through raising your own personal awareness and then helping others around you, he told me. Originally from Long Island, he had been to Occupy Wall Street, and saw people being kettled on the Brooklyn Bridge. However, he did not think protests or people who print their own driver's licenses—so-called "free men on the land"—did any good. Resistance only fed negativity. Spirituality was the only route to free-dom and all he wanted to focus on. We talked about conspiracies, and how it seemed like a few families or groups of people had been in control of the mass of people, resources, and power throughout history concealed under different "nations" and "empires." But it was really the bankers, those with wealth and power, under different names, sometimes cooperating with each other and sometimes fighting with each other, but always exploiting the people for their own gain. Roger said in the end, we should not get attached to this. The only thing we could do about the system now was to follow our spiritual practice because then we could make changes on a deep, karmic level. The practice was all we had, and by changing ourselves, we could change the people around us, and then they would change the people around them, and it would spread out as ripples of positive energy through the universe.

Spirituality is seen as a new way of living that obviates the power structures of society, through promoting self-governance and self-reliance. It is a way of living otherwise from the current norms and systems. The most radical form of this is the "free men on the land," or those living off the grid that try not to depend on utility companies and government services.[61] Even for those in Sedona who took a more moderate path, naturopathic medicine was a means of not depending on the pharmaceutical and insurance companies for healthcare, homeschooling was a way to educate children outside of mainstream education, and buying local and being self-employed were ways not to invest in the corporate-controlled economy. Many advocated living in small-scale communities and not paying tax as a way of not funding the perpetual state of war in the United States. These were mostly held as ideals; however, the majority did pay tax because they did not want to get in trouble. Total self-reliance was utopian; yet, desires for it did express the importance of personal freedom as a goal of the spiritual path.

WHERE'S THE TRUST?

Why is there a lack of trust in the federal government, corporations, media, or the scientific community? One stance is that this is something new, an emergence of a "conspiracy culture" since the 1970s because of the revelation of "real conspiracies" such as Watergate alongside a postmodern "epistemological insecurity."[62] The other is to take the long view, pointing to the presence of conspiracy theories about George III in the Constitution to suggest that they are part of the fabric of American political and social life.[63] There is a longer history of anti-elitism and skepticism of (especially federal government) authority in the United States that has flourished in the state of perpetual social insecurity and economic precarity created by neoliberalism.[64] Part of this insecurity concerns the perceived decline of America. Its status as a superpower and force for good in the global order was once assumed. Now that time is nostalgia, found only on country music stations and among the elderly.[65] There is a feeling on both the political left and right that America is "headed for an abyss."[66] American exceptionalism is felt to be on shaky ground. The Empire is ending, and someone is to blame for the loss of unchallenged supremacy. Fears of imminent economic collapse, civil war, mass destruction, and death are expressed by those involved in spirituality and others who are not. The labeling of conspiracy theories as "fake news" around the 2016 election attests to this growing anxiety, as indeed does the outcome of that election, won as it was on a platform of "make America great again." The desire for halcyonic return is painfully clear.

The fake news controversy surrounding the 2016 election points to the extent to which many of these theories contain implicit or explicit right-wing positions, for example anti-federal government, anti-UN and other supranational institutions, anti-gun control, anti-science and -intellectualism. This is why for some it is surprising that conspiracy theories, so often right-wing and aggressive, should find an eager audience among the ostensibly more left-wing and pacifist spiritual seekers.[67] However, historically there has been a dark side of esotericism, found especially in Traditionalism, which defined itself in opposition to the Establishment in resurrecting the true wisdom that has been suppressed.[68] In rejecting the rationality of the third dimension, my interlocutors were placing themselves in this lineage, seeking out alternative sources of authority on which to found their claims to higher knowledge. This knowledge is stigmatized not because it is wrong or irrational, in their view, but because of a cover-up, because it threatens to subvert the mainstream authorities and their sources of power. The true source of power is found in the self that can use manifestation to create reality and end third-dimensional power structures.

Conspiracy theories are an important part of spirituality because they offer a form of theodicy. I have suggested that they are part of how knowledge is socially constructed in spirituality. Is the continued use of the modifier "conspiracy" justified? What makes a "theory" a "conspiracy theory" is the surfeit of meaning and explanation, overextending the agency and intentionality behind complex socio-political situations. Conspiracy theories suggest that the government often does not work in the people's interests, that corporations put profits above safety, that scientists often do not anticipate the consequences of their innovations, that the average American has very little control over their environment, that the game is rigged against them in so many ways. It is a way of talking about class and power that cloaks inequality in the mystery of conspiracy, granting intention to situations that seem harmful and unfair. It creates someone to blame. There is a reason for the darkness and suffering in the world. There is also a solution to it, awakening and following the spiritual path.

CONCLUSION

All Energy Vibrates at a Certain Frequency

"But I don't want to go among mad people," Alice remarked.

"Oh, you ca'n't [sic] help that," said the Cat: "We're all mad here. I'm mad. You're mad."

"How do you know I'm mad?" said Alice.

"You must be," said the Cat, "or you wouldn't have come here."

—LEWIS CARROLL, *Alice's Adventures in Wonderland,*
2003 ed., p. 55

AT A CONFERENCE HELD AT THE Los Abrigados resort in late October 2012 called "The 2012 Scenario," Graham, a radio and talk show host on ascension and spirituality, spoke about creating a new world. It starts with each of us, individually. How we do this is through manifestation, a process through which anyone can create whatever reality they want. Graham then went into specifics of what he called the "creation formula" for manifestation: intent + stillpoint + action = creation. Intent is prayer, visualization, focus. Stillpoint is bringing intention into the heart and letting it germinate there, then action is pushing it out into the universe to make it happen. This results in creation, which Graham characterized as "cool" results. He then gave the example of when he wanted a new home. He visualized already having a new home, seeing himself inside the rooms, feeling the happiness of being there. In his words, he breathed the creation particles of his home into his being so he became the home, he was one with the home. He held it in his heart, held his breath for seventeen seconds, experienced what he called the stillpoint, then he pushed it out with a breath into the universe. Then he began to look for houses, listening to his intuition as he did. He found a home on the day he needed to move out. He was not frantic or searching listings. His new home was so much better than he imagined. The creation formula worked.

Manifestation is a practice of trust. Graham really needed a place to live, but he felt he had to listen and trust his intuition, rather than desperately reaching for what he needed. It is arguable that he could have just as likely found a home in the time he needed it without this practice. The availability of rental housing stock in his area and his disposable income to pay for monthly rent and a deposit played pivotal roles alongside finding the stillpoint. But the experience of this mundane feat was qualitatively changed by his practice. House-hunting and moving is often stressful. Graham emphasized that through staying in the moment and being present, he found it easier to let go of that fear. Worrying about not getting something does not help you get it, he told us. Manifestation was a way of achieving ordinary things while maintaining a sense of peace, not giving in to the pervasive fear of not having enough or not being enough that seemed endemic among people involved in spirituality.

It was also a way to engender faith that the big changes in the world that the people who attended the conference desired would actually come to pass. There is something almost classically millenarian about this. Graham advised us to trust in the universe. We are powerful creators, he enjoined us, so dream big. Then he asked what actions we were doing now to create the new world. He offered the microphone to the audience and asked someone to describe what the new age looked like for them. A man named Brad immediately raised his hand and stood up and announced that he wanted to see a society free from the need to exchange with monetary accounting, an economy based instead on only the need to give, where there was no need for finances.

This utopian vision of the new age was intimately intertwined with a rejection of the current political economic formation in America. The mode of exchange they lived with was a burden. Finding a house was stressful, earning a wage felt exploitative, they wanted to live in a joyous world where everything that was needed was given freely. Manifestation was a way of easing the strains of this mode of exchange, where what was desired was imagined, and then when it was created, it was figured as exactly what was desired in the first place. It could change a single life, and then if everyone did this, it could change the world. It was significant that change did not come from the people at the conference joining together and working to create the changes they wanted communally; instead, each was enjoined to look within, create what they wanted, and then those small individual changes would cumulatively create sweeping worldwide change. It was also significant that despite these grand visions, manifestation was most often described as useful in connection with quotidian monetary exchanges.

It would be easy to be cynical and dismissive of manifestation as a spiritual practice. And a number of people that I knew in Sedona who did not engage in spirituality were. My friend Tom was a videographer, who had been negotiating with David Icke's ex-partner, Pamela, to make a video about her life experiences, her special relationship with lightning, and her ideas about the Reptilians.[1] Reflecting on potentially editing Pamela's video, he said he half thought it could be really fun, but then again it just "sounds so Sedona." It probably would not become a finished product because she was likely to run out of money. I said people have big ideas in Sedona. He said that was the "master manifesters," they think they can just put their big idea out there and it will work, because they can get people like him to do the nuts and bolts. According to Tom, a million-dollar idea and a cup of coffee are both worth $2.

Tom had never (and would never) go to a conference like the 2012 Scenario, but he accurately summed up the version of manifestation that Graham offered: put the idea out into the universe with focus and intention and it will work. It was the same concept as Vixen du Lac gave me in my first week in Sedona when advising how to find a room to rent. However, Tom located the success of manifestation not in finding the stillpoint, but in the other people that were relied upon, and left unacknowledged, in the process of creation. It was not really a way of creating reality as desired through focus, intuition, and trusting the universe. It was relying on others to help solve the problematic details, and failing when the material basis was not supplied. Then shrugging and accepting this as evidence that it was not really meant to be.

There is something slippery about manifestation as a concept, and this points toward the ambiguities at the heart of spirituality. It was common to hear people warn against expressing negativity because that would manifest more negativity, that what you put out there would come back to you. Yet Saanvi, from chapter four, simply dismissed manifestation, saying she did not believe in it, arguing instead that whatever happens to you, happens, and you have no control over it. The person she said this to accepted it and agreed that since that was what she believed, that was how her reality would be. There is an element of solipsism, where whatever one thinks, that is what is. When thinking about the rumors and conspiracy theories discussed in the previous chapter, this can create a dangerous situation. If you believe vaccines are dangerous, then they are. If I believe they are safe, then they are. What you believe, I call a conspiracy theory. What I believe, you call fake news. A shared consensus on reality is losing ground in America, a problem that goes far beyond spirituality.

There was a denial of material causation in manifestation, a shift into a realm of pure ideas where thought creates matter, and matter is an illusion. Yet if we can all manifest whatever we want, why are there such great disparities between people? Why are some rich and some poor, some healthy and some sick, some happy and some sad? This encapsulates what I have called the tension between equality and hierarchy. While it was theoretically possible to create whatever reality you wanted, some seemed far more successful at this than others. This tension emerged when I explained to people in Sedona what I was doing there. At first when I said I was researching spirituality, they would often say that was what they did too. Then when I explained that this was something I received funding to do, they realized it was not the same. Many of them struggled to maintain a spiritual practice alongside earning money, and my situation was viewed with some envy. A Vedic astrologer and spiritual tour guide that I knew called me a "mama manifester" for being paid to live in Sedona and hang out doing spiritual practice. I embodied what they aspired to: earning a living and doing spiritual practice at the same time.

It quickly transpired that many thought this must in itself be a spiritual achievement on my part. Rahelio told me that I was on a spiritual quest whether I knew it or not. A spiritual tour guide who offered vortex tours, Rahelio practiced what he called Native American and Toltec shamanism, and Western astrology. With long straight black hair that fell to his waist, he was of Mexican ancestry, born and raised in the Midwest, but called himself Toltec.[2] At the age of fifty-four, he had lived in Sedona for twenty-five years, having been able to consistently earn a living from his business, a feat he felt validated his spiritual practice. The Star People from the Pleiades gave him a message to come to Sedona to find his path, he told me. I, too, had been called here to find my path. Even if I did not believe it, that did not matter, because belief was rooted in experience and I was experiencing spirituality. Each person had their own spiritual truth, and I would learn mine here. His intonation was perhaps intended as prophetic, but I found it confusing. I asked him about mad people: were they simply living their unique truth? He said that if people were a danger to themselves or others, they would be locked up, but otherwise whatever you think is your own spiritual truth. But who gets to decide what is madness and what is spiritual truth?

There was an assertion of the priority of experience over belief in Rahelio's words. Even if I did not believe I was on a spiritual path, my experience meant I was. This statement was then followed by an assertion that whatever I thought would be my own spiritual truth. The latter assertion seemed to undermine the former to me. How could I be on a spiritual path whether I knew it or not if everything I thought was my personal, spiritual truth? The solution was in another slippery concept of spirituality, that of truth. Something could be spiritually true that a person could be unaware of, if that person was not sufficiently aware or conscious to grasp it. From where I was when I spoke to Rahelio, in the first months of my fieldwork, I still had to learn my spiritual truth, and for that I had to follow my spiritual path. I would be unable to do the things that I was doing without being affected by it. It was the start of a spiritual path, I was told. I may have entered upon it thinking I was undertaking academic research, but that was a trick of the monkey mind, a way for the spiritual truth to awaken within me while I thought I was doing something else. I was, in my interlocutors' eyes, much the same as they were: seeking, studying, researching about spirituality. Joseph Dumit reflected on the similarities between anthropologists and "new agers" and suggested that the two mirror each other, each playing out relativist colonial fantasies of being the other.[3] Yet the comment about being a "mama manifester" pointed toward one thing that was different for me from many others participating in spiritual activities: I got paid.

I decided to adopt this native framing of my research, directing my participation toward what I intuited as my spiritual path. I spoke to a friend about having to follow one's own spiritual path to learn about spirituality. Spirituality is following your own path and being true to your own highest good, she said. She agreed that it had to be experienced, not just heard about, and so what felt right to me on my spiritual path would be my research. If it did not serve me, stop doing it, she advised. I therefore participated in an array of practices in order to find and follow my spiritual path. I attended yoga classes four or five times a week and practiced casually with friends and acquaintances regularly. For spiritual people this is an everyday social occasion, much like getting a beer in other contexts; you stretch out and do some poses together while you chat. I joined a kung fu group and studied shaolin and baguazhang styles, learning qigong meditation and novel interpretations of Daoist philosophy, eventually leaving when I decided that getting punched in the gut by men with barely repressed misogyny did not serve me. I learned how to spin fire, using a hoop and a staff with wicks wrapped in Kevlar, joining a troupe and performing for tips outside restaurants and bars and at the annual Dia de Muertos festival in Sedona. When I put my back out doing kung fu, I got a series of massages because healing the body and understanding how it is connected with the mind were important spiritually. Massages are called "bodywork," and it is a form of spiritual therapy, not indulgent relaxation. I took weekly meditation classes with Swami Steve, where I would sit in silence for an hour at a time, developing my spiritual awareness and overcoming my chattering mind. I tried a raw food diet, and lasted for a week because I just could not handle that much kale. I went to live off-grid in a solar-powered barn with no running water, digging latrine pits, because the spiritual path led me away from society and its comforts.

To help divine my spiritual path, since I learned early on that it was not simply a case of following my whims, I would go to readers. Most dropped the epithet "psychic," some used cards like tarot or oracle decks, but they all accessed my energy and the energy of the universe and helped me understand how to follow my path. James was a white-haired man living on disability benefits who gave readings for extra cash and to develop his spiritual practice. He started our reading with cards, a mix of the Dragon Tarot, Divine Guidance, Ascended Masters, and Angel Therapy decks, which he could shuffle like a Vegas croupier. Turning over cards that depicted the Star, the Three of Coins, and the Nine of Wands, he advised me that my work was taking lots of energy now. I needed a break, before moving toward change and focusing on my spiritual path. Even though I was doing my research, I was also discovering my own spiritual path.

After participating in one of her neo-shamanic retreats, Lana told me I was leaving my safe place as a researcher and becoming a seeker. Although I had not expected it, Sedona got to me. I was studying Sedona while it was studying me, and it would provide me the answer or the resolution not on my time, but at the right time. She advised me to be patient, like a bear in hibernation. My spiritual path was therefore not just the product of what I decided to do, but prompted and influenced by those I sought advice from, who would use the modalities of spirituality, like tarot and oracle cards, to help divine how I should move forward on my path.

As I reached the midpoint of my fieldwork, as I suspect may be common among ethnographers, I had immersed myself so deeply in spirituality that I became a little lost. I would have my own epiphanies about my spiritual path while doing my practice. I had a realization in yoga that I was not focused on one particular practice because spirituality is not one thing—

it is not yoga or qigong or meditation—it is the selection among these things and none of them, what speaks to you personally as your truth. It is the indi- · vidual spiritual path that is given the label "spirituality" that must be trod in order to learn. I could not learn about spirituality in Sedona without finding and walking my own spiritual path. I was on a spiritual path by virtue of doing the activities I was doing—this had changed me. Spirituality was creating a space for that inner work.

The boundaries began to blur. Saanvi asked me when I had time for school with all the stuff I did, and I told her all the stuff I did *was* my research. I was doing my schoolwork right now. She said that was convenient, with arch skepticism, since it seemed like stuff I wanted to do anyway. I said that was my spiritual path, but I also did boring stuff like going to the Raw Food Expo that I did not enjoy so much. Indeed, it was around this point that I fell out with the kung fu group that I had joined. It had started to take over my routine, spending several hours each day practicing forms, doing push-ups and other conditioning moves, and the two-person drills where one person hit and the other blocked had become punishing. I received swollen bruises the length of my forearms from one such drill, and my teacher was so proud he took a picture and posted it on Facebook, calling me a "badass kung fu girl." What did this have to do with spirituality? It seemed more like I was being valorized for my ability to take abuse. After I quit, I had a listless summer, mostly spinning fire, traveling to visit retreats and festivals frequented by spiritual people in neighboring states, and when I returned I discovered that my friend Jade had died, as related at the end of chapter one.

That spurred my move off-grid.[4] Living self-sufficiently in an earthship or homestead-style house was often spoken of by my interlocutors in Sedona as their dream, the ideal end point of their spiritual path. They could grow their own food, trade and barter for other goods, and generate their own electricity with solar panels or windmills. They would be disconnected from the American political state that they disagreed with and saw as a failure, and they would forego the modes of exchange that they thought had low vibrations. I joined Thom and Benito, introduced in chapter four, whom I met through fire spinning, when they bought an acre of off-grid land two hours' drive from Sedona toward the Grand Canyon in a census-designated place called Valle. There we built a small homestead with solar panels for electricity, a wood stove for heat, a water tank to fill up jugs of potable water, and a latrine toilet. Despite Thom's stated opinion that we were building a commune, there were no more than three or four people there at any one time. Although they built a sweat lodge and an altar for ritual purposes, in

daily life they seemed to share more in common with the preppers, survivalists, and methamphetamine users who also lived in RVs, trailers, and tents
that scattered the undeveloped dirt tracks of the high-desert forest area.[5]

When hearing Thom's rants about the people rising up against the federal
government that wanted to take their guns alternating with his musings
about the special energy of the San Francisco Peaks, I found myself ques-
tioning: what was the difference between spirituality and survivalism?

Both were ways of living otherwise, beyond the current social and political structures of the state. While it might seem like a right-wing/left-wing
split can be read as the difference, this is a misdirection. What might be
called conspiracy theories proliferate among many considered marginal
in America. The key difference between these positions is the solution
offered to the problems diagnosed by those theories. Rather than stockpile
resources, spirituality offered personal enlightenment as the solution to the
problems in contemporary American society. The theories behind those
ills over-attribute agency; there is an individual, or group of individuals, to
blame. They are not systemic or collective social problems. Thus the solution
is also individual, changing personal choices for the better. The result is a
doubling down on individualist answers to social problems.

As I cleared the trash that perennially littered the land off-grid, I thought
about how I had to literally deal with my own shit all the time out there,
like when I sealed up the old latrine pit and moved the toilet seat to the
new hole that Benito dug. I had to look at what we consumed and what that
left behind. It showed where our energy was directed, and the resources we
used. There is a lot to be learned from dealing with your own trash. It makes
you face what you use and how. We drank a lot of beer, mainly the brands
PBR and Budweiser. That was one thing I learned from the trash. I also
thought about this as a metaphor for the spiritual path, a journey through
your own emotional and psychological detritus, sorting it and reusing what
you can, burning what you cannot, and thinking more carefully about what
you use and how you use it in the future. This applied to people as well as
products and places. The purpose of the spiritual path is to learn the truth
about your self.

But what is the self? It seemed that all the practice I did was aimed
at developing some aspect of myself: yoga and kung fu to train the body,
meditation to train the mind, readings to reflect on my choices. Yet this all
seemed focused on an intangible concept that resisted definition, and was
somehow insufficient. This insufficiency was reflected in those I spoke to
who critiqued the self-focused nature of spirituality. The musician who said

that all spiritual practice was worthless without service to others. The yoga teacher who said it was about building community, not just working on the self. Yet I could not help but notice how isolated these voices were, indeed, how isolated the whole "spiritual community" in Sedona was from each other and from those who did not engage with spirituality. Individual practitioners focusing on their individual practice. Enlightenment came through raising your personal vibration, which was meant to lead to oneness with the universe, but that did not seem to connect people with each other in the present. Indeed, the focus on ascension to another dimension subtly, or sometimes overtly, denigrated this world as the fleshy, dense third dimension to be left behind, along with all those other humans not as committed to spiritual development. At the same time, there was a political economy based on waged labor, without meaningful social provision or collective bargaining. As a form of religion without collectivization of resources, spiritual practitioners found themselves balancing a job with their spiritual practice, or selling their spiritual practice to support themselves. If they were successful, like Rahelio, this validated their presence in Sedona and their practice; if not, then it was not meant to be. Thinking that everything happens for a reason and that reason is for the best possible good glossed over systemic inequalities that influenced outcomes.

I learned something else from the trash. The journey I went on through continually cleaning and sorting our garbage could have been avoided entirely if there was a trash collection service in Valle. While moving off-grid entailed going through my own portal, which ended up in a very different location from where I started in Sedona, it was a leap of faith that felt in some ways unnecessary or excessive. Leaving society is an illusion; it was still there in the paved highway that led to the gas station and on to the Grand Canyon National Park. Going off-grid is a fantasy, another diversion from the real into the fake.

Portals that compress spacetime allow the self to connect directly to the universe. Yet doing so skips over the intervening stages. The result is an inability to think at middle scales. Crafting the self through spiritual practice aims to alter the nature of reality without working collectively. The middle scales matter, though. The social, the state, the community matter. These are the social relationships that help constitute the self; the self is part of other selves, and the interconnections between them make them what they are. Trust comes from working on relationships despite difficulties and differences. When I heard about chemtrails, I found it so hard to believe because I knew the sort of people that were impugned as "government scientists."

I worked with them. I could not accept that the people I conversed and collaborated with would knowingly poison the atmosphere, the same air they breathed themselves. Yet I also knew that that was what was happening as carbon emissions increase, as the average global temperature rises. A lack of trust erodes a shared consensus of reality, but a refusal to look at the consequences of social and economic systems creates only a shared delusion.

ACKNOWLEDGMENTS

AS I'M WRITING THIS, BILLIONS of people are under orders to stay at home, including me. The coronavirus pandemic of 2020 redirected so much human activity that one wonders whether anything written before could carry any relevance afterward. Yet the themes addressed in this book still suffuse American social life. Stories spread of coronavirus-carrying bats controlled using 5G towers, invisible waves that cause life-altering consequences, continuing the chemtrail fears in new potent form. Colloidal silver as cure, vaccinations as injury: these claims that loom large in the current crisis festered for years in the online lives of those involved in spirituality described in these pages.

For the existence of which, I would like to thank the series editors at the Class 200 list, University of Chicago Press, Katie Lofton and John Lardas Modern, for their exceptional encouragement, sage suggestions, and enthusiastic support of this project. A special thank you to Kyle Wagner for his hard work and genial advice in transforming the manuscript into a published volume, and to Dylan Montanari, Caterina MacLean, and Marianne Tatom for their excellent assistance. The current form of the words is indebted to two anonymous reviewers, whose direction, advice, and critique were invaluable.

This book would also not exist without a series of conversations over a period of nearly ten years in spoken and written form with Matthew Engelke, beginning at the London School of Economics, and continuing long after I had much right to impose in such a way. Fenella Cannell's guidance was formative to my intellectual development and ethnographic directions. David Graeber's work was a constant source of inspiration, and I was fortunate to have in-person advice from him at the LSE alongside the wonderful Tim Jenkins from the University of Cambridge. What you both said then guided much that followed. At the LSE two people are central to the infrastructure supporting anyone trying to do anthropology: Yanina Hinrichsen and Tom Hinrichsen. I also benefited from conversations with Rita Astuti, Charles Stafford, Michael Scott, Hans Steinmüller, Deborah James, Nick Long, Agustin Diz, Juli Huang, Katharine Fletcher Wolstenholme, Méadhbh McIvor, Philip Proudfoot, Fuad Musallam, Alanna Cant, and Andrew Sanchez. During my "NRM phase" at Inform, I want to acknowledge the support and insight of Eileen Barker, Sarah Harvey, Suzanne Newcombe, Shanon Shah, Silke Steidinger, Aled Jones, and Marat Shterin.

The writing and revision process took place during a postdoctoral fellowship at Ghent University. So many people were engaging, helpful, and inspiring that I will surely miss some, but I would be remiss if I failed to mention Julie Birkholz, Jasper Schelstraete, Koenraad Claes, Shannon Lambert, Gry Ulstein, Marco Caracciolo, Mahlu Mertens, River Ramuglia, Itamar Shachar, Carine Plancke, and Robin Vandenvoort. Farhan Samanani is that guy you meet at a conference and three years later get a Wenner-Gren grant together and is therefore the best. Egil Asprem is that other guy you meet at a conference who continues to make me work harder and better. Also everyone at the Templar castle that time in the South of France—Julian, Manon, Liana, Earl, Korshi, Jenny, Wouter, Matt, et al.

For literature on the history and culture of northern Arizona, I was lucky to have access to the special collections of the Cline Library at Northern Arizona University. Libraries are close to my heart, and without the Cambridge University Library none of this likely would have begun. I will always look for more magical adventures in the stacks. In a material semiotic sense, none of my research or writing would be possible without the financial support of the Economic and Social Research Council (UK) and the European Research Council.

I am forever indebted to the people of Sedona, whose generous hospitality in welcoming me into their homes and lives I will always treasure. I only hope these words can equal the gift you gave to me. There are many I should mention individually, but I will limit myself to Peter, Mynzah, Brad, Jamie, Jim, James, Matthew, Melody/Melanie, Dylan, Emma, Andrea, Sean, and Kimi.

My England family were constant in their love and support, first and foremost Mum and Andrew, and also Judith, Elly, and Richard, in helping me achieve my crazy dream. My Arizona family, especially Oscar, Johnny,

Chelsea, Lynda, Sam, Bruce, Laura, Julian, Nori, and Azami, shared dinners, sofas, safety meetings, cameras, and wifi, and now I hope you see what I was working on all that time. Christopher, this may be worth more than that car. Alexander, as always, is the one for whom I did all of this.

I hope to see you all in the outside soon.

NOTES

INTRODUCTION

1. For John Lardas Modern, spirituality emerged with a specific signification for American Protestantism in the first half of the nineteenth century as an innate human capacity for religion (*Secularism in Antebellum America*, [Chicago: University of Chicago Press, 2011], 121). For Robert Wuthnow, spirituality also gained new meaning in a specific historical period, across religious affiliations, springing from an enhanced focus on the self as the locus of religious insight, in response to increasing uncertainty in the material conditions of living in America in the late twentieth century (*After Heaven: Spirituality in America since the 1950s* [Berkeley: University of California Press, 1998]). Coming from a history of religions perspective, Wouter Hanegraaff attempted to isolate spirituality and religion from contingent contexts and provide clear definitions separating the two ("New Age Religion and Secularization," *Numen* 47, no. 3 [2000]: 200), as does Sandra Marie Schneiders ("Religion vs. Spirituality: A Contemporary Conundrum," *Spiritus: A Journal of Christian Spirituality* 3, no. 2 [2003]: 163–85). Sociologists have used quantitative data on self-identification to construct a category of "spiritual but not religious." See Robert C. Fuller, *Spiritual, But Not Religious: Understanding Unchurched America* (Oxford: Oxford University Press, 2001); Wade Clark Roof, *Spiritual Marketplace: Baby Boomers and the Remaking of American Religion* (Princeton, NJ: Princeton University Press, 1999); Paul Heelas et al., *The Spiritual Revolution: Why Religion Is Giving Way to Spirituality* (Oxford: Wiley-Blackwell, 2005); Heinz Streib and Ralph Hood, "'Spirituality' as Privatized Experience-Oriented Religion: Empirical and Conceptual Perspectives," *Implicit Religion* 14, no. 4 (2011): 433–53. The historical construction of the term is addressed by Walter Principe, "Toward Defining Spirituality," *Studies in Religion/Sciences Religieuses* 12, no. 2 (1983): 127–41; and its more recent permutations by Boaz Huss, "Spirituality: The Emergence of a New Cultural Category and Its Challenge to the Religious and the Secular," *Journal of Contemporary Religion* 29, no. 1 (2014): 47–60. I tend to side with Courtney Bender and Omar McRoberts that the problem of defining spirituality with regard to religion is that spirituality becomes defined by what it lacks, just as religion is reified as normative and unproblematic. See "Mapping a Field: Why and How to Study Spirituality," *SSRC Working Papers* (October

2012): 1–27. It is clear that these terms carry great weight and are pregnant with social as well as scholarly meaning, but how to distribute this weight, and which contingencies are reproduced and why, remains the subject of lively debate.

2. Millenarianism is the core of what scholars of religion have been calling "the new age" since the late 1980s. Although the by now largely sterile debates about what the new age is and how it can be defined are largely passed, the ethnographic and archival material describing the emergence of this phenomenon remains rich in detail and insight. See Steven Sutcliffe, *Children of the New Age: A History of Spiritual Practices* (London: Routledge, 2002); Olav Hammer, *Claiming Knowledge: Strategies of Epistemology from Theosophy to the New Age* (Leiden: Brill, 2004); Wouter J. Hanegraaff, *New Age Religion and Western Culture: Esotericism in the Mirror of Secular Thought* (Leiden: Brill, 1996); Sarah Pike, *New Age and Neopagan Religions in America* (New York: Columbia University Press, 2004); Ruth Prince and David Riches, *The New Age in Glastonbury: The Construction of Religious Movements* (New York: Berghahn Books, 2000); Nicholas Campion, *The New Age in the Modern West: Counterculture, Utopia and Prophecy from the Late Eighteenth Century to the Present Day* (London: Bloomsbury Academic, 2016); Anthony d'Andrea, *Reflexive Religion: The New Age in Brazil and Beyond* (Leiden: Brill, 2018); Paul Heelas, *Spiritualities of Life: New Age Romanticism and Consumptive Capitalism* (Oxford: Blackwell, 2008); Paul Heelas, *The New Age Movement: The Celebration of the Self and the Sacralization of Modernity* (Oxford: Blackwell, 1996).

3. Modern, *Secularism in Antebellum America*, 43.

4. The city of Sedona had 10,397 people as of the 2010 census; see "QuickFacts, Sedona city, Arizona," US Census Bureau, https://www.census.gov/quickfacts/fact/table/sedonacity arizona/PST045216, accessed April 21, 2020. However, the nearby community of the Village of Oak Creek is often included when local people talk about "Sedona." It is only six miles to the south of the Sedona city limits, but it is in unincorporated Yavapai County and so counted separately on the census. It had a population of 6,147 as of 2010; see "QuickFacts, Village of Oak Creek (Big Park) CDP, Arizona," US Census Bureau, https://www.census.gov/quickfacts/fact/table/villageofoakcreekbigparkcdparizona /PST045216, accessed April 21, 2020. The estimate of 17,000 is the aggregate of the two communities' population.

5. The comparison to Mecca is Adrian Ivakhiv's in *Claiming Sacred Ground: Pilgrims and Politics at Glastonbury and Sedona* (Bloomington: Indiana University Press, 2001), 187.

6. The centrality of the individual in spirituality should be taken as an insider framing; too often it is taken at face value and extended to an analytic by scholars. "The individual" is an ideal type in this context, and how this type operates socially is an ongoing thematic in the present work. See also Bender and McRoberts, "Mapping a Field," 11.

7. Congregationalism as a complexion of American religion is ably depicted by Nancy Tatom Ammerman, *Pillars of Faith: American Congregations and Their Partners* (Berkeley: University of California Press, 2005).

8. Courtney Bender, *The New Metaphysicals: Spirituality and the American Religious Imagination* (Chicago: University of Chicago Press, 2010); Alireza Doostdar, *The Iranian Metaphysicals: Explorations in Science, Islam and the Uncanny* (Princeton, NJ: Princeton University Press, 2018); Steven Sutcliffe and Ingvild Sælid Gilhus, *New Age*

Spirituality: Rethinking Religion (Abingdon: Acumen, 2013); Catherine L. Albanese, *A Republic of Mind and Spirit: A Cultural History of American Metaphysical Religion* (New Haven, CT: Yale University Press, 2006).

9. My fieldwork in northern Arizona began in July 2012. I remained in Sedona until late 2013, when I moved to Valle, an off-grid rural area near the Grand Canyon, until April 2014. I returned for six months in 2015 and again in 2016, and for short visits to the places and people I knew well during the summer of 2018.

10. A method demonstrated in the lyrical rendering of extraterrestrial narratives by Susan Lepselter, *The Resonance of Unseen Things: Poetics, Power, Captivity, and UFOs in the American Uncanny* (Ann Arbor: University of Michigan, 2016).

11. I refer here to the "world religions paradigm" so ably deconstructed by Tomoko Masuzawa in *Invention of World Religions: Or, How European Universalism Was Preserved in the Language of Pluralism* (Chicago: University of Chicago Press, 2005).

12. Maurice Bloch calls this "the transcendental social" in "Why Religion Is Nothing Special But Is Central," *Philosophical Transactions of the Royal Society B: Biological Sciences* 363, no. 1499 (June 12, 2008): 2056–58.

13. This is a religious understanding of what in a different frame is at the forefront of scientific theory about the composition of the universe and the nature of consciousness. The connection is strong enough to be humorously remarked upon by scientists in this field, such as Tam Hunt in "The Hippies Were Right: It's All About Vibrations, Man!," *Scientific American*, December 5, 2018, https://blogs.scientificamerican.com/observations/the-hippies-were-right-its-all-about-vibrations-man/, accessed April 21, 2020.

14. This is the hundredth-monkey idea, based on an outdated theory in biological anthropology that if you teach a hundred monkeys a skill, then it spreads to the whole group of monkeys like a chain reaction; see Hanegraaff, *New Age Religion,* 351.

15. And thus, the famous song from the musical *Hair* . . . Pike, *New Age and Neopagan Religions,* 146.

16. Sutcliffe, *Children of the New Age,* 26–27; Albanese, *A Republic of Mind and Spirit,* 465.

17. Claude Lévi-Strauss, *Introduction to the Work of Marcel Mauss* (London: Routledge & Kegan Paul, 1987), 63.

18. Marcel Mauss, *A General Theory of Magic* (London: Routledge, 1972), 133.

19. Émile Durkheim, *The Elementary Forms of Religious Life,* translated by Karen E. Fields (New York: Free Press, 1995), 197.

20. Channeling is receiving messages from a non-human entity, such as the dead, aliens, the higher self in the future, or the universe itself, and relaying it most often verbally, but it can also be accomplished through automatic writing. I attended numerous different types of channeling sessions in Sedona. It is also described in New Mexico in Michael F. Brown, *The Channeling Zone: American Spirituality in an Anxious Age* (Cambridge, MA: Harvard University Press, 1999), and in Israel in Adam Klin-Oron, "How I Learned to Channel: Epistemology, Phenomenology, and Practice in a New Age Course," *American Ethnologist* 41, no. 4 (2014): 635–47.

21. For example by Hanegraaff, *New Age Religion and Western Culture,* 516; and by Jeffrey J. Kripal, *Esalen: America and the Religion of No Religion* (Chicago: University of Chicago Press, 2007), 15.

22. The term "synchronicity" was introduced by the psychoanalyst Carl Gustav Jung to suggest that coincidences could be meaningful even if they were not causally connected; see C. G. Jung, *Synchronicity: An Acausal Connecting Principle*, translated by R. F. C. (Richard Francis Carrington) Hull (Princeton, NJ: Princeton University Press, 1973), and *C. G. Jung on Synchronicity and the Paranormal: Key Readings* (London: Routledge, 1997).

23. Christopher G. White, *Other Worlds: Spirituality and the Search for Invisible Dimensions* (Cambridge, MA: Harvard University Press, 2018), 3.

24. White, *Other Worlds*, 18–24.

25. This discussion of Marcel Duchamp's theory of dimensions is indebted to the anthropological theory of art proposed by Alfred Gell, *Art and Agency: An Anthropological Theory* (Oxford: Clarendon Press, 1998), 243.

26. There is an admirable range of scholarship on the historical crossover of esoteric and scientific discourse; see Hammer, *Claiming Knowledge*, 201–330; Egil Asprem, *The Problem of Disenchantment: Scientific Naturalism and Esoteric Discourse, 1900–1939* (Leiden: Brill, 2014); Kocku von Stuckrad, *The Scientification of Religion: An Historical Study of Discursive Change, 1800–2000* (Berlin: De Gruyter, 2014).

27. Mary-Jane Rubenstein, "Cosmic Singularities: On the Nothing and the Sovereign," *Journal of the American Academy of Religion* 80, no. 2 (2012): 502–3; and at more length, her *Worlds Without End: The Many Lives of the Multiverse* (New York: Columbia University Press, 2014).

28. The concept of the higher self seems to come from Helena P. Blavatsky's theosophical writings, in which she took inspiration from the Hindu *atman* to suggest a dual self, one part of which is material and mortal, the other part of which is immortal and the "true" or higher self; see Hammer, *Claiming Knowledge*, 436.

29. Jeanne Favret-Saada, *Deadly Words: Witchcraft in the Bocage* (Cambridge: Cambridge University Press, 1980), 8–9.

30. Mauss, *General Theory of Magic*, 140–43.

31. Charlotte Hardman, "'He May Be Lying But What He Says Is True': The Sacred Tradition of Don Juan as Reported by Carlos Castaneda, Anthropologist, Trickster, Guru, Allegorist," in *The Invention of Sacred Tradition*, edited by James R. Lewis and Olav Hammer (Cambridge: Cambridge University Press, 2007), 38–55.

32. Leigh Eric Schmidt, *Restless Souls: The Making of American Spirituality* (Berkeley: University of California Press, 2012), 103–4.

33. Such critiques are many, but the most incisive remains Dakota historian Philip J. Deloria's *Playing Indian* (New Haven, CT: Yale University Press, 1998).

34. Talal Asad, *Anthropology and the Colonial Encounter* (Reading: Ithaca Press, 1973).

35. This phrase has both social power and implicit theology, examined with startling honesty by Kate Bowler in *Everything Happens for a Reason: And Other Lies I've Loved* (New York: Random House, 2018).

36. Nancy Tatom Ammerman, *Bible Believers: Fundamentalists in the Modern World* (New Brunswick, NJ: Rutgers University Press, 1987), 17.

37. Susan Harding, *The Book of Jerry Falwell: Fundamentalist Language and Politics* (Princeton, NJ: Princeton University Press, 2001), 230; Robert N. Bellah, *Habits of the*

Heart: Individualism and Commitment in American Life (Berkeley: University of California Press, 1985), 220.

38. The complexities and uncertainties of the category of white people are dissected by John Hartigan, *Odd Tribes: Toward a Cultural Analysis of White People* (Durham, NC: Duke University Press, 2005).

39. Despite the use of the term "karma," in its usage reincarnation more closely reflected the ancient Greek concept of metempsychosis, or transmigration of souls. An outline of this idea is found in the Myth of Er in Plato's *Republic*, translated by Robin Waterfield (Oxford: Oxford University Press, 1993), 371–79, and other dialogues; see R. S. Bluck, "Plato, Pindar, and Metempsychosis," *American Journal of Philology* 79, no. 4 (1958), 412–14. This myth persisted in esoteric circles, influenced by Neoplatonism and combined with ideas that Jesus was a gnostic teacher who taught reincarnation, a hidden truth that was removed from the Bible by the early Church Fathers; see Hanegraaff, *New Age Religion and Western Culture*, 321.

40. Lisbeth Mikaelsson, "Homo Accumulans and the Spiritualization of Money," in *New Age Religion and Globalization*, edited by Mikael Rothstein (Copenhagen: Aarhus University Press, 2001), 94–96.

41. Kate Bowler, *Blessed: A History of the American Prosperity Gospel* (Oxford: Oxford University Press, 2013).

42. Albanese, *A Republic of Mind and Spirit*, 395–447.

43. Gwenda Blair, *The Trumps: Three Generations of Builders and a Presidential Candidate* (New York: Simon and Schuster, 2016).

44. Barbara Ehrenreich, *Bright-Sided: How Positive Thinking Is Undermining America* (London: Picador, 2009).

45. Carl Cederström and André Spicer, *The Wellness Syndrome* (Cambridge: Polity, 2015).

46. Jack Allanach and Osho World Foundation, *Osho, India and Me: A Tale of Sexual and Spiritual Transformation* (New Delhi: Niyogi Books, 2013).

47. Eugene V. Gallagher, *The New Religious Movements Experience in America* (Westport, CT: Greenwood Press, 2004), 112–16.

48. James Cullen, *The American Dream: A Short History of an Idea* (Oxford: Oxford University Press, 2004); Hedrick Smith, *Who Stole the American Dream?* (New York: Random House, 2013).

49. On neoliberalism, the following works have been influential on my thinking: Richard Sennett, *The Culture of the New Capitalism* (New Haven, CT: Yale University Press, 2006); Pierre Bourdieu, *Acts of Resistance: Against the New Myths of Our Time* (Cambridge: Polity Press, 1998); Aihwa Ong, *Neoliberalism as Exception: Mutations in Citizenship and Sovereignty* (Durham, NC: Duke University Press, 2006); David Harvey, *A Brief History of Neoliberalism* (Oxford: Oxford University Press, 2005); Loïc J. D. Wacquant, *Punishing the Poor: The Neoliberal Government of Social Insecurity* (Durham, NC: Duke University Press, 2009).

50. Two of the most well-read expositions of these principles are Esther and Jerry Hicks, *The Law of Attraction: The Basic Teachings of Abraham* (London: Hay House, 2006); and Rhonda Byrne, *The Secret* (New York: Atria, 2006), now in its tenth edition.

51. Of which there are many . . . Kimberly J. Lau, *New Age Capitalism: Making Money East*

of Eden (Philadelphia: University of Pennsylvania Press, 2000); Jeremy Carrette and Richard King, *Selling Spirituality: The Silent Takeover of Religion* (London: Routledge, 2005); Adam Possamai, *In Search of New Age Spiritualities* (Farnham: Ashgate, 2005); Michael York, "New Age Commodification and Appropriation of Spirituality," *Journal of Contemporary Religion* 163, no. 3 (2001): 361–72.

52. I am not suggesting that spirituality is complicit in neoliberalism, as for example in James LoRusso, *Spirituality, Corporate Culture, and American Business: The Neoliberal Ethic and the Spirit of Global Capital* (London: Bloomsbury Academic, 2017), 4. Rather, I am suggesting a co-constitution in line with how feminist science and technology studies scholars, particularly Kim TallBear and Donna Haraway, characterize the relationship between society and science; see Kimberly TallBear, *Native American DNA: Tribal Belonging and the False Promise of Genetic Science* (Minneapolis: University of Minnesota Press, 2013), 23; Donna J. Haraway, "Situated Knowledges: The Science Question in Feminism and the Privilege of Partial Perspective," in her *Simians, Cyborgs, and Women: The Reinvention of Nature* (New York: Routledge, 1991), 189–91.

53. David Graeber, *Debt: The First 5,000 Years* (New York: Melville House, 2011).

54. The culture of risk surrounding this accumulation of immaterial wealth is ably described by Karen Ho, *Liquidated: An Ethnography of Wall Street* (Durham, NC: Duke University Press, 2009).

55. Ilana Gershon, *Down and Out in the New Economy: How People Find (or Don't Find) Work Today* (Chicago: University of Chicago Press, 2017).

56. Richard Sennett, *Respect: The Formation of Character in a World of Inequality* (London: Allen Lane, 2003), 105.

57. The notion of enfolding spacetime is indebted to Karen Barad's feminist post-structuralist analysis of theoretical physics, *Meeting the Universe Halfway: Quantum Physics and the Entanglement of Matter and Meaning* (Durham, NC: Duke University Press, 2007), 177.

58. Mark Rifkin, *Beyond Settler Time: Temporal Sovereignty and Indigenous Self-Determination* (Durham, NC: Duke University Press, 2017), 2.

59. Barad, *Meeting the Universe Halfway*, 3.

CHAPTER ONE

1. On the problematic logistics and supply chains of the city of Phoenix, given its location, see Thomas E. Sheridan, *Arizona: A History* (Tucson: University of Arizona Press, 2012), 2–6, 376–77, 405–9; Andrew Ross, *Bird on Fire: Lessons from the World's Least Sustainable City* (Oxford: Oxford University Press, 2011).

2. The term "vortex" was nearly always pluralized as "vortexes," not "vortices," so I follow the native usage of the term here.

3. On the continuity of land claims and stories in places where Indigenous sovereignty has not gone away but been denied, see Pamela E. Klassen, *The Story of Radio Mind:*

A Missionary's Journey on Indigenous Land (Chicago: University of Chicago Press, 2018), 20.

4. On nature religion, see Catherine L. Albanese, *Nature Religion in America: From the Algonkian Indians to the New Age* (Chicago: University of Chicago Press, 1990) and *Reconsidering Nature Religion* (Harrisburg, PA: Trinity, 2002).

5. The term "natural amenities" comes from Todd W. Ferguson and Jeffrey A. Tamburello, "The Natural Environment as a Spiritual Resource: A Theory of Regional Variation in Religious Adherence," *Sociology of Religion* 76, no. 3 (2015): 295–314. It is a curiously bloodless way of speaking about nature that locates its purpose in servicing human needs, much as the wide body of literature on "ecosystem services" does.

6. Adrian Ivakhiv, "Red Rocks, 'Vortexes' and the Selling of Sedona: Environmental Politics in the New Age," *Social Compass* 44, no. 3 (1997): 367–84.

7. Thomas E. Sheridan, *Landscapes of Fraud: Mission Tumacácori, the Baca Float, and the Betrayal of the O'odham* (Tucson: University of Arizona Press, 2006), 15–16.

8. Richard A. Grusin, *Culture, Technology, and the Creation of America's National Parks* (Cambridge: Cambridge University Press, 2004).

9. Eliza Darling, "The Lorax Redux: Profit Biggering and Some Selective Silences in American Environmentalism," *Culture and Ecology* 12, no. 4 (2001): 51–66.

10. This is a lively and flourishing genre, but see for example Dick Sutphen, *Dick Sutphen Presents Sedona: Psychic Energy Vortexes*, edited by Dawn Abbey (Malibu, CA: Valley of the Sun Publishing, 1986); Dennis Andres, *What Is a Vortex? Sedona's Vortex Sites, a Practical Guide* (Sedona: Meta Adventures, 2000); Richard Dannelley, *Sedona Power Spot, Vortex & Medicine Wheel Guide* (Sedona: Vortex Society, 1992) and *Sedona: Beyond the Vortex: Activating the Planetary Ascension Program* (Flagstaff, AZ: Light Technology Publishing 1995); Toraya Ayres, *The History of New Age Sedona* (Cedar City, UT: High Mountain Training and Publishing, 1997).

11. Ivakhiv, *Claiming Sacred Ground*, 24–25.

12. Interestingly, in online depictions Sedona is not included as one of the earth chakras. Nearby Mount Shasta in California is the root chakra. Glastonbury as the heart chakra is also mentioned in Prince and Riches, *The New Age in Glastonbury*, 59. The energy in Sedona is nearly always described as positive, and Sutphen called the vortexes there "positive vortexes," but there were also "negative vortexes," the most famous of which is the Bermuda triangle (*Sedona*, 82–84). Ivakhiv mentioned two "negative vortexes" in Sedona, at Indian Gardens and the Sedona post office site (*Claiming Sacred Ground*, 185). I did not hear these locations talked about as negative vortexes during my fieldwork.

13. Sutphen, *Sedona*, 82.

14. Andres, *What Is a Vortex?*, 23.

15. Andres, *What Is a Vortex?*, 17.

16. Orbs are the blurry colored circles of light that sometimes show up in photos, caused by lens flare or dust on the lens. In spirituality, these photographic bloopers are interpreted as interdimensional beings, sometimes also called elementals or fairies or aliens, that show up on photographs when they want to. Some people told me they were very

good at getting photographs of orbs, speculating that the orbs must be attracted to their good energy. On the spiritual interpretation of photographic "blobs," see Paolo Apolito, *The Internet and the Madonna: Religious Visionary Experience on the Web* (Chicago: University of Chicago Press, 2005).

17. Ivakhiv, "Red Rocks," 377.

18. This story can also be found in a history of Sedona by a local author, Hoyt C. Johnson, in *The Sedona Story: Settlement to Centennial* (Tucson: AzScene, 2008), 5.

19. Ayres, *History of New Age Sedona*, 4–5.

20. Mary Lou Keller, "Introduction: Echoes of the Past," in *Sedona Vortex Guide Book*, edited by Page Bryant (Sedona: Light Technology Publications, 1991), xvi.

21. Andres, *What Is a Vortex?*, 14; Sutphen, *Sedona*, 21.

22. Ayres, *History of New Age Sedona*, 7.

23. Hammer, *Claiming Knowledge*, 134–38.

24. Ivakhiv, *Claiming Sacred Ground*, 173.

25. Ivakhiv, "Red Rocks," 369–70.

26. Bender and McRoberts, "Mapping a Field," 6.

27. The appropriation and resale of Native American material culture, and the white American practice of calling oneself a "shaman," have been critiqued as colonialist by Native American scholars and scholars of religion. See Deloria, *Playing Indian*; Alice Beck Kehoe, *Shamans and Religion: An Anthropological Exploration in Critical Thinking* (Long Grove, IL: Waveland Press, 2000); Lisa Aldred, "Plastic Shamans and Astroturf Sun Dances: New Age Commercialization of Native American Spirituality," *American Indian Quarterly* 24, no. 3 (2000): 329–52.

28. Joel Myerson, ed., *Transcendentalism: A Reader* (Oxford: Oxford University Press, 2000), xxxi.

29. Kimberly TallBear, "Caretaking Relations, Not American Dreaming," *Kalfou* 6, no. 1 (2019): 31.

30. Ivakhiv, *Claiming Sacred Ground*, 160–61.

31. Gell, *Art and Agency*, 22.

32. Ivakhiv, *Claiming Sacred Ground*, 188.

33. Michaela Benson and Karen O'Reilly, eds., *Lifestyle Migration: Expectations, Aspirations and Experiences* (Farnham: Ashgate, 2009).

34. Sheridan, *Landscapes of Fraud*, 13.

35. Mike Harrison, John Williams, Sigrid Khera, and Carolina C. Butler, *Oral History of the Yavapai* (Phoenix: Acacia Publications, 2012), 40.

36. On who is, can claim to be, and the political and scientific mechanisms through which they can claim to be "Native American" or an enrolled member of particular tribe, see Circe Sturm, *Blood Politics: Race, Culture, and Identity in the Cherokee Nation of Oklahoma* (Berkeley: University of California Press, 2002); TallBear, *Native American DNA*.

37. Sheridan, *Arizona*, 67–108.

38. Robert J. Wallis, *Shamans/Neo-Shamans: Ecstasy, Alternative Archaeologies, and Contemporary Pagans* (London: Routledge, 2003), 205–7.

39. There are many works on this complex and shameful history; a classic is Dee Alexander Brown, *Bury My Heart at Wounded Knee: An Indian History of the American West* (New

York: Vintage, 1991). Activist and historian Vine Deloria's *Custer Died for Your Sins: An Indian Manifesto* (Norman: University of Oklahoma Press, 1969) remains peerless. A few relevant to Arizona include Sheridan, *Landscapes of Fraud* and *Arizona*; Klara B. Kelley and Harris Francis, *Navajo Sacred Places* (Bloomington: Indiana University Press, 1994); Judy Pasternak, *Yellow Dirt: A Poisoned Land and the Betrayal of the Navajos* (New York: Free Press, 2010).

40. Timothy Braatz, *Surviving Conquest: A History of the Yavapai Peoples* (Lincoln: University of Nebraska Press 2003); Ivakhiv, *Claiming Sacred Ground*, 151–52.

41. Kelley and Francis, *Navajo Sacred Places*, 17–18.

42. Dana E. Powell, *Landscapes of Power: Politics of Energy in the Navajo Nation* (Durham, NC: Duke University Press, 2018), 8.

43. Andrei A. Znamenski, *The Beauty of the Primitive: Shamanism and the Western Imagination* (Oxford: Oxford University Press, 2007), 275–305; Adam Kuper, *The Reinvention of Primitive Society: Transformations of a Myth*, 2nd ed. (London: Routledge, 2005), 206.

44. Deloria, *Playing Indian*, 3–5.

45. Deloria, *Playing Indian*, 5.

46. TallBear, "Caretaking Relations," 31.

47. TallBear, *Native American DNA*, 36; Rifkin, *Beyond Settler Time*, 39.

48. David Chidester and Edward T. Linenthal, "Introduction," in *American Sacred Space* (Bloomington: Indiana University Press, 1995), 12–13.

49. Sara M. Patterson, "The Plymouth Rock of the American West: Remembering, Forgetting, and Becoming American in Utah," *Material Religion* 11, no. 3 (July 3, 2015): 329–53.

50. Sheridan, *Landscapes of Fraud*, 6.

51. Klassen, *Story of Radio Mind*, 24.

52. Vine Deloria, *God Is Red: A Native View of Religion*, 3rd ed. (Golden, CO: Fulcrum Publications, 2003), 61–75, 275–85.

53. Deloria, *God Is Red*, 66–67.

54. Hanegraaff, *New Age Religion and Western Culture*, 309–12; Hammer, *Claiming Knowledge*, 99–101.

55. This mythology can be placed in the context of race-shifting, or pretendianism, in which white Americans spuriously claim Native American identity, most often Cherokee, in order to enhance their own spiritual authenticity, Sturm, *Blood Politics*, 58–59; TallBear, *Native American DNA*, 134–35.

56. Hammer, *Claiming Knowledge*, 89.

57. On spirituality and Mount Shasta, see Helen McCarthy, "Assaulting California's Sacred Mountains: Shamans vs. New Age Merchants of Nirvana," in *Beyond Primitivism: Indigenous Religious Traditions and Modernity*, edited by Jacob Olupona (London: Routledge, 2003), 172–78; and on Hawaii, see Mikael Rothstein, "Hawaii in New Age Imaginations: A Case of Religious Inventions," in *Handbook of New Age*, edited by Daren Kemp and James R. Lewis (Leiden: Brill, 2007), 315–40.

58. Mircea Eliade, *The Sacred and the Profane: The Nature of Religion*, translated by Willard R. Trask (New York: Harcourt, 1959), 26.

59. Durkheim, *The Elementary Forms of Religious Life*, 34–44.

60. Ivakhiv, *Claiming Sacred Ground*, 45.

61. Michael Harner developed core-shamanism, principally through his work *The Way of the Shaman* (New York: Harper and Row, 1990), in which he described it as the essential, universal elements of all shamanistic practices cross-culturally, an idea that he subsequently marketed through further books and through founding the Institute of Shamanic Studies. It has been heavily critiqued by scholars of shamanism; see Paul C. Johnson, "Shamanism from Ecuador to Chicago: A Case Study in New Age Ritual Appropriation," *Religion* 25, no. 2 (1995): 163–78.

62. Arturo Escobar, "After Nature: Steps to an Antiessentialist Political Ecology," *Current Anthropology* 40, no. 1 (1999): 4–7.

63. Albanese, *Reconsidering Nature Religion*, 1.

64. On the Transcendentalists, see John Gatta, *Making Nature Sacred: Literature, Religion, and Environment in America from the Puritans to the Present* (Oxford: Oxford University Press, 2004), 71–141; Myerson, *Transcendentalism*; Lance Newman, *Our Common Dwelling: Henry Thoreau, Transcendentalism, and the Class Politics of Nature* (New York: Palgrave Macmillan, 2005).

65. Catherine L. Albanese, "Introduction: Awash in a Sea of Metaphysics," *Journal of the American Academy of Religion* 75, no. 3 (2007): 582–88.

66. William Cronon, *Uncommon Ground: Rethinking the Human Place in Nature* (New York: W. W. Norton, 1996), 80.

67. He used "great valley" in the meaning given to it in the *Land Before Time* animated children's movies, where a group of young dinosaurs go looking for a mythical "great valley" with plentiful water and vegetation all year round, habitable and safe from the monsters that destroyed their home.

68. Immanuel Kant, *Observations on the Feeling of the Beautiful and Sublime and Other Writings*, edited by Patrick Frierson and Paul Guyer (Cambridge: Cambridge University Press, 2011); Cornelia Klinger, "The Concepts of the Sublime and the Beautiful In Kant and Lyotard," *Constellations* 2, no. 2 (1995): 207–23.

69. Sheridan, *Arizona*, 241.

70. Richard Sennett, *The Craftsman* (New Haven, CT: Yale University Press, 2008), 140–41.

71. Cronon, *Uncommon Ground*, 51.

72. Cronon, *Uncommon Ground*, 76.

73. Eliza Darling, "City in the Country: Wilderness Gentrification and the Rent Gap," *Environment and Planning A* 37 (2005): 1029–30.

74. James Siegel, "Academic Work: The View from Cornell," *Diacritics* 11, no. 1 (1981): 68–83.

75. It was reported on often in the local news, for example George Heckerd, "Sedona Pleads with ADOT after Increase of Bridge Suicides," *12 News,* March 16, 2016, https://www.12news.com/article/news/local/arizona/sedona-pleads-with-adot-after-increase-of-bridge-suicides/84290013, accessed April 23, 2020.

76. Kelley McMillan, "Here's Why Ski Towns Are Seeing More Suicides," *National Geographic* online, May 16, 2016, https://www.nationalgeographic.com/adventure/adventure-blog/2016/05/16/why-are-ski-towns-suicides-happening-at-such-an-alarming-rate/, accessed April 23, 2020.

77. A document produced by the Coconino County Public Health Services provides detailed information on suicide in the county, based on data from the Centers for

Disease Control. The county has a higher rate of suicide than the state of Arizona as a whole; however, the towns that are most frequently the site of suicide for both residents and non-residents of the county are Flagstaff, Tuba City, and Page. These latter two towns are in the Navajo Nation reservation, and Flagstaff is the largest city in the county and also near the border with the reservation. Native Americans were also found to be disproportionately at risk from suicide in the county; see Public Health Services Coconino County, "Suicide in Coconino County 2017: An Overview of Suicide Trends from 2010–2016," http://www.coconino.az.gov/DocumentCenter/View/20418 /Coconino-County-Suicide-Report-12018?bidId=.

CHAPTER TWO

1. On New Age reinterpretations of the Mayan calendar and its emergence as a new form of millenarianism in the early twenty-first century, see Robert K. Sitler, "The 2012 Phenomenon: New Age Appropriation of an Ancient Mayan Calendar," *Nova Religio* 9, no. 3 (2006): 24–38; Anthony Aveni, *The End of Time: The Maya Mystery of 2012* (Boulder: University Press of Colorado, 2009); Joseph Gelfer, *2012: Decoding the Countercultural Apocalypse* (London: Taylor and Francis, 2014); Kevin A. Whitesides, "2012 Millennialism Becomes Conspiracist Teleology: Overlapping Alternatives in Late Twentieth Century Cultic Milieu," *Nova Religio: The Journal of Alternative and Emergent Religions* 19, no. 2 (2015): 30–48; Andrew Fergus Wilson, "From Mushrooms to the Stars: 2012 and the Apocalyptic Milieu," in *Prophecy in the New Millennium: When Prophecies Persist*, edited by Sarah Harvey and Suzanne Newcombe, 225–38 (Farnham: Ashgate, 2013); Suzanne Rough, "Remembering the Future: 2012 as Planetary Transition," in *Prophecy in the New Millennium: When Prophecies Persist*, edited by Sarah Harvey and Suzanne Newcombe, 255–60 (Farnham: Ashgate, 2013).
2. This is a well-known book of channeled material by Tom Kenyon and Virginia Essene, *The Hathor Material: Messages from an Ascended Civilization* (Nicosia: ORB Communications, 1996).
3. Rainbow Gatherings are annual meetings of the Rainbow Family, a loose network of self-identifying "family members" in America and Europe who tend to live outside formal economic and political systems, and come together to create temporary settlements at their gatherings that run on cooperative and consensus-based organizational practices. See Chelsea Schelly, *Crafting Collectivity: American Rainbow Gatherings and Alternative Forms of Community* (London: Routledge, 2015).
4. Peter called the idea that the world ended at the end of the Mayan Long Count calendar a "misassumption"; the calendar ended only to begin again, as calendars do. Instead, he saw the significance of the date in the fact that the winter solstice was at 11:11, and talk of a "Mayan apocalypse" was just a clue pointing him in the right direction through wrong information. Solstices were considered significant events in Sedona because the energy was said to have a high vibration on those dates; numerous ceremonies were held on the solstices and equinoxes throughout the year.

5. The video has been archived and accessed through this link: https://vimeo.com /38445566.

6. He was interviewed for a Norwegian magazine, *Pløt*, and for documentaries by Australian and Canadian broadcasters, as well as written about in numerous newspapers and websites, for example Eric Tsetsi, "Sedona Vortex Jumper Peter Gersten Wanders Home After Vortex Fails to Open," *Phoenix New Times*, December 22, 2012, http:// www.phoenixnewtimes.com/news/sedona-vortex-jumper-peter-gersten-wanders -home-after-vortex-fails-to-open-6648932, accessed April 23, 2020; Robert Sheaffer, "2012: Peter Gersten's 'Leap of Faith,'" *Bad UFOs*, February 10, 2011, http://badufos .blogspot.com/2011/02/2012-peter-gerstens-leap-of-faith.html, accessed April 23, 2020; "Doubting That Leap of Faith," *Ground Zero Media*, December 10, 2012, https://www .groundzeromedia.org/doubting-that-leap-of-faith/, accessed April 23, 2020; "Mayan Calendar Vortex Jumper Costs County $838," *Sedona Red Rock News*, December 29, 2012, http://redrocknews.com/news/13-top-news/8968-vortex-jumper-costs-838, accessed April 23, 2020.

7. Jerome Bruner, "The Narrative Construction of Reality," *Critical Inquiry* 18, no. 1 (1991): 6.

8. Bruner, "The Narrative Construction of Reality," 6–19.

9. In America, around 95 percent of legal cases are resolved through plea deals, the colloquial term used for what legal scholars call plea bargaining. It is a process whereby a defendant pleads guilty to a lesser charge, foregoing their right to trial, but receiving a reduced sentence in return; see Bruce P. Smith, "Plea Bargaining and the Eclipse of the Jury," *Annual Review of Law and Social Science* 1, no. 1 (December 4, 2005): 131–49. It saves the cost of a trial, and for defendants, gets them out of jail quicker; however, the process has been critiqued for encouraging the innocent to plead guilty out of fear of staying in jail while awaiting trial (which can take months or years). All of my interlocutors who had been convicted of a criminal offense had accepted a plea deal. Some expressed the opinion that police piled on as many charges as possible in order to intimidate them into accepting a plea deal, which would be for a lesser charge, but at the same time the full list of charges would have been unlikely to proceed in a trial. This situation persists because many of those subject to it cannot afford adequate legal representation, and instead use public defenders, such as Peter, who encouraged them to sign the plea deal, and get through the system as quickly as possible.

10. Bruner, "The Narrative Construction of Reality," 14.

11. Harding, *The Book of Jerry Falwell*, 140.

12. G. Thomas Couser, *Altered Egos: Authority in American Autobiography* (Oxford: Oxford University Press, 1989): 12–13; Michael Bérubé, "Autobiography as Performative Utterance," *American Quarterly* 52, no. 2 (2000): 341.

13. Couser, *Altered Egos*, 248.

14. Vine Deloria and Clifford M. Lytle, *American Indians, American Justice* (Austin: University of Texas Press, 1983).

15. David Robertson attributed the "11:11" symbol to Solara An-Ra, a Montana-based channeler who also popularized the term "ascension" for the imminent spiritual enlightenment of humanity [*UFOs, Conspiracy Theories and the New Age: Millennial Conspira-*

cism (London: Bloomsbury, 2016), 83]. Solara said that when people see 11:11, they are seeing the overlaps between the physical and divine realms. When I asked Peter about this, he said that Solara was one of a number of bloggers and writers who were talking about 11:11 in the 1990s and early 2000s who influenced him around the time of his epiphany. Others in Sedona who attributed significance to 11:11 told me that if you were noticing this number repeatedly, it meant extradimensional beings were already trying to contact you. Yet others just said it was a synchronicity meant to make you pay attention to where the energy of the universe was flowing.

16. Bruner, "The Narrative Construction of Reality," 7–8.

17. Nick Bostrom, "Are You Living in a Computer Simulation?," *Philosophical Quarterly* 53, no. 211 (2003): 243–55; John D. Barrow, "Living in a Simulated Universe" (2007), unpublished paper, https://www.simulation-argument.com/barrowsim.pdf, accessed April 27, 2020.

18. Rubenstein, "Cosmic Singularities," –507.

19. Bruner, "The Narrative Construction of Reality," 13.

20. Richard Dawkins, "Viruses of the Mind," in *Dennett and His Critics: Demystifying Mind,* edited by Bo Dahlbom, 13–27 (Oxford: Blackwell, 1993).

21. Kathleen Stewart and Susan Harding, "Bad Endings: American Apocalypsis," *Annual Review of Anthropology* 28 (1999): 285–310; James D. Faubion, *The Shadows and Lights of Waco: Millennialism Today* (Princeton, NJ: Princeton University Press, 2001); David Chidester, *Salvation and Suicide: Jim Jones, the Peoples Temple, and Jonestown* (Bloomington: Indiana University Press, 2003); Jeffrey Kaplan, *Radical Religion in America: Millenarian Movements from the Far Right to the Children of Noah* (Syracuse, NY: Syracuse University Press, 1997); Catherine Wessinger, *How the Millennium Comes Violently: From Jonestown to Heaven's Gate* (New York: Seven Bridges Press, 2000); Charles B. Strozier and Michael Flynn, *The Year 2000: Essays on the End* (New York: New York University Press, 1997).

22. A galactic astrologer uses astronomical bodies beyond the twelve zodiac constellations of Western astrology for divination; see Susannah Crockford, "A Mercury Retrograde Kind of Day: Exploring Astrology in Contemporary New Age Spirituality and American Social Life," *Correspondences* 6, no. 1 (2018): 47–75.

23. Ivakhiv, *Claiming Sacred Ground,* 174.

24. On UFO stories about these locations in southwest America, see David Darlington, *Area 51: The Dreamland Chronicles* (New York: H. Holt, 1997); Lepselter, *Resonance of Unseen Things.*

25. Harding, *The Book of Jerry Falwell,* 233; Joel Robbins, "'When Do You Think the World Will End?' Globalization, Apocalypticism, and the Moral Perils of Fieldwork in 'Last New Guinea,'" *Anthropology and Humanism* 22, no. 1 (1997): 14; Richard Eves, "'Great Signs from Heaven': Christian Discourses of the End of the World from New Ireland," *Asia Pacific Journal of Anthropology* 12, no. 1 (2011): 19; Kent Eaton, "Beware the Trumpet of Judgement! John Nelson Darby and the Nineteenth-Century Brethren," in *The Coming Deliverer: Millennial Themes in World Religions* (Cardiff: University of Wales Press, 1997), 141–42.

26. Bruner, "The Narrative Construction of Reality," 18–19.

27. Melissa Ames, "Introduction: Television Studies in the 21st Century," in *Time in Television Narrative: Exploring Temporality in Twenty-First Century Programming*, edited by Melissa Ames, 4–19 (Jackson: University Press of Mississippi, 2012); Sarah Himsel Burcon, "*Lost* in Our Middle Hour: Faith, Fate, and Redemption Post-9/11," in *Time in Television Narrative: Exploring Temporality in Twenty-First Century Programming*, edited by Melissa Ames, 125–38 (Jackson: University Press of Mississippi, 2012); Lucy Bennett, "Lost in Time? *Lost* Fan Engagement with Temporal Play," in *Time in Television Narrative: Exploring Temporality in Twenty-First Century Programming*, edited by Melissa Ames, 297–308 (Jackson: University Press of Mississippi, 2012).

28. Timothy Jenkins, *Of Flying Saucers and Social Scientists: A Re-Reading of When Prophecy Fails and of Cognitive Dissonance* (London: Palgrave Macmillan, 2013), 52–53.

29. Jenkins, *Of Flying Saucers*, 54–66; Leon Festinger, Henry Riecken, and Stanley Schachter, *When Prophecy Fails* (Minneapolis: University of Minnesota Press, 1956).

30. Festinger et al., *When Prophecy Fails*, 237.

31. Festinger et al., *When Prophecy Fails*, 26.

32. Jenkins, *Of Flying Saucers*, 66.

33. Festinger et al., *When Prophecy Fails*, 244.

34. Festinger et al., *When Prophecy Fails*, 246.

35. Jenkins, *Of Flying Saucers*, 3–4.

36. Stewart and Harding, "Bad Endings," 287.

37. Michael Barkun, "Reflections after Waco: Millennialists and the State," in *From the Ashes: Making Sense of Waco*, edited by James R. Lewis (Lanham: Rowman & Littlefield, 1994), 44.

38. Joseph Dumit, "Playing Truths: Logics of Seeking and Persistence of the New Age," *Focaal* 37 (2001): 72.

39. At one point I even tried to describe it to him in terms of Arnold van Gennep's rite of passage, where the ascent was separation from ordinary life, being on the top was liminality, and the descent was reincorporation. Arnold van Gennep, *The Rites of Passage* (Chicago: University of Chicago Press, 1960); Victor Turner, *The Ritual Process: Structure and Anti-Structure* (Piscataway, NJ: Aldine Transaction, 1969).

40. Bruner, "The Narrative Construction of Reality," 7.

41. Bruner, "The Narrative Construction of Reality," 16.

42. Jenkins, *Of Flying Saucers*, 15.

43. Norman Cohn, *The Pursuit of the Millennium: Revolutionary Millenarians and Mystical Anarchists of the Middle Ages* (London: Random House, 1993), 14–15.

44. Cohn, *The Pursuit of the Millennium*, 15.

45. Maurice Bloch, "The Blob," *Anthropology of This Century*, no. 1 (2011), online version.

46. Slavoj Žižek, *Living in the End Times* (London: Verso, 2010), ix–xiii.

47. Jean Baudrillard, *The Ecstasy of Communication* (Los Angeles: Semiotext(e), 2012), 31.

48. Jean Baudrillard, *Simulations* (Los Angeles: Semiotext(e), 1983), 152.

49. Scott Ross, "Being Real on Fake Instagram: Likes, Images, and Media Ideologies of Value," *Journal of Linguistic Anthropology* 29, no. 3 (2019): 359–74.

50. Bruner, "The Narrative Construction of Reality," 13.

51. Sennett, *Craftsman*, 72; Sennett, *Respect*, 28.

CHAPTER THREE

---

1. Susan A. Clancy, *Abducted: How People Come to Believe They Were Kidnapped by Aliens* (Cambridge, MA: Harvard University Press, 2005); Brenda Denzler, *The Lure of the Edge: Scientific Passions, Religious Beliefs, and the Pursuit of UFOs* (Berkeley: University of California Press, 2001); Bridget Brown, *They Know Us Better Than We Know Ourselves: The History and Politics of Alien Abduction* (New York: New York University Press, 2007); Jodi Dean, *Aliens in America: Conspiracy Cultures from Outerspace to Cyberspace* (Ithaca, NY: Cornell University Press, 1998); Debbora Battaglia, ed., *E.T. Culture: Anthropology in Outerspaces* (Durham, NC: Duke University Press, 2005); Lepselter, *Resonance of Unseen Things.*

2. Christopher Partridge, ed., *UFO Religions* (London: Routledge, 2003); Benjamin E. Zeller, "At the Nexus of Science and Religion: UFO Religions," *Religion Compass* 5, no. 11 (2011): 666–74; James R. Lewis, ed., *The Gods Have Landed: New Religions from Other Worlds* (Albany: State University of New York Press, 1995) and *Encyclopedic Sourcebook of UFO Religions* (Amherst, MA: Prometheus Books, 2003); Susan J. Palmer, *Aliens Adored: Raël's UFO Religion* (New Brunswick, NJ: Rutgers University Press, 2004); John A. Saliba, "The Study of UFO Religions," *Nova Religio: The Journal of Alternative and Emergent Religions* 10, no. 2 (2006): 103–23.

3. Brown, *The Channeling Zone,* 24.

4. Zeller, "At the Nexus of Science and Religion," 670.

5. Nasir Khan, *Development of the Concept and Theory of Alienation in Marx's Writings: March 1843 to August 1844* (Oslo: Solum Forlag, 1995), 36.

6. Jean Comaroff and John L. Comaroff, "Naturing the Nation: Aliens, Apocalypse and the Postcolonial State," *Journal of Southern African Studies* 27, no. 3 (2001): 627–51, and "Alien-Nation: Zombies, Immigrants, and Millennial Capitalism," *South Atlantic Quarterly* 101, no. 4 (2002): 779–805.

7. Elizabeth A. Povinelli, "The Will to Be Otherwise/The Effort of Endurance," *South Atlantic Quarterly* 111, no. 3 (2012): 459.

8. Kundalini in spirituality is a term analogous to energy. Specifically, the kundalini rises from the root chakra at the base of the spine to the crown chakra above the head, culminating in spiritual enlightenment. It takes the form of two coiled snakes gradually or rapidly unraveling. Kundalini yoga aims to engage this process through movement and breathing exercises. The term "Kundalini" is derived from the name of a Hindu goddess, a consort of Shiva, who could appear as a vital force coiled at the base of the spine. Olav Hammer traces how this concept, along with that of the chakras, is a reformulation of Tantric doctrine by theosophical writers in the late nineteenth century, specifically Charles Leadbeater, which has been combined with scientific concepts of "energy" by late twentieth-century "new age" authors (*Claiming Knowledge*, 183–90).

9. Merkabah is a form of Jewish mysticism, based on the Old Testament Book of Ezekiel. The word in Hebrew translates as "chariot." In the passage in Ezekiel, God is seen in a vision seated on his throne or chariot; see Gerschom Scholem, *Major Trends in Jewish Mysticism* (New York: Knopf Doubleday, 1960). In spirituality, the term is used

most often in connection with spaceships. Those espousing beliefs in ancient aliens, that ancient peoples had contact with UFOs and recorded them in their sacred texts, interpret the biblical merkabah as a UFO. They translate the term as Mer = Light, Ka = Spirit, Ba = body; see for example http://www.crystalinks.com/merkaba.html.

10. The data for this chapter on Mynzah comes primarily from my interview with him and subsequent informal conversations with him during my fieldwork period. He also wrote his own version and published it online, which contained the same narrative as he gave in our interview but with more detail; see https://mynzahosiris.wordpress.com/.

11. See Mynzah's autobiography on kundalini awakening; Mynzah, "Mynzah Kundalini Awakening Story," July 9, 2015, https://mynzahosiris.wordpress.com/2015/07/09/mynzah-kundalini-awakening-story/, accessed April 24, 2020.

12. Heaven's Gate, a UFO religion that committed mass suicide in 1997, talked about aliens from the Next Level planting seeds in humans on this planet that spur spiritual evolution. Christopher Partridge connected this imagery to the Justinian doctrine of *spermatic logos*, where prior to Christ humans contained seeds of the Word and could therefore come to partial awareness of God; see Partridge, "Alien Demonology: The Christian Roots of the Malevolent Extraterrestrial in UFO Religions and Abduction Spiritualities," *Religion* 34, no. 3 (2004): 176–77.

13. Mynzah, "Chapter One—In the Beginning (autobiography book by Mynzah)," July 9, 2015, https://mynzahosiris.wordpress.com/2015/07/09/chapter-one-in-the-beginning-autobiography-book-by-mynzah/, accessed April 24, 2020.

14. Autobiography, "Chapter Z, The Last Day on Earth," https://mynzahosiris.wordpress.com/2015/07/09/chapter-z-the-last-day-on-earth-autobiography-book-by-mynzah/.

15. Frank Lambert, *Inventing the "Great Awakening"* (Princeton, NJ: Princeton University Press, 1999); Alan Heimert, *Religion and the American Mind: From the Great Awakening to the Revolution* (Cambridge, MA: Harvard University Press, 1966); Neil Meyer, "Falling for the Lord: Shame, Revivalism, and the Origins of the Second Great Awakening," *Early American Studies: An Interdisciplinary Journal* 9, no. 1 (2011): 169–93.

16. Steve Turner, *Amazing Grace: The Story of America's Most Beloved Song* (New Yok: Ecco, 2002).

17. D. Bruce Hindmarsh, *The Evangelical Conversion Narrative: Spiritual Autobiography in Early Modern England* (Oxford: Oxford University Press, 1999), 915.

18. Hindmarsh, *The Evangelical Conversion Narrative*, 920.

19. I. M. Lewis, *Ecstatic Religion: A Study of Shamanism and Spirit Possession*, 2nd ed. (London: Routledge, 1989); Piers Vitebsky, "Shamanism," in *Indigenous Religions: A Companion*, edited by Graham Harvey, 55–67 (London: Cassell, 2000).

20. Susan Harding, "Representing Fundamentalism: The Problem of the Repugnant Cultural Other," *Social Research* 58 (1991): 373–93; Joel Robbins, *Becoming Sinners: Christianity and Moral Torment in a Papua New Guinea Society* (Berkeley: University of California Press, 2004).

21. Matthew Engelke, "Discontinuity and the Discourse of Conversion," *Journal of Religion in Africa* 34, no. 1/2 (2004): 105–6.

22. Matthew Engelke, "Christianity and the Anthropology of Secular Humanism," *Current Anthropology* 55, no. S10 (2014): S293.

23. Engelke, "Christianity and the Anthropology of Secular Humanism," S296.

24. Erin F. Johnston, "'I Was Always This Way . . .': Rhetorics of Continuity in Narratives of Conversion," *Sociological Forum* 28, no. 3 (2013): 561.

25. Tanya M. Luhrmann, *Persuasions of a Witches' Craft: Ritual Magic in Contemporary England*, 2nd ed. (Cambridge, MA: Harvard University Press, 1991), 307–23.

26. "NAFPS Forum," begun October 21, 2013, last updated March 10, 2016, http://www.newagefraud.org/smf/index.php?topic=4211.0. Sierra also seemed to be involved in the medical marijuana industry. A CNBC news report from 2010 featured her mother and grandmother, an account of her military service that reflected what was written about her on newagefraud.org rather than what she said at the conference, and a medical history ascribed to the side effects of Advil rather than government experiments; see Rob Reuteman, "Life Of Pain Drives Medical Marijuana Clinic Owner," *CNBC News*, April 19, 2010, https://www.cnbc.com/id/36179432.

27. Barbara Bodenhorn and Gabriele Vom Bruck, "'Entangled in Histories': An Introduction to the Anthropology of Names and Naming," in *The Anthropology of Names and Naming*, edited by Gabriele Vom Bruck and Barbara Bodenhorn (Cambridge: Cambridge University Press, 2009), 2.

28. John L. Austin, *How to Do Things with Words*, edited by J. O. Urmson and Marina Sbisà, 2nd ed. (Cambridge, MA: Harvard University Press, 1975); Bodenhorn and vom Bruck, "'Entangled in Histories,'" 11; Michael Lambek, "What's in a Name? Name Bestowal and the Identity of Spirits in Mayotte and Northwest Madagascar," in *The Anthropology of Names and Naming*, edited by Gabriele Vom Bruck and Barbara Bodenhorn (Cambridge: Cambridge University Press, 2009), 125.

29. Lambek, "What's in a Name?," 116.

30. Lambek, "What's in a Name?," 119.

31. Michael Lambek, "Kinship, Modernity, and the Immodern," in *Vital Relations: Modernity and the Persistent Life of Kinship*, edited by Susan McKinnon and Fenella Cannell (Santa Fe, NM: School for Advanced Research Press, 2013), 253–54.

32. Bodenhorn and vom Bruck, "'Entangled in Histories,'" 3.

33. Or even before; see Linda Layne, "'Your Child Deserves a Name': Possessive Individualism and the Politics of Memory of Pregnancy Loss," in *The Anthropology of Names and Naming*, edited by Gabriele vom Bruck and Barbara Bodenhorn, 31–50 (Cambridge: Cambridge University Press, 2009).

34. Bodenhorn and vom Bruck, "'Entangled in Histories,'" 22.

35. Landmark Forum is one of the organizations that combine spirituality with positive thinking, personal well-being, and corporate profitability. A number of my interlocutors had involvements with it during my fieldwork, describing it variously as "life-changing" and "cult-like"; see Renee Lockwood, "Religiosity Rejected: Exploring the Religio-Spiritual Dimensions of Landmark Education," *International Journal for the Study of New Religions* 2, no. 2 (2011): 225–54.

36. David M. Schneider, *American Kinship: A Cultural Account*, 2nd ed. (Chicago: University of Chicago Press, 1980), 21–27.

37. Fenella Cannell, "The Re-Enchantment of Kinship," in *Vital Relations: Modernity and the Persistent Life of Kinship*, edited by Susan McKinnon and Fenella Cannell, 217–

40 (Santa Fe, NM: School for Advanced Research Press, 2013); Kath Weston, *Families We Choose: Lesbians, Gays, Kinship* (New York: Columbia University Press, 1991); Jane Collier, Michelle Z. Rosaldo, and Sylvia Junko Yanagisako, "Is There a Family? New Anthropological Views," in *The Gender/Sexuality Reader: Culture, History, Political Economy*, edited by Roger N. Lancaster and Micaela Di Leonardo, 71–77 (London: Routledge, 1997); Margaret K. Nelson, "Single Mothers 'Do' Family," *Journal of Marriage and Family* 68, no. 4 (2006): 781–95; Carol B. Stack, *All Our Kin: Strategies for Survival in a Black Community* (London: Harper & Row, 1974); Sylvia J. Yanagisako and Carol L. Delaney, eds., *Naturalizing Power: Essays in Feminist Cultural Analysis* (London: Routledge, 1995).

38. Weston, *Families We Choose*, 26–29.

39. Weston, *Families We Choose*, 127.

40. Weston, *Families We Choose*, 126.

41. Cannell, "The Re-Enchantment of Kinship," 225.

42. Nelson, "Single Mothers 'Do' Family," 786.

43. Roof, *Spiritual Marketplace*, 294; Wuthnow, *After Heaven*, 7; Richard Cimino and Don Lattin, *Shopping for Faith: American Religion in the New Millennium* (San Francisco: Jossey-Bass, 2002), 21.

44. Janet Carsten, *After Kinship* (Cambridge: Cambridge University Press, 2004), 17.

45. Richard Sennett and Jonathan Cobb, *The Hidden Injuries of Class* (New York: Norton, 1972), 100.

46. Mynzah, "Chapter Four—3rd to the 4th Power (Autobiography Book by Mynzah)," July 9, 2015, https://mynzahosiris.wordpress.com/2015/07/09/chapter-four-3rd-to-the-4th-power-autobiography-book-by-mynzah/, accessed April 24, 2020. His framing echoed Peter's belief system in the second chapter, although the two did not know each other.

47. Mynzah, "Chapter A—Awakened (Autobiography Book by Mynzah)," July 9, 2015, https://mynzahosiris.wordpress.com/2015/07/09/chapter-a-awakened-autobiography-book-by-mynzah/, accessed April 24, 2020.

48. Clancy, *Abducted*, 94.

49. Sherry B. Ortner, "Identities: The Hidden Life of Class," *Journal of Anthropological Research* 54, no. 1 (1998): 8.

50. Arlie Russell Hochschild, *Strangers in Their Own Land: Anger and Mourning on the American Right* (New York: New Press, 2016).

51. Sherry B. Ortner, *Not Hollywood: Independent Film at the Twilight of the American Dream* (Durham, NC: Duke University Press, 2013), 194–98.

52. Selina Todd, *The People: The Rise and Fall of the Working Class, 1910–2010* (London: John Murray, 2014), 4.

53. Sennett and Cobb, *Hidden Injuries*, 10.

54. Ivakhiv, *Claiming Sacred Ground*, 161–65.

55. David Wachsmuth and Alexander Weisler, "Airbnb and the Rent Gap: Gentrification through the Sharing Economy," *Environment and Planning A: Economy and Space* 50, no. 6 (2018): 1147–70.

56. Walt Disney owned a ranch near the creek in West Sedona on the street that was later

called "Disney Lane." Thunder Mountain in Sedona was said by locals to be the model for the Big Thunder Mountain Railroad ride in Disney World, Florida.

57. Katherine S. Newman, *Falling from Grace: Downward Mobility in the Age of Affluence* (Berkeley: University of California Press,1988), 233.

58. Sennett, *Respect*, 12.

59. David R. Roediger, *The Wages of Whiteness: Race and the Making of the American Working Class* (London: Verso, 2007); Edward E. Baptist, *The Half Has Never Been Told: Slavery and the Making of American Capitalism* (New York: Basic Books, 2014); Sven Beckert, *Empire of Cotton: A Global History* (New York: Vintage, 2015).

60. Ortner, "Identities," 7. It is interesting to think through Ortner's point in relation to the recent discursive emergence of the white working class. Of course, Ortner wrote this paper nearly two decades before the 2016 election. However, there is perhaps a relationship between the deployment of a reified category of white working class and the white supremacist backlash against the first black president. In a sense, it is a reclamation of subjugated status for white people against perceived "advantages" given to blacks and Hispanics based on their subjugated status; see Hochschild, *Strangers in Their Own Land*, 221–30.

61. Sennett and Cobb, *Hidden Injuries*, 193.

62. Khan, *Development of the Concept*, 76–103; Ernest Mandel, "The Causes of Alienation," in *The Marxist Theory of Alienation: Three Essays*, edited by Ernest Mandel and George Novack (Atlanta: Pathfinder, 1970), 13–16.

63. Khan, *Development of the Concept*, 28–29.

64. Sennett and Cobb, *Hidden Injuries*, 208.

65. Before Elizabeth's speech, I approached her, introduced myself, and explained why I was in Sedona and where I was from. She was amazed, as not many people do PhDs in anthropology at LSE. She was only the 200th in its 100-year history. It was too eerie of a coincidence, she claimed; it must be "an incredible synchronicity." Conferring with the conference organizer, who said it gave her chills, they said this meeting was meant to happen and we had something to do here.

66. Krista's YouTube channel: https://www.youtube.com/channel/UCgcLitnZO-nGpOyeS8jck5g, and her Etsy store: https://www.etsy.com/uk/shop/kristasangels?ref=pr_shop_more, where products include crystal jewelry, a hat that says "starseed," and a font called "galactic faery."

67. For example, "What Is a Real Friend?" and "Find Your Starseed Origins Exercise."

68. Ra had his own YouTube channel with Arcturan channelings: https://www.youtube.com/user/SIRIUSSTARSEED, and the Sa-Ra key was available here: http://www.sovereign-alliance.com/products/practitioner-tools/sara-key/.

69. Wacquant, *Punishing the Poor*, 76–109.

70. Ortner, "Identities," 8.

71. Jean Burgess and Joshua Green, *YouTube: Online Video and Participatory Culture*, 2nd ed. (Cambridge: Polity, 2018), 4–6.

72. Julian Hopkins, *Monetising the Dividual Self: The Emergence of the Lifestyle Blog and Influencers in Malaysia* (New York: Berghahn Books, 2019).

73. Gershon, *Down and Out*, 14–16.

74. Khan, *Development of the Concept*; Ernest Mandel and George Edward Novack, *The Marxist Theory of Alienation: Three Essays* (Atlanta: Pathfinder, 1970).

75. Mandel, "Causes of Alienation," 16.

76. Max Horkheimer and Theodor W. Adorno, *Dialectic of Enlightenment: Philosophical Fragments*, translated by Gunzelin Schmid Noerr and Edmund Jephcott (Palo Alto: Stanford University Press, 2002), 94.

77. Christopher F. Roth, "Ufology as Anthropology: Race, Extraterrestrials, and the Occult," in *E.T. Culture: Anthropology in Outerspaces*, edited by Debbora Battaglia (Durham, NC: Duke University Press, 2005), 89–92.

78. J. Gordon Melton, "The Contactees: A Survey," in *The Gods Have Landed: New Religions from Other Worlds*, edited by James R. Lewis (Albany: State University of New York Press, 1995), 1–12.

CHAPTER FOUR

1. Elizabeth Pleck, "The Making of the Domestic Occasion: The History of Thanksgiving in the United States," *Journal of Social History* 32, no. 4 (1999): 773–89.

2. Lauren Berlant, "Slow Death (Sovereignty, Obesity, Lateral Agency)," *Critical Inquiry* 33, no. 4 (2007): 772.

3. Berlant, "Slow Death," 764.

4. Berlant, "Slow Death," 766.

5. Berlant, "Slow Death," 775.

6. Berlant, "Slow Death," 779.

7. Janet Carsten, *The Heat of the Hearth: The Process of Kinship in a Malay Fishing Community* (Oxford: Clarendon Press, 1997), 12.

8. Carsten, *The Heat of the Hearth*, 166.

9. Carsten, *The Heat of the Hearth*, 175.

10. Maurice Bloch, "Commensality and Poisoning," *Social Research* 66, no. 1 (1999): 133–49.

11. On the religious overtones of gluten-free diets and the lack of scientific basis for the health claims for people without celiac disease, see Alan Levinovitz, *The Gluten Lie: And Other Myths about What You Eat* (New York: Reagan Arts, 2015).

12. Soy is an interesting case of a foodstuff that has fallen in and out of favor with the organic and artisanal food movements. Originally imported from Japan by Buddhist-influenced hippies in the 1960s, soy was marketed as a more environmentally friendly protein source than meat. Later its association with genetic modification and the level of industrial processing that goes into production has led to its ill repute among the same sorts of consumers; see Samuel Fromartz, *Organic, Inc.: Natural Foods and How They Grew* (San Diego, CA: Harcourt, 2006), 157–67.

13. Claude Lévi-Strauss, *The Raw and the Cooked* (London: Cape, 1970).

14. Claude Lévi-Strauss, "The Culinary Triangle," in *Food and Culture: A Reader*, edited by Carole Counihan and Penny Van Esterik, 3rd ed. (London: Routledge, 2013), 41; see

also Dylan Clark, "The Raw and the Rotten: Punk Cuisine," *Ethnology* 43, no. 1 (2004): 19–31.

15. Jennifer Brady and Matthew Ventresca, "'Officially A Vegan Now': On Meat and Renaissance Masculinity in Pro Football," *Food and Foodways* 22, no. 4 (October 2, 2014): 310.

16. On veganism and vegetarianism in American culture as a way to distance oneself from normative values, see Annie Blazer, "Hallelujah Acres: Christian Raw Foods and the Quest for Health," in *Religion, Food, and Eating in North America*, edited by Benjamin E. Zeller (New York: Columbia University Press, 2014), 68–85; Benjamin E. Zeller, "Quasi-Religious American Foodways: The Cases of Vegetarianism and Locavorism," in *Religion, Food, and Eating in North America*, edited by Benjamin E. Zeller (New York: Columbia University Press, 2014), 294–320.

17. Mary Douglas, *Purity and Danger: An Analysis of Concept of Pollution and Taboo* (London: Routledge, 1984), 3–5.

18. Blazer, "Hallelujah Acres."

19. Amit Desai, "Subaltern Vegetarianism: Witchcraft, Embodiment and Sociality in Central India," *South Asia: Journal of South Asian Studies* 31, no. 1 (2008): 96–117.

20. Desai, "Subaltern Vegetarianism," 97.

21. James Laidlaw, "A Life Worth Leaving: Fasting to Death as Telos of a Jain Religious Life," *Economy and Society* 34, no. 2 (2005): 178–99.

22. Laidlaw, "A Life Worth Leaving," 185.

23. Caroline Walker Bynum, "Fast, Feast, and Flesh: The Religious Significance of Food to Medieval Women," in *Food and Culture: A Reader*, edited by Carole Counihan and Penny Van Esterik, 3rd ed. (London: Routledge, 2013), 253.

24. This again points to the mythic quality of breatharianism. A breatharian in Scotland did indeed starve to death trying to follow this diet; see "Woman 'Starved Herself to Death,'" *BBC News*, September 21, 1999, http://news.bbc.co.uk/1/hi/scotland/453661 .stm. She was part of the "new age" Findhorn community described in Sutcliffe, *Children of the New Age*. See also Susannah Crockford, "Becoming a Being of Pure Consciousness: Fasting and New Age Spirituality," *Nova Religio* 23, no. 1 (2019): 38–59.

25. Douglas, *Purity and Danger*, 8.

26. Findal and Buttercup acknowledged its fractional percentage of alcohol as a benefit; it could act as an alcohol substitute and so raise one's vibration while "detoxifying" the body from the poison of alcohol.

27. "Quest for the Philosopher's Stone," *ORMUS*, http://www.subtleenergies.com/ormus /ormus/ormus.htm, describes ormus from a believer's perspective. As a substance with no scientifically established functional value, it has garnered particular scorn from the skeptic movement; see "Ormus," *Rational Wiki*, http://rationalwiki.org/wiki/Ormus.

28. *Prima materia*, or first matter, is the starting material for all alchemical operations, particularly the creation of the philosopher's stone, the substance used to turn lead into gold, sometimes also thought to be the "elixir of life" that granted immortality. See Stanton J. Linden, *The Alchemy Reader: From Hermes Trismegistus to Isaac Newton* (Cambridge: Cambridge University Press, 2003).

29. C. G. Jung, *Psychology and Alchemy*, 2nd ed. (London: Routledge & Kegan Paul, 1989).

30. Sennett, *Craftsman*, 62.

31. On the crossovers between self-help, spirituality, and business, see Heelas, *Spiritualities of Life*, 151–64; LoRusso, *Spirituality, Corporate Culture, and American Business*, 81–96.

32. Heather Paxson, *The Life of Cheese: Crafting Food and Value in America* (Berkeley: University of California Press, 2013).

33. Heather Paxson, "The 'Art' and 'Science' of Handcrafting Cheese in the United States," *Endeavour* 35, no. 2–3 (2011): 116.

34. Carole M. Counihan, "Food Rules in the United States: Individualism, Control, and Hierarchy," *Anthropological Quarterly* 65, no. 2 (1992): 60–61.

35. Sidney W. Mintz, *Tasting Food, Tasting Freedom: Excursions into Eating, Culture, and the Past* (Boston: Beacon Press, 1996), 85.

36. Paxson, "'Art' and 'Science,'" 116.

37. Heather Paxson, "Post-Pasteurian Cultures: The Microbiopolitics of Raw-Milk Cheese in the United States," *Cultural Anthropology* 23, no. 1 (2008): 16.

38. Fromartz, *Organic*, 204.

39. Allison James, "Eating Green(s): Discourses of Organic Food," in *Environmentalism: The View from Anthropology*, edited by Kay Milton, 2nd ed. (London: Routledge, 2005), 204; Fromartz, *Organic*, 201–5; Julie Guthman, "Fast Food/Organic Food: Reflexive Tastes and the Making of 'Yuppie Chow,'" *Social & Cultural Geography* 4, no. 1 (2003): 46.

40. Guthman, "Fast Food/Organic Food," 51.

41. Blazer, "Hallelujah Acres," 68.

42. Jack Goody, "Industrial Food: Towards the Development of a World Cuisine," in *Food and Culture: A Reader*, edited by Carole Counihan and Penny Van Esterik (London: Routledge, 2013), 74.

43. Sidney W. Mintz, *Sweetness and Power: The Place of Sugar in Modern History* (New York: Viking, 1985).

44. Robert Albritton, "Between Obesity and Hunger: The Capitalist Food Industry," in *Food and Culture: A Reader*, edited by Carole Counihan and Penny Van Esterik, 3rd ed. (New York: Routledge, 2013), 342–52.

45. A GED is the most basic form of qualification obtainable in the American education system. It is for those who do not complete the high school diploma and can be attained through sitting for an exam.

46. In 2019, she posted on Facebook that during this time she had been suffering from an eating disorder, which she concealed from those she knew, binge-eating thousands of calories in secret.

47. Pierre Bourdieu, *Distinction: A Social Critique of the Judgement of Taste* (London: Routledge & Kegan Paul, 1984).

48. Guthman, "Fast Food/Organic Food," 54–55.

49. On the "libertarian spirituality" underpinning the Whole Foods Market brand, see LoRusso, *Spirituality, Corporate Culture, and American Business*, 108–14.

50. For more on the widespread opposition to the addition of fluoride to drinking water as a public health measure, see Gretchen Ann Reilly, "'Not a So-Called Democracy': Anti-Fluoridationists and the Fight over Drinking Water," in *The Politics of Healing: Histories of Alternative Medicine in Twentieth-Century North America*, edited by Robert D. Johnston (London: Routledge, 2004), 131–49.

51. Guthman, "Fast Food/Organic Food," 46.

52. Marion Nestle, "Hunger in America: A Matter of Policy," *Social Research* 66, no. 1 (1999): 261.

53. Nestle, "Hunger in America," 260; Albritton, "Between Obesity and Hunger," 342–43.

54. Jerry Shannon, "Food Deserts: Governing Obesity in the Neoliberal City," *Progress in Human Geography* 38, no. 2 (2014): 248–66; Sarah Whitley, "Changing Times in Rural America: Food Assistance and Food Insecurity in Food Deserts," *Journal of Family Social Work* 16, no. 1 (2013): 36–52.

55. James E. McWilliams, *A Revolution in Eating: How the Quest for Food Shaped America* (New York: Columbia University Press, 2005), 5–16.

56. On slow food, see Wendy Parkins and Geoffrey Craig, *Slow Living* (Oxford: Berg, 2006); Wendy Parkins, "Out of Time," *Time & Society* 13, no. 2–3 (2004): 363–82; Alison Leitch, "Slow Food and the Politics of Pork Fat: Italian Food and European Identity," *Ethnos* 68, no. 4 (2003): 437–62.

57. See the moving account by Sarah S. Lochlann Jain, *Malignant: How Cancer Becomes Us* (Oakland: University of California Press, 2013).

58. Diet as a cure for cancer has been touted since at least the Gerson Therapy and macrobiotic diets gained popularity in the 1920s and 1930s; see Albanese, *A Republic of Mind and Spirit*, 484–87. At the Raw Food Expo in Sedona that I attended in 2013, one of the speakers claimed to have cured his cancer through a raw vegetable and fruit juice diet; however, he made clear that although he believed this, he was not legally allowed to make such a claim. At the alchemy workshop, where one of the attendees claimed to have cured her inoperable liver and bowel with a plant-based, alkaline diet, Findal was careful not to make medical claims about the elixirs he brewed when questioned about cancer.

59. Counihan, "Food Rules"; Helen Gremillion, "The Cultural Politics of Body Size," *Annual Review of Anthropology* 34, no. 1 (2005): 13–32; Susie Orbach, *Hunger Strike: The Anorectic's Struggle as a Metaphor for Our Age* (London: Faber, 1986).

60. On the religious roots of the American culture of physical improvement, see R. Marie Griffiths, *Born Again Bodies: Flesh and Spirit in American Christianity* (Berkeley: University of California Press, 2004); Mary Elizabeth Lelwica, *Shameful Bodies: Religion and the Culture of Physical Improvement* (London: Bloomsbury, 2017).

61. Antoine Faivre, *Access to Western Esotericism* (Albany: State University of New York Press, 1994), 10–11.

CHAPTER FIVE

1. Karl Popper, *The Open Society and Its Enemies*, 5th rev. ed. (Princeton, NJ: Princeton University Press, 1966), 297; Alfred Moore, "Conspiracy and Conspiracy Theories in Democratic Politics," *Critical Review* 28, no. 1 (2016): 3.

2. Richard Hofstadter, *The Paranoid Style in American Politics, and Other Essays* (New York: Knopf, 1965); Ted Goertzel, "Belief in Conspiracy Theories," *Political Psychology*

15, no. 4 (1994): 731–42; Jovan Byford, *Conspiracy Theories: A Critical Introduction* (London: Palgrave Macmillan, 2011); Joseph E. Uscinski and Joseph M. Parent, *American Conspiracy Theories* (Oxford: Oxford University Press, 2014); Cass R. Sunstein and Adrian Vermeule, "Conspiracy Theories: Causes and Cures," *Journal of Political Philosophy* 17, no. 2 (2009): 202–27; Russell Muirhead and Nancy L. Rosenblum, "Speaking Truth to Conspiracy: Partisanship and Trust," *Critical Review* 28, no. 1 (2016): 63–88.

3. Moore, "Conspiracy and Conspiracy Theories," 6.

4. Moore, "Conspiracy and Conspiracy Theories," 7.

5. Mathijs Pelkmans and Rhys Machold, "Conspiracy Theories and Their Truth Trajectories," *Focaal* 59 (2011): 66–80; Didier Fassin, "The Politics of Conspiracy Theories: On AIDS in South Africa and a Few Other Global Plots," *Brown Journal of World Affairs* 17, no. 2 (2011): 39–50; Todd Sanders and Harry G. West, "Power Revealed and Concealed in the New World Order," in *Transparency and Conspiracy: Ethnographies of Suspicion in the New World Order*, edited by Harry G. West and Todd Sanders (Durham, NC: Duke University Press, 2003); Nayanika Mathur, "'It's a Conspiracy Theory *and* Climate Change': Of Beastly Encounters and Cervine Disappearances in Himalayan India," *HAU: Journal of Ethnographic Theory* 5, no. 1 (2015): 87; Judith Bovensiepen, "Visions of Prosperity and Conspiracy in Timor-Leste," *Focaal*, no. 75 (2016): 75–88; Leslie Butt, "'Lipstick Girls' and 'Fallen Women': AIDS and Conspiratorial Thinking in Papua, Indonesia," *Cultural Anthropology* 20, no. 3 (2005): 412–42.

6. Michael T. Taussig, *Shamanism, Colonialism, and the Wild Man: A Study in Terror and Healing* (Chicago: University of Chicago Press, 1987); Jean Comaroff and John L. Comaroff, eds., *Millennial Capitalism and the Culture of Neoliberalism* (Durham, NC: Duke University Press, 2001); Nancy Scheper-Hughes, *Death Without Weeping: The Violence of Everyday Life in Brazil* (Berkeley: University of California Press, 1993); Karen A. Kroeger, "AIDS Rumors, Imaginary Enemies, and the Body Politic in Indonesia," *American Ethnologist* 30, no. 2 (2003): 243–57; Karen Dubinsky, *Babies Without Borders: Adoption and Migration across the Americas* (New York: New York University Press, 2010); Eirik Saethre and Jonathan Stadler, "Malicious Whites, Greedy Women, and Virtuous Volunteers: Negotiating Social Relations through Clinical Trial Narratives in South Africa," *Medical Anthropology Quarterly* 27, no. 1 (2013): 103–20; Jane Parish, "The Age of Anxiety," in *The Age of Anxiety: Conspiracy Theory and the Human Sciences*, edited by Martin Parker and Jane Parish (Oxford: Blackwell/Sociological Review, 2001), 1–16.

7. Butt, "'Lipstick Girls' and 'Fallen Women,'" 414.

8. Sanders and West, "Power Revealed and Concealed," 13.

9. Pelkmans and Machold, "Conspiracy Theories," 68.

10. Robertson, *UFOs, Conspiracy Theories and the New Age*, 210–12.

11. The example given by Alfred Gell is of stones believed to grant wishes and answer prayers, which are not mistaken for persons but granted special properties in specific situations revealed only through initiation (*Art and Agency*, 123).

12. Sanders and West, "Power Revealed and Concealed," 14.

13. Taussig, *Shamanism, Colonialism, and the Wild Man*.

14. David Graeber, *The Utopia of Rules: On Technology, Stupidity, and the Secret Joys of Bureaucracy* (New York: Melville House, 2015), 167.

15. Justine M. Bakker, "Hidden Presence: Race and/in the History, Construct, and Study of Western Esotericism," *Religion* 49 (2019): 14–15.

16. Ian Hacking, *The Emergence of Probability: A Philosophical Study of Early Ideas about Probability, Induction and Statistical Inference*, 2nd ed. (Cambridge: Cambridge University Press, 2006), 32.

17. Jason Ānanda Josephson-Storm, *The Myth of Disenchantment: Magic, Modernity, and the Birth of the Human Sciences* (Chicago: University of Chicago Press, 2017); Wouter J. Hanegraaff, *Esotericism and the Academy: Rejected Knowledge in Western Culture* (Cambridge: Cambridge University Press, 2012).

18. Dustin Tingley and Gernot Wagner, "Solar Geoengineering and the Chemtrails Conspiracy on Social Media," *Palgrave Communications* 3, no. 1 (2017): 1–7; Andrea Ballatore, "Google Chemtrails: A Methodology to Analyze Topic Representation in Search Engine Results," *First Monday* 20, no. 7 (2015): 1–21.

19. "Contrails Factsheet" released by the Environmental Protection Agency (EPA) in 2000; Stephen Fraser, "Phantom Menace? Are Conspirators Using Aircraft to Pollute the Skies?," *Current Science* 94, no. 14 (2009): 8–9; "Contrail Facts" released by the US Air Force; Canadian government response: http://holmestead.ca/chemtrails/response-en.html; UK government response: https://www.publications.parliament.uk/pa/cm200506/cmhansrd/vo051108/text/51108w11.htm.

20. An alternative explanation that was rumored by performers in her show was that she did not have any money left and had no choice but to return to her parents' home in Minnesota.

21. Sedona has a small private airport, which is itself subject to conspiracy theories that pilots dump jet fuel in order to take off because the runway is too short, as mentioned in chapter one. A petition was circulated online against this: https://www.change.org/p/stop-jet-fuel-dumping-save-the-sedona-sanctuary. Sedona is, however, in the flight path between Phoenix and Las Vegas, and Phoenix and Flagstaff, as well as other cities to the northwest. Due to the prevalence of domestic air travel, there are few areas in the continental United States that are not subject to overhead air traffic.

22. Lawrence Quill, "Technological Conspiracies: Comte, Technology, and Spiritual Despotism," *Critical Review* 28, no. 1 (2016): 92.

23. Water vapor, which is what constitutes contrails, is a greenhouse gas, and the lingering cirrus clouds result in radiative forcing, which means more of the sun's heat is trapped in the atmosphere; see Lisa Bock and Ulrike Burkhardt, "Contrail Cirrus Radiative Forcing for Future Air Traffic," *Atmospheric Chemistry and Physics* 19 no. 12 (2019): 8163–74.

24. On the politics and economics of climate change, see Kate Ervine, *Carbon* (Cambridge: Polity, 2018); William T. Vollmann, *No Immediate Danger: Volume One of Carbon Ideologies* (New York: Viking, 2018); Naomi Klein, *This Changes Everything: Capitalism vs. the Climate* (New York: Simon and Schuster, 2014).

25. Fassin, "Politics of Conspiracy Theories," 42.

26. Alexandra Bakalaki, "Chemtrails, Crisis, and Loss in an Interconnected World," *Visual Anthropology Review* 32, no. 1 (2016): 12–23.

27. Kevin Surprise, "Stratospheric Imperialism: Liberalism, (Eco)Modernization, and Ideologies of Solar Geoengineering Research," *Environment and Planning E: Nature and Space* (April 2019), 1–23; Rose Cairns, "Climates of Suspicion: 'Chemtrail' Conspiracy Narratives and the International Politics of Geoengineering," *Geographical Journal* 182, no. 1 (2016): 70–84.

28. For instance, an Aurora Flight Sciences report from the University of Calgary published in 2011 of a cost-benefit analysis of geoengineering was linked by worldtruth.tv as confirming chemtrails were real. See Luemas, "Chemtrail Whistleblower Speaks," *World Truth TV*, http://worldtruth.tv/chemtrail-whistleblower-speaks/, accessed April 25, 2020.

29. Tamzy J. House, James B. Near, William B. Shields, Ronald J. Celentano, David M. Husband, Ann E. Mercer, and James E. Pugh, "Weather as a Force Multiplier: Owning the Weather in 2025" (1996).

30. Clyde Haberman, "Agent Orange's Long Legacy, for Vietnam and Veterans," *New York Times*, May 12, 2014, https://www.nytimes.com/2014/05/12/us/agent-oranges-long-legacy-for-vietnam-and-veterans.html?_r=0, accessed April 25, 2020.

31. Robert Alan Goldberg, *Enemies Within: The Culture of Conspiracy in Modern America* (New Haven, CT: Yale University Press, 2001), ix; Mark Fenster, *Conspiracy Theories: Secrecy and Power in American Culture*, rev. ed. (Minneapolis: University of Minnesota Press, 2008), 9.

32. Uscinski and Parent, *American Conspiracy Theories*, 2.

33. On Icke and Reptilians, see Michael Barkun, *A Culture of Conspiracy: Apocalyptic Visions in Contemporary America* (Berkeley: University of California Press, 2003), 98–108; Robertson, *UFOs, Conspiracy Theories and the New Age*, 139–44.

34. Byford, *Conspiracy Theories*, 72.

35. Robertson, *UFOs, Conspiracy Theories and the New Age*, 10–11.

36. Dan Frosch and Kirk Johnson, "Shooting at Colorado Theater Showing Batman Movie," *New York Times*, July 21, 2012, http://www.nytimes.com/2012/07/21/us/shooting-at-colorado-theater-showing-batman-movie.html, accessed April 25, 2020.

37. This quote was originally taken from the Sedona 30 website, www.sedona30.com, which has since been taken down; it has been archived here: https://web.archive.org/web/20160324011256/http://sedona30.com/history.html. See also "Sedona 30 Launches Website," *Sedona.biz*, July 5, 2012, http://www.sedona.biz/news-from-sedona/sedona-30-launches-website/, accessed April 26, 2020.

38. Ryan Randazzo, "State Settles 'Smart' Meter Debate," *Arizona Republic*, December 19, 2014, http://www.azcentral.com/story/money/business/2014/12/12/state-settles-smart-meter-debate/20343257/, accessed April 26, 2020.

39. Sennett and Cobb, *Hidden Injuries*, 159.

40. Quill, "Technological Conspiracies," 2016; Susan Harding and Kathleen Stewart, "Anxieties of Influence: Conspiracy Theory and Therapeutic Culture in Millennial America," in *Transparency and Conspiracy: Ethnographies of Suspicion in the New World Order*,

edited by Harry G. West and Todd Sanders (Durham, NC: Duke University Press, 2003), 258–86; Daniel Hellinger, "Paranoia, Conspiracy, and Hegemony in American Politics," in *Transparency and Conspiracy: Ethnographies of Suspicion in the New World Order*, edited by Harry G. West and Todd Sanders (Durham, NC: Duke University Press, 2003), 204–32.

41. Stef Aupers, "'Trust No One': Modernization, Paranoia and Conspiracy Culture," *European Journal of Communication* 27, no. 1 (2012): 27; Quill, "Technological Conspiracies," 89; Fenster, *Conspiracy Theories*, 1.

42. Jessica Johnson, "The Self-Radicalization of White Men: 'Fake News' and the Affective Networking of Paranoia," *Communication, Culture and Critique* 11, no. 1 (2018): 100–115.

43. Interestingly, in response to "fake news" criticisms, Google de-indexed Natural News, so it no longer showed up in search results. Natural News responded with claims that this was a "conspiracy" against them; see "Why Did Google Penalize NaturalNews.com in February 2017?," *Telapost*, February 22, 2017, https://www.telapost.com/natural-news -google-penalty/. It has subsequently been removed from a range of internet platforms, including Twitter and Facebook; see Beth Mole, "Facebook Bans Health and Conspiracy Site Natural News," *Ars Technica*, June 10, 2019, https://arstechnica.com/science /2019/06/natural-news-hawker-of-vitamins-and-far-right-conspiracies-banned-from -facebook/. Following an investigation into its slide from selling supplements to focusing primarily on conspiracy theories, see Kelly Weill, "The New Infowars Is a Vitamin Site Predicting the Apocalypse," *Daily Beast*, June 8, 2019 [updated January 20, 2020], https://www.thedailybeast.com/how-natural-news-became-a-conspiracy-hub-rivaling -infowars.

44. For example, a frequent post made by my interlocutors was articles claiming that 75 percent of doctors would refuse chemotherapy themselves. It was used to claim that chemotherapy was ineffective and only offered to the masses to make money for "Big Pharma"; see S. D. Wells, "75% of Physicians in the World Refuse Chemotherapy for Themselves," *Natural News*, January 3, 2012, http://www.naturalnews.com/036054 _chemotherapy_physicians_toxicity.html; and the rebuttal of the cited study, "Do Doctors Refuse Chemotherapy on Themselves?," *Anaximperator Blog*, May 6, 2010, https:// anaximperator.wordpress.com/2010/05/06/do-75-of-doctors-refuse-chemotherapy-on -themselves/.

45. For example, see Mike Adams, "Shameless Health Authorities Keep Pushing Flu Vaccines Even after Openly Admitting They Don't Work," *Natural News*, December 20, 2014, http://www.naturalnews.com/048063_flu_vaccines_junk_science_zealotry.html, where it is claimed that "vaccines are a religion."

46. Egil Asprem, "How Schrödinger's Cat Became a Zombie," *Method & Theory in the Study of Religion* 28, no. 2 (2016): 113–40; Hammer, *Claiming Knowledge*, 201–330.

47. Hammer, *Claiming Knowledge*, 206.

48. Byford, *Conspiracy Theories*, 89.

49. Uscinski and Parent, *American Conspiracy Theories*, 50.

50. Pelkmans and Machold, "Conspiracy Theories," 69.

51. Uscinski and Parent, *American Conspiracy Theories*, 33.

52. Dan Sperber, *Explaining Culture: A Naturalistic Approach* (Oxford: Blackwell, 1996), 96.

53. Hugh Gusterson, "How Rumors Tap and Fuel Anxieties in the Internet Age," *Sapiens*, January 2017, http://www.sapiens.org/column/conflicted/power-of-rumors/.

54. Russell Muirhead and Nancy L. Rosenblum, *A Lot of People Are Saying: The New Conspiracism and the Assault on Democracy* (Princeton, NJ: Princeton University Press, 2019).

55. Uscinski and Parent, *American Conspiracy Theories*, 2–4.

56. Charlotte Ward and David Voas, "The Emergence of Conspirituality," *Journal of Contemporary Religion* 26, no. 1 (2011): 103–21; Egil Asprem and Asbjørn Dyrendal, "Conspirituality Reconsidered: How Surprising and How New Is the Confluence of Spirituality and Conspiracy Theory?," *Journal of Contemporary Religion* 30, no. 3 (2015): 367–82; Aupers, "'Trust No One,'" 31; Whitesides, "2012 Millennialism Becomes Conspiracist Teleology," 30–48; Asbjørn Dyrendal, David G. Robertson, and Egil Asprem, eds., *Handbook of Conspiracy Theory and Contemporary Religion* (Leiden: Brill, 2018).

57. Barkun, *Culture of Conspiracy*, 2.

58. Byford, *Conspiracy Theories*, 23.

59. Ward and Voas, "The Emergence of Conspirituality," 104; Aupers, "'Trust No One,'" 30.

60. Robertson, *UFOs, Conspiracy Theories and the New Age*, 5–6.

61. Susannah Crockford, "Thank God for the Greatest Country on Earth: White Supremacy, Vigilantes, and Survivalists in the Struggle to Define the American Nation," *Religion, State and Society* 46, no. 3 (2018): 224–42; "Becoming a Being of Pure Consciousness," 46–50.

62. Aupers, "'Trust No One,'" 24.

63. Uscinski and Parent, *American Conspiracy Theories*, 2–3.

64. Volker Heins, "Critical Theory and the Traps of Conspiracy Thinking," *Philosophy & Social Criticism* 33, no. 7 (2007): 790.

65. One of the two country music stations in northern Arizona had a break from their scheduled airplay at noon each day to "thank god that we live in the greatest country on earth," and then played the opening bars of the "Star-Spangled Banner."

66. Uscinksi and Parent, *American Conspiracy Theories*, 13.

67. Ward and Voas, "The Emergence of Conspirituality," 104.

68. Asprem and Dyrendal, "Conspirituality Reconsidered," 374.

CONCLUSION

1. Pamela lived in Sedona, where I met her. She had been struck by lightning several times, and had a metal plate in her head. On her relationship with Icke, see Robertson, *UFOs, Conspiracy Theories and the New Age*, 139–40.

2. Toltec is the name given to the archaeological remains of a Mesoamerican state found in what is now Hidalgo, Mexico. Toltec shamanism was popularized as a form of neo-shamanism drawing on Mexican cultural history and cosmologies of spirituality by Don Miguel Ruiz, an author and shaman who has appeared on Oprah Winfrey's and

Ellen de Generes's television programs. See Brett Hendrickson, "Neo-Shamans, *Curanderismo* and Scholars: Metaphysical Blending in Contemporary Mexican American Folk Healing," *Nova Religio* 19, no. 1 (2015), 39–40.

3. Dumit, "Playing Truths," 73.

4. Off-grid generally means not connected to the power, water, or sewage grids. On off-grid living and the forms this can take, see Phillip Vannini and Jonathan Taggart, *Off the Grid: Re-Assembling Domestic Life* (London: Routledge, 2015).

5. For further discussion of Valle, survivalism, and off-grid social life, see Crockford, "Thank God for the Greatest Country on Earth," 235–37; "Digging Holes, Posting Signs, Loading Guns: Constructing Home Near the Grand Canyon," in *Home: Ethnographic Encounters*, edited by Johannes Lenhard and Farhan Samanani (London: Bloomsbury Academic, 2020), 87–100.

BIBLIOGRAPHY

Albanese, Catherine L. 2007. "Introduction: Awash in a Sea of Metaphysics." *Journal of the American Academy of Religion* 75 (3): 582–88.

———. 1990. *Nature Religion in America: From the Algonkian Indians to the New Age.* Chicago: University of Chicago Press.

———. 2002. *Reconsidering Nature Religion.* Harrisburg, PA: Trinity.

———. 2006. *A Republic of Mind and Spirit: A Cultural History of American Metaphysical Religion.* New Haven, CT: Yale University Press.

Albritton, Robert. 2013. "Between Obesity and Hunger: The Capitalist Food Industry." In *Food and Culture: A Reader,* edited by Carole Counihan and Penny Van Esterik, 3rd ed., 342–52. New York: Routledge.

Aldred, Lisa. 2000. "Plastic Shamans and Astroturf Sun Dances: New Age Commercialization of Native American Spirituality." *American Indian Quarterly* 24 (3): 329–52.

Allanach, Jack, and Osho World Foundation. 2013. *Osho, India and Me: A Tale of Sexual and Spiritual Transformation.* New Delhi: Niyogi Books.

Ames, Melissa. 2012. "Introduction: Television Studies in the 21st Century." In *Time in Television Narrative: Exploring Temporality in Twenty-First Century Programming,* edited by Melissa Ames, 4–19. Jackson: University Press of Mississippi.

Ammerman, Nancy Tatom. 1987. *Bible Believers: Fundamentalists in the Modern World.* New Brunswick, NJ: Rutgers University Press.

———. 2005. *Pillars of Faith: American Congregations and Their Partners.* Berkeley: University of California Press.

Andres, Dennis. 2000. *What Is a Vortex? Sedona's Vortex Sites, a Practical Guide.* Sedona, AZ: Meta Adventures.

Apolito, Paolo. 2005. *The Internet and the Madonna: Religious Visionary Experience on the Web.* Chicago: University of Chicago Press.

Asad, Talal. 1973. *Anthropology and the Colonial Encounter.* Reading: Ithaca Press.

Asprem, Egil. 2016. "How Schrödinger's Cat Became a Zombie." *Method & Theory in the Study of Religion* 28 (2): 113–40.

———. 2014. *The Problem of Disenchantment: Scientific Naturalism and Esoteric Discourse, 1900–1939.* Leiden: Brill.

Asprem, Egil, and Asbjørn Dyrendal. 2015. "Conspirituality Reconsidered: How Surpris-
    ing and How New Is the Confluence of Spirituality and Conspiracy Theory?" *Journal
    of Contemporary Religion* 30 (3): 367–82.
Aupers, Stef. 2012. "'Trust No One': Modernization, Paranoia and Conspiracy Culture."
    European Journal of Communication 27 (1): 22–34.
Austin, John Langshaw. 1975. *How to Do Things with Words*. Edited by J. O. Urmson and
    Marina Sbisà. 2nd ed. Cambridge, MA: Harvard University Press.
Aveni, Anthony. 2009. *The End of Time: The Maya Mystery of 2012*. Boulder: University
    Press of Colorado.
Ayres, Toraya. 1997. *The History of New Age Sedona*. Cedar City, UT: High Mountain
    Training and Publishing.
Bakalaki, Alexandra. 2016. "Chemtrails, Crisis, and Loss in an Interconnected World."
    Visual Anthropology Review 32 (1): 12–23.
Bakker, Justine M. 2019. "Hidden Presence: Race and/in the History, Construct, and
    Study of Western Esotericism." *Religion* 49: 1–25.
Ballatore, Andrea. 2015. "Google Chemtrails: A Methodology to Analyze Topic Represen-
    tation in Search Engine Results." *First Monday* 20 (7): 1–21.
Baptist, Edward E. 2014. *The Half Has Never Been Told: Slavery and the Making of
    American Capitalism*. New York: Basic Books.
Barad, Karen Michelle. 2007. *Meeting the Universe Halfway: Quantum Physics and the En-
    tanglement of Matter and Meaning*. Durham, NC: Duke University Press.
Barkun, Michael. 2003. *A Culture of Conspiracy: Apocalyptic Visions in Contemporary
    America*. Berkeley: University of California Press.
———. 1994. "Reflections after Waco: Millennialists and the State." In *From the Ashes:
    Making Sense of Waco*, edited by James R. Lewis, 41–50. Lanham, MD: Rowman &
    Littlefield.
Barrow, John D. 2007. "Living in a Simulated Universe." Unpublished paper, https://www
    .simulation-argument.com/barrowsim.pdf, accessed April 27, 2020.
Battaglia, Debbora, ed. 2005. *E.T. Culture: Anthropology in Outerspaces*. Durham, NC:
    Duke University Press.
Baudrillard, Jean. 2012. *The Ecstasy of Communication*. Los Angeles: Semiotext(e).
———. 1983. *Simulations*. Los Angeles: Semiotext(e).
Beckert, Sven. 2015. *Empire of Cotton: A Global History*. New York: Vintage.
Bellah, Robert N. 1985. *Habits of the Heart: Individualism and Commitment in American
    Life*. Berkeley: University of California Press.
Bender, Courtney. 2010. *The New Metaphysicals: Spirituality and the American Religious
    Imagination*. Chicago: University of Chicago Press.
Bender, Courtney, and Omar McRoberts. 2012. "Mapping a Field: Why and How to Study
    Spirituality." *SSRC Working Papers* (October): 1–27.
Bennett, Lucy. 2012. "Lost in Time? *Lost* Fan Engagement with Temporal Play." In *Time
    in Television Narrative: Exploring Temporality in Twenty-First Century Programming*,
    edited by Melissa Ames, 297–308. Jackson: University Press of Mississippi.
Benson, Michaela, and Karen O'Reilly, eds. 2009. *Lifestyle Migration: Expectations, Aspi-
    rations and Experiences*. Farnham: Ashgate.

Berlant, Lauren. 2007. "Slow Death (Sovereignty, Obesity, Lateral Agency)." *Critical Inquiry* 33 (4): 754–80.

Bérubé, Michael. 2000. "Autobiography as Performative Utterance." *American Quarterly* 52 (2): 339–43.

Blair, Gwenda. 2016. *The Trumps: Three Generations of Builders and a Presidential Candidate*. New York: Simon & Schuster.

Blazer, Annie. 2014. "Hallelujah Acres: Christian Raw Foods and the Quest for Health." In *Religion, Food, and Eating in North America*, edited by Benjamin E. Zeller, 68–85. New York: Columbia University Press.

Bloch, Maurice. 2011. "The Blob." *Anthropology of This Century*, no. 1, online version.

———. 1999. "Commensality and Poisoning." *Social Research* 66 (1): 133–49.

———. 2008. "Why Religion Is Nothing Special but Is Central." *Philosophical Transactions of the Royal Society B: Biological Sciences* 363 (1499 [June 12]): 2055–61.

Bluck, R. S. 1958. "Plato, Pindar, and Metempsychosis." *American Journal of Philology* 79 (4): 405–14.

Bock, Lisa, and Ulrike Burkhardt. 2019. "Contrail Cirrus Radiative Forcing for Future Air Traffic." *Atmospheric Chemistry and Physics* 19 (12): 8163–74.

Bodenhorn, Barbara, and Gabriele vom Bruck. 2009. "'Entangled in Histories': An Introduction to the Anthropology of Names and Naming." In *The Anthropology of Names and Naming*, edited by Gabriele vom Bruck and Barbara Bodenhorn, 1–30. Cambridge: Cambridge University Press.

Bostrom, Nick. 2003. "Are You Living in a Computer Simulation?" *Philosophical Quarterly* 53 (211): 243–55.

Bourdieu, Pierre. 1998. *Acts of Resistance: Against the New Myths of Our Time*. Cambridge: Polity Press.

———. 1984. *Distinction: A Social Critique of the Judgement of Taste*. London: Routledge & Kegan Paul.

Bovensiepen, Judith. 2016. "Visions of Prosperity and Conspiracy in Timor-Leste." *Focaal* 75: 75–88.

Bowler, Kate. 2013. *Blessed: A History of the American Prosperity Gospel*. Oxford: Oxford University Press.

———. 2018. *Everything Happens for a Reason: And Other Lies I've Loved*. New York: Random House.

Braatz, Timothy. 2003. *Surviving Conquest: A History of the Yavapai Peoples*. Lincoln: University of Nebraska Press.

Brady, Jennifer, and Matthew Ventresca. 2014. "'Officially A Vegan Now': On Meat and Renaissance Masculinity in Pro Football." *Food and Foodways* 22 (4 [October 2]): 300–321.

Brown, Bridget. 2007. *They Know Us Better Than We Know Ourselves: The History and Politics of Alien Abduction*. New York: New York University Press.

Brown, Dee Alexander. 1991. *Bury My Heart at Wounded Knee: An Indian History of the American West*. New York: Vintage.

Brown, Michael F. 1999. *The Channeling Zone: American Spirituality in an Anxious Age*. Cambridge, MA: Harvard University Press.

Bruner, Jerome. 1991. "The Narrative Construction of Reality." *Critical Inquiry* 18 (1): 1–21.

Burgess, Jean, and Joshua Green. 2018. *YouTube: Online Video and Participatory Culture.* 2nd ed. Cambridge: Polity.

Butt, Leslie. 2005. "'Lipstick Girls' and 'Fallen Women': AIDS and Conspiratorial Thinking in Papua, Indonesia." *Cultural Anthropology* 20 (3): 412–42.

Byford, Jovan. 2011. *Conspiracy Theories: A Critical Introduction.* London: Palgrave Macmillan.

Bynum, Caroline Walker. 2013. "Fast, Feast, and Flesh: The Religious Significance of Food to Medieval Women." In *Food and Culture: A Reader*, edited by Carole Counihan and Penny Van Esterik, 3rd ed., 245–64. London: Routledge.

Byrne, Rhonda. 2006. *The Secret.* 10th ed. New York: Atria Books/Beyond Worlds.

Cairns, Rose. 2016. "Climates of Suspicion: 'Chemtrail' Conspiracy Narratives and the International Politics of Geoengineering." *Geographical Journal* 182 (1): 70–84.

Campion, Nicholas. 2016. *The New Age in the Modern West: Counterculture, Utopia and Prophecy from the Late Eighteenth Century to the Present Day.* London: Bloomsbury Academic.

Cannell, Fenella. 2013. "The Re-Enchantment of Kinship." In *Vital Relations: Modernity and the Persistent Life of Kinship*, edited by Susan McKinnon and Fenella Cannell, 217–40. Santa Fe, NM: School for Advanced Research Press.

Carrette, Jeremy, and Richard King. 2005. *Selling Spirituality: The Silent Takeover of Religion.* London: Routledge.

Carsten, Janet. 2004. *After Kinship.* Cambridge: Cambridge University Press.

———. 1997. *The Heat of the Hearth: The Process of Kinship in a Malay Fishing Community.* Oxford: Clarendon Press.

Cederström, Carl, and André Spicer. 2015. *The Wellness Syndrome.* Cambridge: Polity.

Chidester, David. 2003. *Salvation and Suicide: Jim Jones, the Peoples Temple, and Jonestown.* Bloomington: Indiana University Press.

Chidester, David, and Edward T. Linenthal. 1995. "Introduction." In *American Sacred Space*, edited by Edward T. Linenthal and David Chidester, 1–42. Bloomington: Indiana University Press.

Cimino, Richard, and Don Lattin. 2002. *Shopping for Faith: American Religion in the New Millennium.* San Francisco: Jossey-Bass.

Clancy, Susan A. 2005. *Abducted: How People Come to Believe They Were Kidnapped by Aliens.* Cambridge, MA: Harvard University Press.

Clark, Dylan. 2004. "The Raw and the Rotten: Punk Cuisine." *Ethnology* 43 (1): 19–31.

Cohn, Norman. 1993. *The Pursuit of the Millennium: Revolutionary Millenarians and Mystical Anarchists of the Middle Ages.* London: Random House.

Collier, Jane, Michelle Z. Rosaldo, and Sylvia Junko Yanagisako. 1997. "Is There a Family? New Anthropological Views." In *The Gender/Sexuality Reader: Culture, History, Political Economy*, edited by Roger N. Lancaster and Micaela Di Leonardo, 71–77. London: Routledge.

Comaroff, Jean, and John L. Comaroff. 2002. "Alien-Nation: Zombies, Immigrants, and Millennial Capitalism." *South Atlantic Quarterly* 101 (4): 779–805.

———. 2001. "Naturing the Nation: Aliens, Apocalypse and the Postcolonial State." *Journal of Southern African Studies* 27 (3): 627–51.

Comaroff, Jean, and John L. Comaroff, eds. 2001. *Millennial Capitalism and the Culture of Neoliberalism*. Durham, NC: Duke University Press.

Counihan, Carole M. 1992. "Food Rules in the United States: Individualism, Control, and Hierarchy." *Anthropological Quarterly* 65 (2): 55–66.

Couser, G. Thomas. 1989. *Altered Egos: Authority in American Autobiography*. Oxford: Oxford University Press.

Crockford, Susannah. 2019. "Becoming a Being of Pure Consciousness: Fasting and New Age Spirituality." *Nova Religio* 23 (1): 38–59.

———. 2020. "Digging Holes, Posting Signs, Loading Guns: Constructing Home Near the Grand Canyon." In *Home: Ethnographic Encounters*, edited by Johannes Lenhard and Farhan Samanani, 87–100. London: Bloomsbury Academic.

———. 2018. "A Mercury Retrograde Kind of Day: Exploring Astrology in Contemporary New Age Spirituality and American Social Life." *Correspondences* 6 (1): 47–75.

———. 2018. "Thank God for the Greatest Country on Earth: White Supremacy, Vigilantes, and Survivalists in the Struggle to Define the American Nation." *Religion, State and Society* 46 (3): 224–42.

Cronon, William. 1996. *Uncommon Ground: Rethinking the Human Place in Nature*. New York: W. W. Norton.

Cullen, James. 2004. *The American Dream: A Short History of an Idea*. Oxford: Oxford University Press.

D'Andrea, Anthony. 2018. *Reflexive Religion: The New Age in Brazil and Beyond*. Leiden: Brill.

Dannelley, Richard. 1995. *Sedona: Beyond the Vortex: Activating the Planetary Ascension Program*. Flagstaff, AZ: Light Technology Publishing.

———. 1992. *Sedona Power Spot, Vortex & Medicine Wheel Guide*. Sedona, AZ: Vortex Society.

Darling, Eliza. 2005. "City in the Country: Wilderness Gentrification and the Rent Gap." *Environment and Planning A* 37: 1015–32.

———. 2001. "The Lorax Redux: Profit Biggering and Some Selective Silences in American Environmentalism." *Culture and Ecology* 12 (4): 51–66.

Darlington, David. 1997. *Area 51: The Dreamland Chronicles*. New York: H. Holt.

Dawkins, Richard. 1993. "Viruses of the Mind." In *Dennett and His Critics: Demystifying Mind*, edited by Bo Dahlbom, 13–27. Oxford: Blackwell.

Dean, Jodi. 1998. *Aliens in America: Conspiracy Cultures from Outerspace to Cyberspace*. Ithaca, NY: Cornell University Press.

Deloria, Philip Joseph. 1998. *Playing Indian*. New Haven, CT: Yale University Press.

Deloria, Vine. 1969. *Custer Died for Your Sins: An Indian Manifesto*. Norman: University of Oklahoma Press.

———. 2003. *God Is Red: A Native View of Religion*. 3rd ed. Golden, CO: Fulcrum Publications.

Deloria, Vine, and Clifford M. Lytle. 1983. *American Indians, American Justice*. Austin: University of Texas Press.

Denzler, Brenda. 2001. *The Lure of the Edge: Scientific Passions, Religious Beliefs, and the Pursuit of UFOs*. Berkeley: University of California Press.

Desai, Amit. 2008. "Subaltern Vegetarianism: Witchcraft, Embodiment and Sociality in Central India." *South Asia: Journal of South Asian Studies* 31 (1): 96–117.

Doostdar, Alireza. 2018. *The Iranian Metaphysicals: Explorations in Science, Islam, and the Uncanny*. Princeton, NJ: Princeton University Press.

Douglas, Mary. 1984. *Purity and Danger: An Analysis of Concept of Pollution and Taboo*. London: Routledge.

Dubinsky, Karen. 2010. *Babies Without Borders: Adoption and Migration across the Americas*. New York: New York University Press.

Dumit, Joseph. 2001. "Playing Truths: Logics of Seeking and Persistence of the New Age." *Focaal* 37: 63–75.

Durkheim, Émile. 1995. *The Elementary Forms of Religious Life*. Translated by Karen E. Fields. New York: Free Press.

Dyrendal, Asbjørn, David G. Robertson, and Egil Asprem, eds. 2018. *Handbook of Conspiracy Theory and Contemporary Religion*. Leiden: Brill.

Eaton, Kent. 1997. "Beware the Trumpet of Judgement! John Nelson Darby and the Nineteenth-Century Brethren." In *The Coming Deliverer: Millennial Themes in World Religions*, 119–54. Cardiff: University of Wales Press.

Ehrenreich, Barbara. 2009. *Bright-Sided: How Positive Thinking Is Undermining America*. London: Picador.

Eliade, Mircea. 1959. *The Sacred and the Profane: The Nature of Religion*. Translated by Willard R. Trask. New York: Harcourt.

Engelke, Matthew. 2014. "Christianity and the Anthropology of Secular Humanism." *Current Anthropology* 55 (S10): S292–301.

———. 2004. "Discontinuity and the Discourse of Conversion." *Journal of Religion in Africa* 34 (1/2): 82–109.

Ervine, Kate. 2018. *Carbon*. Cambridge: Polity.

Escobar, Arturo. 1999. "After Nature: Steps to an Antiessentialist Political Ecology." *Current Anthropology* 40 (1): 1–30.

Eves, Richard. 2011. "'Great Signs from Heaven': Christian Discourses of the End of the World from New Ireland." *Asia Pacific Journal of Anthropology* 12 (1): 13–28.

Faivre, Antoine. 1994. *Access to Western Esotericism*. Albany: State University of New York Press.

Fassin, Didier. 2011. "The Politics of Conspiracy Theories: On AIDS in South Africa and a Few Other Global Plots." *Brown Journal of World Affairs* 17 (2): 39–50.

Faubion, James D. 2001. *The Shadows and Lights of Waco: Millennialism Today*. Princeton, NJ: Princeton University Press.

Favret-Saada, Jeanne. 1980. *Deadly Words: Witchcraft in the Bocage*. Cambridge: Cambridge University Press.

Fenster, Mark. 2008. *Conspiracy Theories: Secrecy and Power in American Culture*. Rev. ed. Minneapolis: University of Minnesota Press.

Ferguson, Todd W., and Jeffrey A. Tamburello. 2015. "The Natural Environment as a Spiritual Resource: A Theory of Regional Variation in Religious Adherence." *Sociology of Religion* 76 (3): 295–314.

Festinger, Leon, Henry Riecken, and Stanley Schachter. 1956. *When Prophecy Fails*. Minneapolis: University of Minnesota Press.

Fraser, Stephen. 2009. "Phantom Menace? Are Conspirators Using Aircraft to Pollute the Skies?" *Current Science* 94 (14): 8–9.

Fromartz, Samuel. 2006. *Organic, Inc.: Natural Foods and How They Grew*. San Diego, CA: Harcourt.

Fuller, Robert C. 2001. *Spiritual, But Not Religious: Understanding Unchurched America*. Oxford: Oxford University Press.

Gallagher, Eugene V. 2004. *The New Religious Movements Experience in America*. Westport, CT: Greenwood Press.

Gatta, John. 2004. *Making Nature Sacred: Literature, Religion, and Environment in America from the Puritans to the Present*. Oxford: Oxford University Press.

Gelfer, Joseph. 2014. *2012: Decoding the Countercultural Apocalypse*. London: Taylor and Francis.

Gell, Alfred. 1998. *Art and Agency: An Anthropological Theory*. Oxford: Clarendon Press.

Gennep, Arnold van. 1960. *The Rites of Passage*. Chicago: University of Chicago Press.

Gershon, Ilana. 2017. *Down and Out in the New Economy: How People Find (or Don't Find) Work Today*. Chicago: University of Chicago Press.

Goertzel, Ted. 1994. "Belief in Conspiracy Theories." *Political Psychology* 15 (4): 731–42.

Goldberg, Robert Alan. 2001. *Enemies Within: The Culture of Conspiracy in Modern America*. New Haven, CT: Yale University Press.

Goody, Jack. 2013. "Industrial Food: Towards the Development of a World Cuisine." In *Food and Culture: A Reader*, edited by Carole Counihan and Penny Van Esterik, 72–90. London: Routledge.

Graeber, David. 2011. *Debt: The First 5,000 Years*. New York: Melville House.

———. 2015. *The Utopia of Rules: On Technology, Stupidity, and the Secret Joys of Bureaucracy*. New York: Melville House.

Gremillion, Helen. 2005. "The Cultural Politics of Body Size." *Annual Review of Anthropology* 34 (1): 13–32.

Griffiths, R. Marie. 2004. *Born Again Bodies: Flesh and Spirit in American Christianity*. Berkeley: University of California Press.

Grusin, Richard A. 2004. *Culture, Technology, and the Creation of America's National Parks*. Cambridge: Cambridge University Press.

Gusterson, Hugh. 2017. "How Rumors Tap and Fuel Anxieties in the Internet Age." *Sapiens* (January). http://www.sapiens.org/column/conflicted/power-of-rumors/.

Guthman, Julie. 2003. "Fast Food/Organic Food: Reflexive Tastes and the Making of 'Yuppie Chow.'" *Social & Cultural Geography* 4 (1): 45–58.

Hacking, Ian. 2006. *The Emergence of Probability: A Philosophical Study of Early Ideas about Probability, Induction and Statistical Inference*. 2nd ed. Cambridge: Cambridge University Press.

Hammer, Olav. 2004. *Claiming Knowledge: Strategies of Epistemology from Theosophy to the New Age*. Leiden: Brill.

Hanegraaff, Wouter J. 2012. *Esotericism and the Academy: Rejected Knowledge in Western Culture*. Cambridge: Cambridge University Press.

———. 2000. "New Age Religion and Secularization." *Numen* 47: 3: 288–312.

———. 1996. *New Age Religion and Western Culture: Esotericism in the Mirror of Secular Thought*. Leiden: Brill.

Haraway, Donna J. 1991. *Simians, Cyborgs and Women: The Reinvention of Nature*. New York: Routledge.

Harding, Susan. 2001. *The Book of Jerry Falwell: Fundamentalist Language and Politics*. Princeton, NJ: Princeton University Press.

———. 1991. "Representing Fundamentalism: The Problem of the Repugnant Cultural Other." *Social Research* 58: 373–93.

Harding, Susan, and Kathleen Stewart. 2003. "Anxieties of Influence: Conspiracy Theory and Therapeutic Culture in Millennial America." In *Transparency and Conspiracy: Ethnographies of Suspicion in the New World Order*, edited by Harry G. West and Todd Sanders, 258–86. Durham, NC: Duke University Press.

Hardman, Charlotte. 2007. "'He May Be Lying But What He Says Is True': The Sacred Tradition of Don Juan as Reported by Carlos Castaneda, Anthropologist, Trickster, Guru, Allegorist." In *The Invention of Sacred Tradition*, edited by James R. Lewis and Olav Hammer, 38–55. Cambridge: Cambridge University Press.

Harner, Michael J. 1990. *The Way of the Shaman*. New York: Harper & Row.

Harrison, Mike, John Williams, Sigrid Khera, and Carolina C. Butler. 2012. *Oral History of the Yavapai*. Phoenix: Acacia Publications.

Hartigan, John. 2005. *Odd Tribes: Toward a Cultural Analysis of White People*. Durham, NC: Duke University Press.

Harvey, David. 2005. *A Brief History of Neoliberalism*. Oxford: Oxford University Press.

Heelas, Paul. 1996. *The New Age Movement: The Celebration of the Self and the Sacralization of Modernity*. Oxford: Blackwell.

———. 2008. *Spiritualities of Life: New Age Romanticism and Consumptive Capitalism*. Oxford: Blackwell.

Heelas, Paul, Linda Woodhead, Benjamin Seel, Bronislaw Szerszynski, and Karen Tusting. 2005. *The Spiritual Revolution: Why Religion is Giving Way to Spirituality*. Oxford: Wiley-Blackwell.

Heimert, Alan. 1966. *Religion and the American Mind: From the Great Awakening to the Revolution*. Cambridge, MA: Harvard University Press.

Heins, Volker. 2007. "Critical Theory and the Traps of Conspiracy Thinking." *Philosophy & Social Criticism* 33 (7): 787–801.

Hellinger, Daniel. 2003. "Paranoia, Conspiracy, and Hegemony in American Politics." In *Transparency and Conspiracy: Ethnographies of Suspicion in the New World Order*, edited by Harry G. West and Todd Sanders, 204–32. Durham, NC: Duke University Press.

Hendrickson, Brett. 2015. "Neo-Shamans, *Curanderismo* and Scholars: Metaphysical Blending in Contemporary Mexican American Folk Healing." *Nova Religio* 19 (1): 25–44.

Hicks, Esther, and Jerry Hicks. 2006. *The Law of Attraction: The Basics of the Teachings of Abraham*. London: Hay House.

Himsel Burcon, Sarah. 2012. "*Lost* in Our Middle Hour: Faith, Fate, and Redemption Post-9/11." In *Time in Television Narrative: Exploring Temporality in Twenty-First Century Programming*, edited by Melissa Ames, 125–38. Jackson: University Press of Mississippi.

Hindmarsh, D. Bruce. 1999. *The Evangelical Conversion Narrative: Spiritual Autobiography in Early Modern England*. Oxford: Oxford University Press.

Ho, Karen Zouwen. 2009. *Liquidated: An Ethnography of Wall Street*. Durham, NC: Duke University Press.

Hochschild, Arlie Russell. 2016. *Strangers in Their Own Land: Anger and Mourning on the American Right*. New York: New Press.

Hofstadter, Richard. 1965. *The Paranoid Style in American Politics, and Other Essays*. New York: Knopf.

Hopkins, Julian. 2019. *Monetising the Dividual Self: The Emergence of the Lifestyle Blog and Influencers in Malaysia*. New York: Berghahn Books.

Horkheimer, Max, and Theodor W. Adorno. 2002. *Dialectic of Enlightenment: Philosophical Fragments*. Translated by Gunzelin Schmid Noerr and Edmund Jephcott. Palo Alto, CA: Stanford University Press.

House, Tamzy J., James B. Near, William B. Shields, Ronald J. Celentano, David M. Husband, Ann E. Mercer, and James E. Pugh. 1996. "Weather as a Force Multiplier: Owning the Weather in 2025." Research paper presented to Air Force 2025.

Huss, Boaz. 2014. "Spirituality: The Emergence of a New Cultural Category and Its Challenge to the Religious and the Secular." *Journal of Contemporary Religion* 29 (1): 47–60.

Ivakhiv, Adrian. 2001. *Claiming Sacred Ground: Pilgrims and Politics at Glastonbury and Sedona*. Bloomington: Indiana University Press.

———. 1997. "Red Rocks, 'Vortexes' and the Selling of Sedona: Environmental Politics in the New Age." *Social Compass* 44 (3): 367–84.

Jain, Sarah S. Lochlann. 2013. *Malignant: How Cancer Becomes Us*. Oakland: University of California Press.

James, Allison. 2005. "Eating Green(s): Discourses of Organic Food." In *Environmentalism: The View from Anthropology*, edited by Kay Milton, 2nd ed., 204–13. London: Routledge.

Jenkins, Timothy. 2013. *Of Flying Saucers and Social Scientists: A Re-Reading of When Prophecy Fails and of Cognitive Dissonance*. London: Palgrave Macmillan.

Johnson, Hoyt C. 2008. *The Sedona Story: Settlement to Centennial*. Tucson: AzScene Pub. Co.

Johnson, Jessica. 2018. "The Self-Radicalization of White Men: 'Fake News' and the Affective Networking of Paranoia." *Communication, Culture and Critique* 11 (1): 100–115.

Johnson, Paul C. 1995. "Shamanism from Ecuador to Chicago: A Case Study in New Age Ritual Appropriation." *Religion* 25 (2): 163–78.

Johnston, Erin F. 2013. "'I Was Always This Way . . .': Rhetorics of Continuity in Narratives of Conversion." *Sociological Forum* 28 (3): 549–73.

Josephson-Storm, Jason Ānanda. 2017. *The Myth of Disenchantment: Magic, Modernity, and the Birth of the Human Sciences.* Chicago: University of Chicago Press.

Jung, C. G. (Carl Gustav). 1997. *C. G. Jung on Synchronicity and the Paranormal: Key Readings.* London: Routledge.

——. 1989. *Psychology and Alchemy.* 2nd ed. London: Routledge & Kegan Paul.

——. 1973. *Synchronicity: An Acausal Connecting Principle.* Translated by R. F. C. (Richard Francis Carrington) Hull. Princeton, NJ: Princeton University Press.

Kant, Immanuel. 2011. *Observations on the Feeling of the Beautiful and Sublime and Other Writings.* Edited by Patrick Frierson and Paul Guyer. Cambridge: Cambridge University Press.

Kaplan, Jeffrey. 1997. *Radical Religion in America: Millenarian Movements from the Far Right to the Children of Noah.* Syracuse, NY: Syracuse University Press.

Kehoe, Alice Beck. 2000. *Shamans and Religion: An Anthropological Exploration in Critical Thinking.* Long Grove, IL: Waveland Press.

Keller, Mary Lou. 1991. "Introduction: Echoes of the Past." In *Sedona Vortex Guide Book*, edited by Page Bryant, vi–xvi. Sedona: Light Technology Publications.

Kelley, Klara B., and Harris Francis. 1994. *Navajo Sacred Places.* Bloomington: Indiana University Press.

Kemp, Daren, and James R. Lewis, eds. 2007. *Handbook of New Age.* Leiden: Brill.

Kenyon, Tom, and Virginia Essene. 1996. *The Hathor Material: Messages from an Ascended Civilization.* Nicosia: ORB Communications.

Khan, Nasir. 1995. *Development of the Concept and Theory of Alienation in Marx's Writings: March 1843 to August 1844.* Oslo: Solum Forlag.

Klassen, Pamela E. 2018. *The Story of Radio Mind: A Missionary's Journey on Indigenous Land.* Chicago: University of Chicago Press.

Klein, Naomi. 2014. *This Changes Everything: Capitalism vs. the Climate.* New York: Simon and Schuster.

Klinger, Cornelia. 1995. "The Concepts of the Sublime and the Beautiful in Kant and Lyotard." *Constellations* 2 (2): 207–23.

Klin-Oron, Adam. 2014. "How I Learned to Channel: Epistemology, Phenomenology, and Practice in a New Age Course." *American Ethnologist* 41 (4): 635–47.

Kripal, Jeffrey J. 2007. *Esalen: America and the Religion of No Religion.* Chicago: University of Chicago Press.

Kroeger, Karen A. 2003. "AIDS Rumors, Imaginary Enemies, and the Body Politic in Indonesia." *American Ethnologist* 30 (2): 243–57.

Kuper, Adam. 2005. *The Reinvention of Primitive Society: Transformations of a Myth.* 2nd ed. London: Routledge.

Laidlaw, James. 2005. "A Life Worth Leaving: Fasting to Death as Telos of a Jain Religious Life." *Economy and Society* 34 (2): 178–99.

Lambek, Michael. 2013. "Kinship, Modernity, and the Immodern." In *Vital Relations: Modernity and the Persistent Life of Kinship*, edited by Susan McKinnon and Fenella Cannell, 241–60. Santa Fe, NM: School for Advanced Research Press.

——. 2009. "What's in a Name? Name Bestowal and the Identity of Spirits in Mayotte and Northwest Madagascar." In *The Anthropology of Names and Naming*, edited by

Gabriele vom Bruck and Barbara Bodenhorn, 115–38. Cambridge: Cambridge University Press.

Lambert, Frank. 1999. *Inventing the "Great Awakening."* Princeton, NJ: Princeton University Press.

Lau, Kimberly J. 2000. *New Age Capitalism: Making Money East of Eden.* Philadelphia: University of Pennsylvania Press.

Layne, Linda. 2009. "'Your Child Deserves a Name': Possessive Individualism and the Politics of Memory of Pregnancy Loss." In *The Anthropology of Names and Naming,* edited by Gabriele vom Bruck and Barbara Bodenhorn, 31–50. Cambridge: Cambridge University Press.

Leitch, Alison. 2003. "Slow Food and the Politics of Pork Fat: Italian Food and European Identity." *Ethnos* 68 (4): 437–62.

Lelwica, Mary Elizabeth. 2017. *Shameful Bodies: Religion and the Culture of Physical Improvement.* London: Bloomsbury.

Lepselter, Susan. 2016. *The Resonance of Unseen Things: Poetics, Power, Captivity, and UFOs in the American Uncanny.* Ann Arbor: University of Michigan.

Levinovitz, Alan. 2015. *The Gluten Lie: And Other Myths about What You Eat.* New York: Reagan Arts.

Lévi-Strauss, Claude. 2013. "The Culinary Triangle." In *Food and Culture: A Reader,* edited by Carole Counihan and Penny Van Esterik, 3rd ed., 40–47. London: Routledge.

———. 1987. *Introduction to the Work of Marcel Mauss.* London: Routledge & Kegan Paul.

———. 1970. *The Raw and the Cooked.* London: Cape.

Lewis, I. M. 1989. *Ecstatic Religion: A Study of Shamanism and Spirit Possession.* 2nd ed. London: Routledge.

Lewis, James R., ed. 2003. *Encyclopedic Sourcebook of UFO Religions.* Amherst, MA: Prometheus Books.

———. 1995. *The Gods Have Landed: New Religions from Other Worlds.* Albany: State University of New York Press.

Linden, Stanton J. 2003. *The Alchemy Reader: From Hermes Trismegistus to Isaac Newton.* Cambridge: Cambridge University Press.

Lockwood, Renee. 2011. "Religiosity Rejected: Exploring the Religio-Spiritual Dimensions of Landmark Education." *International Journal for the Study of New Religions* 2 (2): 225–54.

LoRusso, James Dennis. 2017. *Spirituality, Corporate Culture, and American Business: The Neoliberal Ethic and the Spirit of Global Capital.* London: Bloomsbury Academic.

Luhrmann, Tanya M. 1991. *Persuasions of a Witches' Craft: Ritual Magic in Contemporary England.* 2nd ed. Cambridge, MA: Harvard University Press.

Mandel, Ernest. 1970. "The Causes of Alienation." In *The Marxist Theory of Alienation: Three Essays,* edited by Ernest Mandel and George Novack, 13–30. Atlanta: Pathfinder.

Mandel, Ernest, and George Edward Novack. 1970. *The Marxist Theory of Alienation: Three Essays.* Atlanta: Pathfinder.

Masuzawa, Tomoko. 2005. *Invention of World Religions: Or, How European Universalism Was Preserved in the Language of Pluralism.* Chicago: University of Chicago Press.

Mathur, Nayanika. 2015. "'It's a Conspiracy Theory *and* Climate Change': Of Beastly

Encounters and Cervine Disappearances in Himalayan India." *HAU: Journal of Ethnographic Theory* 5 (1): 87.

Mauss, Marcel. 1972. *A General Theory of Magic*. London: Routledge.

McCarthy, Helen. 2003. "Assaulting California's Sacred Mountains: Shamans vs. New Age Merchants of Nirvana." In *Beyond Primitivism: Indigenous Religious Traditions and Modernity*, edited by Jacob Olupọna, 172–78. London: Routledge.

McWilliams, James E. 2005. *A Revolution in Eating: How the Quest for Food Shaped America*. New York: Columbia University Press.

Melton, J. Gordon. 1995. "The Contactees: A Survey." In *The Gods Have Landed: New Religions from Other Worlds*, edited by James R. Lewis, 1–12. Albany: State University of New York Press.

Meyer, Neil. 2011. "Falling for the Lord: Shame, Revivalism, and the Origins of the Second Great Awakening." *Early American Studies: An Interdisciplinary Journal* 9 (1): 169–93.

Mikaelsson, Lisbeth. 2001. "Homo Accumulans and the Spiritualization of Money." In *New Age Religion and Globalization*, edited by Mikael Rothstein, 94–110. Copenhagen: Aarhus University Press.

Mintz, Sidney W. 1985. *Sweetness and Power: The Place of Sugar in Modern History*. New York: Viking.

———. 1996. *Tasting Food, Tasting Freedom: Excursions into Eating, Culture, and the Past*. Boston: Beacon Press.

Modern, John Lardas. 2011. *Secularism in Antebellum America*. Chicago: University of Chicago Press.

Moore, Alfred. 2016. "Conspiracy and Conspiracy Theories in Democratic Politics." *Critical Review* 28 (1): 1–23.

Muirhead, Russell, and Nancy L. Rosenblum. 2019. *A Lot of People Are Saying: The New Conspiracism and the Assault on Democracy*. Princeton, NJ: Princeton University Press.

———. 2016. "Speaking Truth to Conspiracy: Partisanship and Trust." *Critical Review* 28 (1): 63–88.

Myerson, Joel, ed. 2000. *Transcendentalism: A Reader*. Oxford: Oxford University Press.

Nelson, Margaret K. 2006. "Single Mothers 'Do' Family." *Journal of Marriage and Family* 68 (4): 781–95.

Nestle, Marion. 1999. "Hunger in America: A Matter of Policy." *Social Research* 66 (1): 257–82.

Newman, Katherine S. 1988. *Falling from Grace: Downward Mobility in the Age of Affluence*. Berkeley: University of California Press.

Newman, Lance. 2005. *Our Common Dwelling: Henry Thoreau, Transcendentalism, and the Class Politics of Nature*. New York: Palgrave Macmillan.

Ong, Aihwa. 2006. *Neoliberalism as Exception: Mutations in Citizenship and Sovereignty*. Durham, NC: Duke University Press.

Orbach, Susie. 1986. *Hunger Strike: The Anorectic's Struggle as a Metaphor for Our Age*. London: Faber.

Ortner, Sherry B. 1998. "Identities: The Hidden Life of Class." *Journal of Anthropological Research* 54 (1): 1–17.

———. 2013. *Not Hollywood: Independent Film at the Twilight of the American Dream.* Durham, NC: Duke University Press.

Palmer, Susan J. 2004. *Aliens Adored: Raël's UFO Religion.* New Brunswick, NJ: Rutgers University Press.

Parish, Jane. 2001. "The Age of Anxiety." In *The Age of Anxiety: Conspiracy Theory and the Human Sciences*, edited by Martin Parker and Jane Parish, 1–16. Oxford: Blackwell/Sociological Review.

Parkins, Wendy. 2004. "Out of Time." *Time & Society* 13 (2–3): 363–82.

Parkins, Wendy, and Geoffrey Craig. 2006. *Slow Living.* Oxford: Berg.

Partridge, Christopher. 2004. "Alien Demonology: The Christian Roots of the Malevolent Extraterrestrial in UFO Religions and Abduction Spiritualities." *Religion* 34 (3): 163–89.

Partridge, Christopher, ed. 2003. *UFO Religions.* London: Routledge.

Pasternak, Judy. 2010. *Yellow Dirt: A Poisoned Land and the Betrayal of the Navajos.* New York: Free Press.

Patterson, Sara M. 2015. "The Plymouth Rock of the American West: Remembering, Forgetting, and Becoming American in Utah." *Material Religion* 11 (3 [July 3]): 329–53.

Paxson, Heather. 2011. "The 'Art' and 'Science' of Handcrafting Cheese in the United States." *Endeavour* 35 (2–3): 116–24.

———. 2013. *The Life of Cheese: Crafting Food and Value in America.* Berkeley: University of California Press.

———. 2008. "Post-Pasteurian Cultures: The Microbiopolitics of Raw-Milk Cheese in the United States." *Cultural Anthropology* 23 (1): 15–47.

Pelkmans, Mathijs, and Rhys Machold. 2011. "Conspiracy Theories and Their Truth Trajectories." *Focaal* 59: 66–80.

Pike, Sarah. 2004. *New Age and Neopagan Religions in America.* New York: Columbia University Press.

Plato. 1993. *Republic.* Translated by Robin Waterfield. Oxford: Oxford University Press.

Pleck, Elizabeth. 1999. "The Making of the Domestic Occasion: The History of Thanksgiving in the United States." *Journal of Social History* 32 (4): 773–89.

Popper, Karl. 1966. *The Open Society and Its Enemies.* 5th rev. ed. Princeton, NJ: Princeton University Press.

Possamai, Adam. 2005. *In Search of New Age Spiritualities.* Farnham: Ashgate.

Povinelli, Elizabeth A. 2012. "The Will to Be Otherwise/The Effort of Endurance." *South Atlantic Quarterly* 111 (3): 453–75.

Powell, Dana E. 2018. *Landscapes of Power: Politics of Energy in the Navajo Nation.* Durham, NC: Duke University Press.

Prince, Ruth, and David Riches. 2000. *The New Age in Glastonbury: The Construction of Religious Movements.* New York: Berghahn Books.

Principe, Walter. 1983. "Toward Defining Spirituality." *Studies in Religion/Sciences Religieuses* 12 (2): 127–41.

Quill, Lawrence. 2016. "Technological Conspiracies: Comte, Technology, and Spiritual Despotism." *Critical Review* 28 (1): 89–111.

Reilly, Gretchen Ann. 2004. "'Not a So-Called Democracy': Anti-Fluoridationists and the Fight over Drinking Water." In *The Politics of Healing: Histories of Alternative Medicine in Twentieth-Century North America*, edited by Robert D. Johnston, 131–49. London: Routledge.

Rifkin, Mark. 2017. *Beyond Settler Time: Temporal Sovereignty and Indigenous Self-Determination*. Durham, NC: Duke University Press.

Robbins, Joel. 2004. *Becoming Sinners: Christianity and Moral Torment in a Papua New Guinea Society*. Berkeley: University of California Press.

———. 1997. "'When Do You Think the World Will End?' Globalization, Apocalypticism, and the Moral Perils of Fieldwork in 'Last New Guinea.'" *Anthropology and Humanism* 22 (1): 6–30.

Robertson, David G. 2016. *UFOs, Conspiracy Theories and the New Age: Millennial Conspiracism*. London: Bloomsbury.

Roediger, David R. 2007. *The Wages of Whiteness: Race and the Making of the American Working Class*. London: Verso.

Roof, Wade Clark. 1999. *Spiritual Marketplace: Baby Boomers and the Remaking of American Religion*. Princeton, NJ: Princeton University Press.

Ross, Andrew. 2011. *Bird on Fire: Lessons from the World's Least Sustainable City*. Oxford: Oxford University Press.

Ross, Scott. 2019. "Being Real on Fake Instagram: Likes, Images, and Media Ideologies of Value." *Journal of Linguistic Anthropology* 29 (3): 359–74.

Roth, Christopher F. 2005. "Ufology as Anthropology: Race, Extraterrestrials, and the Occult." In *E.T. Culture: Anthropology in Outerspaces*, edited by Debbora Battaglia, 38–93. Durham, NC: Duke University Press.

Rothstein, Mikael. 2007. "Hawaii in New Age Imaginations: A Case of Religious Inventions." In *Handbook of New Age*, edited by Daren Kemp and James R. Lewis, 315–40. Leiden: Brill.

Rough, Suzanne. 2013. "Remembering the Future: 2012 as Planetary Transition." In *Prophecy in the New Millennium: When Prophecies Persist*, edited by Sarah Harvey and Suzanne Newcombe, 255–60. Farnham: Ashgate.

Rubenstein, Mary-Jane. 2012. "Cosmic Singularities: On the Nothing and the Sovereign." *Journal of the American Academy of Religion* 80 (2): 485–517.

———. 2014. *Worlds Without End: The Many Lives of the Multiverse*. New York: Columbia University Press.

Saethre, Eirik, and Jonathan Stadler. 2013. "Malicious Whites, Greedy Women, and Virtuous Volunteers: Negotiating Social Relations through Clinical Trial Narratives in South Africa." *Medical Anthropology Quarterly* 27 (1): 103–20.

Saliba, John A. 2006. "The Study of UFO Religions." *Nova Religio: The Journal of Alternative and Emergent Religions* 10 (2): 103–23.

Sanders, Todd, and Harry G. West. 2003. "Power Revealed and Concealed in the New World Order." In *Transparency and Conspiracy: Ethnographies of Suspicion in the New World Order*, edited by Harry G. West and Todd Sanders, 1–37. Durham, NC: Duke University Press.

Schelly, Chelsea. 2015. *Crafting Collectivity: American Rainbow Gatherings and Alternative Forms of Community*. London: Routledge.

Scheper-Hughes, Nancy. 1993. *Death Without Weeping: The Violence of Everyday Life in Brazil*. Berkeley: University of California Press.

Schmidt, Leigh Eric. 2012. *Restless Souls: The Making of American Spirituality*. Berkeley: University of California Press.

Schneider, David Murray. 1980. *American Kinship: A Cultural Account*. 2nd ed. Chicago: University of Chicago Press.

Schneiders, Sandra Marie. 2003. "Religion vs. Spirituality: A Contemporary Conundrum." *Spiritus: A Journal of Christian Spirituality* 3 (2): 163–85.

Scholem, Gershom. 1960. *Major Trends in Jewish Mysticism*. New York: Knopf Doubleday.

Sennett, Richard. 2008. *The Craftsman*. New Haven, CT: Yale University Press.

———. 2006. *The Culture of the New Capitalism*. New Haven, CT: Yale University Press.

———. 2003. *Respect: The Formation of Character in a World of Inequality*. Northwood: Allen Lane.

Sennett, Richard, and Jonathan Cobb. 1972. *The Hidden Injuries of Class*. New York: Norton.

Shannon, Jerry. 2014. "Food Deserts: Governing Obesity in the Neoliberal City." *Progress in Human Geography* 38 (2): 248–66.

Sheridan, Thomas E. 2012. *Arizona: A History*. Tucson: University of Arizona Press.

———. 2006. *Landscapes of Fraud: Mission Tumacácori, the Baca Float, and the Betrayal of the O'odham*. Tucson: University of Arizona Press.

Siegel, James. 1981. "Academic Work: The View from Cornell." *Diacritics* 11 (1): 68–83.

Sitler, Robert K. 2006. "The 2012 Phenomenon: New Age Appropriation of an Ancient Mayan Calendar." *Nova Religio* 9 (3): 24–38.

Smith, Bruce P. 2005. "Plea Bargaining and the Eclipse of the Jury." *Annual Review of Law and Social Science* 1 (1 [December 4]): 131–49.

Smith, Hedrick. 2013. *Who Stole the American Dream?* New York: Random House.

Sperber, Dan. 1996. *Explaining Culture: A Naturalistic Approach*. Oxford: Blackwell.

Stack, Carol B. 1974. *All Our Kin: Strategies for Survival in a Black Community*. London: Harper & Row.

Stewart, Kathleen, and Susan Harding. 1999. "Bad Endings: American Apocalypsis." *Annual Review of Anthropology* 28: 285–310.

Streib, Heinz, and Ralph Hood. 2011. "'Spirituality' as Privatized Experience-Oriented Religion: Empirical and Conceptual Perspectives." *Implicit Religion* 14 (4): 433–53.

Strozier, Charles B., and Michael Flynn. 1997. *The Year 2000: Essays on the End*. New York: New York University Press.

Stuckrad, Kocku von. 2014. *The Scientification of Religion: An Historical Study of Discursive Change, 1800–2000*. Berlin: De Gruyter.

Sturm, Circe. 2002. *Blood Politics: Race, Culture, and Identity in the Cherokee Nation of Oklahoma*. Berkeley: University of California Press.

Sunstein, Cass R., and Adrian Vermeule. 2009. "Conspiracy Theories: Causes and Cures." *Journal of Political Philosophy* 17 (2): 202–27.

Surprise, Kevin. 2019. "Stratospheric Imperialism: Liberalism, (Eco)Modernization, and Ideologies of Solar Geoengineering Research." *Environment and Planning E: Nature and Space* (April): 1–23.

Sutcliffe, Steven. 2002. *Children of the New Age: A History of Spiritual Practices*. London: Routledge.

Sutcliffe, Steven, and Ingvild Sælid Gilhus. 2013. *New Age Spirituality: Rethinking Religion*. Abingdon: Acumen.

Sutphen, Dick. 1986. *Dick Sutphen Presents Sedona: Psychic Energy Vortexes*. Edited by Dawn Abbey. Malibu, CA: Valley of the Sun Publishing.

TallBear, Kimberly. 2019. "Caretaking Relations, Not American Dreaming." *Kalfou* 6 (1): 24–41.

———. 2013. *Native American DNA: Tribal Belonging and the False Promise of Genetic Science*. Minneapolis: University of Minnesota Press.

Taussig, Michael T. 1987. *Shamanism, Colonialism, and the Wild Man: A Study in Terror and Healing*. Chicago: University of Chicago Press.

Tingley, Dustin, and Gernot Wagner. 2017. "Solar Geoengineering and the Chemtrails Conspiracy on Social Media." *Palgrave Communications* 3 (1): 1–7.

Todd, Selina. 2014. *The People: The Rise and Fall of the Working Class, 1910–2010*. London: John Murray.

Turner, Steve. 2002. *Amazing Grace: The Story of America's Most Beloved Song*. New York: Ecco.

Turner, Victor. 1969. *The Ritual Process: Structure and Anti-Structure*. Piscataway, NJ: Aldine Transaction.

Uscinski, Joseph E., and Joseph M. Parent. 2014. *American Conspiracy Theories*. Oxford: Oxford University Press.

Vannini, Phillip, and Jonathan Taggart. 2015. *Off the Grid: Re-Assembling Domestic Life*. London: Routledge.

Vitebsky, Piers. 2000. "Shamanism." In *Indigenous Religions: A Companion*, edited by Graham Harvey, 55–67. London: Cassell.

Vollmann, William T. 2018. *No Immediate Danger: Volume One of Carbon Ideologies*. New York: Viking.

Wachsmuth, David, and Alexander Weisler. 2018. "Airbnb and the Rent Gap: Gentrification through the Sharing Economy." *Environment and Planning A: Economy and Space* 50 (6): 1147–70.

Wacquant, Loïc J. D. 2009. *Punishing the Poor: The Neoliberal Government of Social Insecurity*. Durham, NC: Duke University Press.

Wallis, Robert J. 2003. *Shamans/Neo-Shamans: Ecstasy, Alternative Archaeologies, and Contemporary Pagans*. London: Routledge.

Ward, Charlotte, and David Voas. 2011. "The Emergence of Conspirituality." *Journal of Contemporary Religion* 26 (1): 103–21.

Wessinger, Catherine Lowman. 2000. *How the Millennium Comes Violently: From Jonestown to Heaven's Gate*. New York: Seven Bridges Press.

Weston, Kath. 1991. *Families We Choose: Lesbians, Gays, Kinship*. New York: Columbia University Press.

White, Christopher G. 2018. *Other Worlds: Spirituality and the Search for Invisible Dimensions*. Cambridge, MA: Harvard University Press.

Whitesides, Kevin A. 2015. "2012 Millennialism Becomes Conspiracist Teleology: Overlapping Alternatives in Late Twentieth Century Cultic Milieu." *Nova Religio: The Journal of Alternative and Emergent Religions* 19 (2): 30–48.

Whitley, Sarah. 2013. "Changing Times in Rural America: Food Assistance and Food Insecurity in Food Deserts." *Journal of Family Social Work* 16 (1): 36–52.

Wilson, Andrew Fergus. 2013. "From Mushrooms to the Stars: 2012 and the Apocalyptic Milieu." In *Prophecy in the New Millennium: When Prophecies Persist*, edited by Sarah Harvey and Suzanne Newcombe, 225–38. Farnham: Ashgate.

Wuthnow, Robert. 1998. *After Heaven: Spirituality in America since the 1950s*. Berkeley: University of California Press.

Yanagisako, Sylvia Junko, and Carol Lowery Delaney, eds. 1995. *Naturalizing Power: Essays in Feminist Cultural Analysis*. London: Routledge.

York, Michael. 2001. "New Age Commodification and Appropriation of Spirituality." *Journal of Contemporary Religion* 163 (3): 361–72.

Zeller, Benjamin E. 2011. "At the Nexus of Science and Religion: UFO Religions." *Religion Compass* 5 (11): 666–74.

———. 2014. "Quasi-Religious American Foodways: The Cases of Vegetarianism and Locavorism." In *Religion, Food, and Eating in North America*, edited by Benjamin E. Zeller, 294–320. New York: Columbia University Press.

Žižek, Slavoj. 2010. *Living in the End Times*. London: Verso.

Znamenski, Andrei A. 2007. *The Beauty of the Primitive: Shamanism and the Western Imagination*. Oxford: Oxford University Press.

INDEX

ideology, 24, 25, 113, 155
Illuminati, 165
illusion: of leaving society, 187; mass, 13, 35, 134; matter, 12, 182; of perspective, 123; reality, 124; separation, 15, 16, 31, 152; third dimension, 30, 161
imperialism, 20, 36, 56, 126
incarnation, 5, 15, 21–22, 105, 113, 120; as aliens, 95, 98, 101, 102; group, 106, 107, 108; third dimension, 134
Indigenous peoples, 35–36, 40–48, 50–52
individual, 77–79, 86–90, 93, 113; agency, 22; freedom of, 21; responses to cancer, 149; responsibility, 27, 127, 152; rights, 173; in spirituality, 9, 10, 25, 29–31, 129, 166, 167, 181, 185–87
individualism, 10, 30, 87, 113, 127, 173; meritocratic, 111; radical, 89; of spiritual path, 31
individuation, 115, 119
inequality: class, 30, 112, 178; economic, 27, 28; social, 114, 122, 167
Infowars, 170
initiation, 44, 155
inspiration, 19, 20, 89
intuition, 13, 18, 21, 38, 58, 169, 173, 174, 181; divine communication, 56; as feeling, 52; from higher self, 19; listening to, 180
invisibility cloak, 113

Jesus Christ, 11, 13, 50, 70, 77, 133
Joseph, 67, 70, 73

Kant, Immanuel, 58
karma, 23, 105, 176
Kate, 141–44, 146, 150, 152
kinship, 104–9, 127; biology as symbol, 106–9; brotherhood, 105–7, 110; families, 106–9, 117; family, 87, 92, 93; father, 80, 109, 110, 142, 147, 175; mother, 11, 98, 99, 109, 110, 114, 142; name, 104; soul family, 105–7; star family, 99, 116
kombucha, 128, 131, 135, 139
Krishna Prem, 26
Krista Raisa, 116

kundalini: awakening, 97, 98, 101; yoga, 67, 129, 130
kung fu, 48, 61, 80, 144, 157, 183–86

labor, 156; alienation, 114, 120–21; deregulation, 96, 119; as value, 140, 152; waged, 187
Lakota, 48, 54
Lana, 54–56, 60, 184
landscape, 36, 38, 40, 49; agency, 12; divinity in, 57; as nature, 44, 54; social construction, 35; sublime, 58, 60, 63
language: models, 83; of spirituality, 77, 130, 136; of technology, 80
Law of Attraction, 27
legitimation, 169; of food system, 128; of knowledge, 154, 156, 157, 173; of science, 171; use of Native Americans, 40, 44, 52
Lemuria, 51, 52
Lévi-Strauss, Claude, 14, 131
levitation, 14, 16, 136
light: in alchemy, 136–38; bodies as, 134, 150–53; city of, 99; and dark, 117; and love, 6–8, 130; in spirituality, 95, 98, 116, 122, 140
lightworker, 102, 104, 130, 137

mainstream, 171, 173, 174; media, 163, 164, 170
manifestation, 3, 5, 10, 11, 16, 30, 31, 43, 79, 52, 163, 179–82; abundance, 28, 177, 113, 182, 183; of money, 13, 24, 181; positivity, 15; and theodicy, 13, 175; and vortexes, 37
Marx, Karl, 114, 120, 121
materialism, 13, 29, 96, 171, 174, 175
materiality, 28, 29
matter, 16, 29, 32, 42, 85, 182; consciousness, 37; transformation into energy, 77
Mauss, Marcel, 14
Mayan: Long Count calendar, 3, 65, 68, 81; zodiac cards, 117
media: alternative, 169, 170, 173, 177; attention, 71, 74; hostility to, 157, 170; mainstream, 163, 164, 169–70, 173; mass, 120; new, 8; reality, 87; representation in, 121; social, 30, 74, 77, 86, 90, 91, 104, 123, 160; as source material, 82, 116